ENCOUNTERING BLISS

My Journey through India with Ānandamayī Mā

Ānandamayī Mā

ENCOUNTERING BLISS

My Journey through India with Ānandamayī Mā

Eine ganz gewöhnliche Heilige Dir große Seele der Ānandamayī Mā Indienfahrt mit der bedeutendsten Hindu-Heiligen der Neuzeit

---

MELITA MASCHMANN

Rendered into English by

SHRIDHAR B. SHROTRI

MOTILAL BANARSIDASS PUBLISHERS
PRIVATE LIMITED • DELHI

*Reprint: Delhi, **2006***
First Edition: Delhi, 2002

ISBN: 81-208-1541-6 (Cloth)
ISBN: 81-208-1571-8 (Paper)

MOTILAL BANARSIDASS
41 U.A. Bungalow Road, Jawahar Nagar, Delhi 110 007
8 Mahalaxmi Chamber, 22 Bhulabhai Desai Road, Mumbai 400 026
236, 9th Main III Block, Jayanagar, Bangalore 560 011
203 Royapettah High Road, Mylapore, Chennai 600 004
Sanas Plaza, 1302 Baji Rao Road, Pune 411 002
8 Camac Street, Kolkata 700 017
Ashok Rajpath, Patna 800 004
Chowk, Varanasi 221 001

Printed in India
BY JAINENDRA PRAKASH JAIN AT SHRI JAINENDRA PRESS,
A-45 NARAINA, PHASE-I, NEW DELHI 110 028
AND PUBLISHED BY NARENDRA PRAKASH JAIN FOR
MOTILAL BANARSIDASS PUBLISHERS PRIVATE LIMITED,
BUNGALOW ROAD, DELHI 110 007

Acknowledgements

I am extremely grateful to Mr. N.P. Jain, Director, Motilal Banarsidass Indological Publishers and Distributors, Delhi for giving me an opportunity of rendering this book on Ānandamayī Mā.

My thanks are due to Prof. Dr. M.K. Naik, retired Professor of English, Karnatak University, Dharwad for his help in this rendition.

Words fail me to express my gratitude to the author Melita Maschmann and her friend, Sister Bridget for their invaluable guidance in preparing the final copy. I shall ever be indebted to them.

Shridhar B. Shrotri

C-9,
Garden Estate,
Aundh,
Pune-411 007

Publisher's Note

Melita Maschmann blissful encounter with Mā Ānandamayī was purely a chance meeting, during the latters travels in India, in the summer of 1962. The meeting proved so fascinating that instead of leaving the country shortly for the home in Germany she accompanied Mā in her travel in India for the next almost two years and finally made India her home.

The following account of her experience with Mā, which is not a product of a mere credulous devotees mind but the report of a critical-minded and cautioned journalist, is so impressive and enlightening, at times thrilling, elegant in style, objective in approach, that we could not resist the temptation of making it available in English to our readers.

The book, as the reader will see for himself, for excels other existing books on the subject in quality, readability, style and spontaneous appeal, and we are happy to present it to our readers.

Contents

Chapter 1

Ānandamayī Mā—Her Life and Work

Mā was born on 30 April, 1896 in a village called Kheora in East Bengal. She was named Nirmalā Sundarī Devī. Nirmalā means "the pure one", Sundarī, "the beautiful one", and Devī means "goddess". This "Devī" is often given as an *epitheton ornans* following the name of a Brāhmaṇa-girl. Her parents came from a high Brāhmaṇa-caste. Several erudite *paṇḍitas* are said to have come from her mother's family. It is told that one woman from the family put her finger into the fire, while the mortal remains of her husband were consigned to the flames, to find out whether she felt pain and then flung herself singing into the flames. According to tradition, such (self-)immolation is regarded as redeeming, only when a woman who follows her husband in death, has reached such a level of religious perfection that she does not feel any pain in the process.

The house in which Mā was born was surrounded by the houses of poor Muslim farmers with whom the Hindu family lived in amity. Two facts are repeatedly reported about Mā's childhood. I am quoting some examples: The family had noticed that the child Nirmalā, after having learnt to speak, sometimes mentioned things which had occurred shortly after her birth, like the visit of a relative or felling of a tree. I also heard that her parents were worried about the girl, because, unlike other children, she spoke with animals and plants, apparently with invisible creatures also and was often absent-minded for relatively long periods.

When Nirmalā was approaching thirteen, she was married to a Bengali Brāhmaṇa by name Srijut Ramani Mohan

Chakrawarty. He was considerably older than her and she named him Bholānāth (one of the names of Śiva; i.e. "Lord of the humble"). He died of smallpox in 1938 in the *āśrama* of Kishenpur (Dehradun). During his illness Mā herself had looked after him alone and made everyone else leave the house, as she did not want them to lament or wail over his loss. Mā and Bholānāth had led a life of sexual abstinence from the beginning. On his death-bed, he called her his mother. He must have recognized the mysterious mission of the childlike girl who was entrusted to him in marriage, and it is said that early once he called himself her first disciple and servant and had always lived as such.

It is true that the religious ecstasies of his young wife became more and more noticeable to others. This fact must have disturbed Bholānāth. I read a report in which it was said that he consulted a physician, Dr. Mahendra Chandra Nandi who came from a family of sages and exorcists. The doctor was shocked and expressed his helplessness – here it was not a question of releasing one who was possessed, but of worshipping a soul liberated from ignorance (*jīvanmukta*).

Bholānāth came to Dhaka in 1923 and took over the supervision of Shahbag, a large garden belonging to a nawāb. Mā was then 27-years-old. Gradually a growing circle of believing Hindus, who felt drawn to her, gathered in this garden almost every evening. Her family had witnessed her going into a trance during *kīrtana* for over ten years. Now the news of her religious ecstasy spread from mouth to mouth. At the same time, her ecstasies appeared to have become more and more intense and increasingly polymorphous.

I want to write about what I was told and what corresponds to the printed, official accounts. But I shall skip many statements which, I think, are too subjective or which are palpably exaggerated. I am not under the illusion that I can give even a partial or reasonably fair description of the relevant events – either chronologically or in their complexity. Nor can I claim to give an accurate description of how these influenced Mā's friends. There are two reasons for this: only a fraction of the Bengali account of Mā's life has been translated into English, and again only a small selection of English reports was made available to me. What I was told by those whose reminiscences go back to her early days, is limited in its documentary value.

And yet having checked the soundness of many of the facts recorded here to the best of my ability, I am convinced, they correspond to the truth of the events of this time, as this has been corroborated in many ways and by trustworthy people. If I cannot reproduce them as perfectly as I would like, it is because of their Asian characteristics. By this I mean that they concern spheres of experience which are almost completely alien to someone from the West as much for myself as for the reader. And yet I ask the reader to begin with the assumption that what he reads – however unbelievable it seems – is perhaps possible in a world where the spiritual foundations are radically different from those of the contemporary West.

When Mā came to Dhaka with her husband, she had already spent one year in complete silence and she maintained this silence for two more years. There is an account given by herself from the time before this, written by an academic. I am translating it literally:

> "At that time, this body cooked, cleaned and carried out all sorts of household manual work to look after father, mother and Bholānāth. But in reality, it served no one else but God. For, when I served my father, my mother, Bholānāth or others, I considered them as different manifestations of the Almighty and served them as such. When I sat down to prepare the food, I did it as if it was a religious ritual, for the food was after all meant for God. I had only one wish: to serve God in everything and to do everything for the sake of God."

Mā says in another account that she subordinated herself in absolute obedience to her husband at that time. She had carried out, in minutest detail, what he ordered, and she had never opposed him while doing so. What Mā did for her husband, is done by countless other Indian women. However, during this everyday life her religious ecstasies occurred increasingly which were naturally aroused by the *kīrtanas.* For example:

> "Mā got up suddenly, standing on her toes, she raised her arms and tilted her head backwards. She stood in this position for a long time. Her eyes were focussed on an object on the horizon. She was drawn towards it so strongly that her body all but rose from the ground. Gradually she began to move her feet, slowly dancing, following the music like a puppet drawn by an invisible hand. Her eyes were oblivious to her surroundings. But her face shone with rapturous joy."
>
> It says again and again: "Suddenly light flowed out of her."

One of the observers says, "We were convinced that a Divine Power had taken possession of her body. She was swept along through changing dance forms of great beauty. I was struck by its trivial detail: the hair of her body stood on end during this ecstatic experience. When one looked into her eyes, one had the impression that she was completely detached from these manifestations. For, what was happening to her was on another plane altogether. All of a sudden, her eyes would close slowly, and her body would sink to the ground. She remained lying there with her head thrown back. She would regain her senses only on the next day at about 10 a.m. Sometimes, she would come out of her trance even sooner. And on waking up, she would laugh and weep all at once. Her body would assume a Yogic posture. At that time, we heard a deep humming in her throat. A little later, the sound turned into a rumbling and finally emerged as a flow of extremely melodious chanting. Countless Vedic hymns sprang to her lips on such occasions.

Only a few erudite persons have learnt to speak Sanskrit so effortlessly and freely as she did then, although she had no education at all."

Yet it was impossible to write down the hymns because Mā spoke so rapidly. When she was asked later to verify the correctness of the texts which were written down, she refused. "I cannot remember any of them." When she poured out all these prayers, tears would start rolling down her cheeks, but her face would be blissfully transfigured.

Here is an example of a prayer now published:

"You are the light of the universe and the spirit ruling over it. Appear among us. Banish all anxieties. Appear before us. You are the existence in which I live; you are present in the hearts of all these devotees. You are the incarnation of all deities and you have indeed emerged from me . . . I seek shelter in you. You are my refuge and my last resting place. Take my whole existence into you. You appear in two forms: as a redeemer and as a believer who seeks redemption . . . I have created all after my image. I sent all into the world, and they found their last refuge in me. The faith in me is the cause of *mokṣa.* All belong to me. Rudra owes all his power to me alone, and at the same time, I sing Rudra's praise which is revealed in all creation and which is the cause of all creation. . ."

According to Hindu thought, the enlightened one realizes the unity without making any distinction between the devotee, the prayer and the object of worship. Such an experience is expressed here in the sudden "change of role" between the worshipper and the one who is worshipped.

Although Mā was never instructed by a teacher, her body is said to have "assumed" at that time a number of different and extremely complex Yoga-postures. She was not actually "performing" Yoga-exercises, but her body adopted such postures effortlessly and unconsciously on her part. What other people achieved after years of training, blossomed in her instantly and repeatedly.

It was quite often mentioned that Mā was spiritually charged at that time with the result that sensitive people, on touching her feet, fell down unconscious. Mā herself said, "An electric shock went through me at that time, when someone touched my feet. Sometimes, I became suddenly rigid."

There is a mention of a further physical phenomenon. For long periods Mā's body became totally insensitive to pain. This state is typical at a certain stage in Yoga. For example: one day she put a piece of burning coal on her foot and observed with amused interest how it burnt a deep hole through her skin. The wound healed only after months of suppuration. One of her close associates had doubted her insensitiveness.

Mā had become capable of producing all forms of *samādhi* for years. "In the midst of a conversation, her eyes suddenly dilated and took an expression of Infinity; her limbs relaxed and she seemed to be totally self-absorbed; her breath became slower and finally stopped; her body became cold; her hands and feet turned to stone. Still, everything in her gave an impression of great tenderness and frailness. Her face lost all freshness and liveliness: it expressed neither joy nor sorrow. We often feared that life would ebb away permanently. Sometimes, this death-like rigidity of body went on for four or five days; in spite of all our efforts, we could not revive her earlier.

When Mā woke up, she took a little food. She could only move slowly and walk with great effort, but every cell of her body was filled with joy from which the *union* with the Divine continued to shine forth. We felt that she had returned from an extraterrestrial region. There was an expression of universal love in her eyes."

Urged by her devotees, Mā celebrated religious rites during her years in Shahbag. Her friends had every reason to be filled with admiration and amazement at the way she carried out very complicated and lengthy rites exactly according to the *śāstras.* While performing them, she also recited *mantras* which she had never learnt before like the priests. There is an account of *Kālī-pūjā* in Dhaka which has something eerie about it:

"Like lightning, Mā crossed the crowded room and sat so close to the idol of the Goddess that she touched it. Her *sārī* had slipped from her shoulder and her skin, which was otherwise golden-brown, suddenly appeared jet-black (*kālī* = "The Black One"). Her tongue hung from her mouth (like the tongue of the Goddess in her picture). She immediately ordered us: 'Close your eyes'. When we opened them again, we saw that Mā was covered with flowers (like the idols of the gods which are decorated with garlands during the *pūjā*), and Bholānāth celebrated the *pūjā* in front of her, as if she were the idol of the Goddess."

Here is another account:

"Mā sat for a long time withdrawn to herself beside the idol (of the Goddess). Then she began the *pūjā.* It seemed once more that all her movements were guided by a mysterious hand, whereas she herself was lost in a deep trance. She chanted *mantras,* put the flowers on her own head, applied sandalpaste to herself instead of doing it to the idol. Only occasionally, she placed some flowers on it.

After bathing the goat that was to be sacrificed, we placed it in Mā's lap. She wept as she stroked it. Then she chanted the *mantras* and touched all the parts of the animal's body and blessed them. Finally she whispered a *mantra* in its ear. When the goat was taken from her, she seized a knife and lay supine for a long time on the ground. When she applied the knife to her neck, she gave out a cry three times. It sounded like the fear of a sacrificial animal. When the goat was sacrificed later, it did not move, nor did it make any sound. Only with great difficulty, a single drop of blood emerged from the wound."

Here also, we have a manifestation of unity. I am the one who brings the sacrifice, the one to whom the sacrifice is brought and the one who is sacrificed.

Between the second and the third decades of her life, Mā often abstained from taking food for a long period. One of the monks told me that Mā at that time could live without any food. However, she herself said, "Always give me once a day a very small quantity, otherwise I shall completely forget to eat." A further account tells:

> "Mā ate only a handful of rice daily, nothing at night, for five months. For eight to nine months, she took only three morsels of rice during the day and the same quantity during the night. For five to six months, her only diet consisted of a fruit and water twice daily; for four to five months, only a fingerful of food once during the day and once during the night. For five to six months: every morning and evening three grains of rice, and in the course of the day, two to three fruits. There were intervals between these periods of fasting when she ate normally."

Once in a conversation, she herself talked about the time when she lived on a few measured rice-grains. "It appeared like a miracle. But I could also only do it because it is just not impossible. The body does not really need everything we usually eat. As it is, it excretes the most after it has retained the essence." As a consequence of *sādhana*, the body can adjust itself in such a way that it can live from what it absorbs from the air and other components of its surroundings, apart from its own reserves.

From the year 1924, Mā never took anything solid or liquid with her own hands; she was fed. One day–someone who had witnessed this told me–her hand became limp when she wanted to take food as usual, but she couldn't do it although she could use her hand for other tasks. Mā's explanation was: 'I always eat with my own hand. Everyone's hand is my hand." Perhaps, we should remember in this context that the idols of the gods in the temples are fed, as if they were human. I could not find any other explanation for this phenomenon.

Viewing the matter superficially, one has the impression that Mā went through a kind of "School of Wisdom" in the years when she practised Yoga, silence, fasting, etc. But she says explicitly, "I have only pretended to do *sādhana.*" – "Man must be born again and again to reach a certain level of enlightenment on one of the paths of *sādhana.* (One life is not enough for it.) But for this body it is only play."

Mā says elsewhere: "Let me tell you that what I am today, I was from my childhood. But when the different stages of *sādhana* were manifested through this body, something happened to it like the disguising of the true nature of the self. How ignorant was it then? It was in reality knowledge that had disguised itself as ignorance (which played ignorant). I have heard people frequently talking about the secret of this 'act of dualism' that Mā played to tempt her friends into a multifarious and intensive *sādhana.* But all the same, I wonder, if this is not too glib an interpretation."

I must mention one incident here: Mā's husband and several friends met her, when she was praying near the grave of a Fakir according to the tenets of the Koran. Occasionally similar situations were repeated. And Mā was completely fluent in the complexity of the Muslim prayer, although she said, "she knew" nothing about this, when asked. She also said then that she communicated with the spirits of the deceased Muslim sages and saints, as she was often visited by beings no longer alive among us.

I have often heard that Mā was repeatedly subjected to a sort of "inquisition" by a circle of learned *puṇḍits* in the years she became famous on account of her wonderful spiritual capacity. She was asked questions which only the man well-versed in the scriptures could answer. She used to answer without a moment's hesitation. This amazed the scholars, and nobody could explain how she could do it. I personally was not able to speak to an eye-witness at such an occasion.

Several people related their own experience to me of how Mā had appeared to them at a place where she had never "really" been, to console them, to give them advice or to warn them of some danger. I also remember an account of an Army officer who had heard Mā's voice when he was in extreme danger: "Leave this place at once"; he obeyed; a granade exploded then a minute later. A few people told me that Mā had given them *dīkṣā* or advice in a dream. I have also heard that during her years when she "pretended" to practise Yoga, she often predicted events which took place later exactly as foretold.

The written and oral accounts of that time are full of her miraculous cures. They were, however, only cursorily mentioned, like: "This happened in the week in which Mā cured a leper in X. . ." These are indeed exciting events for the Indians, but such miracles happen in a certain stage of the spiritual development of every yogī.

Mā says, "As for my capability of curing, the whole thing had developed on its own. I suddenly noticed that my body had absorbed the pains of others, quite without intention and without the slightest effort on my part. One day, I visited a sick man who was suffering from serious infection of his stomach and intestines. When I came home, I found that I was suffering from the same malady. It lasted exactly for twelve hours, and it raged like a storm through my body, and then everything was normal. The man, who had been suffering for a long time from the malady, was cured the moment I became ill. Similar things started to happen after that. I noticed that a patient was immediately cured, whom I touched without any intention on my part. Later, my capability was put to test, and I knew from that moment that a light touch of my hand was sufficient to cure a patient."

It must have been towards the end of the period when Mā led the life of a *sādhaka* that her condition changed into what is often called "feigned petrification". Obviously, it concerns a phase every person practising *sādhana* undergoes more or less intensely. While his spiritual experiences let him progress in the expanse and depth of the inner dimension, which becomes increasingly mysterious, a kind of paralysis sets in. I shall reproduce here what I have heard:

"Mā had severed all connections with her surroundings at that time. Not only did she not say anything, she even ceased to communicate through signs or gestures. Often for days, she did not move even a limb. She used to lie down, or at times, she would sit motionless for a long period. Only her eyes showed anything of life. Her companions had to guess what she needed. This was particularly difficult because she did not feed herself. She would never have taken any food on her own, even if she had felt hungry. When she did not want anything, she did not indicate at all, she simply let the food particles fall from her lips. If she needed hot water, one had to know it from the expression in her eyes. Of course, there were misunderstandings. At that time, she never bothered about her appearance. She scarcely took a bath" (Among certain *yogīs,* negligence of physical cleanliness is a part of asceticism, whereas bathing is regarded as a religious duty.) But I was repeatedly assured that Mā, in spite of not taking bath, radiated health and cleanliness, which is quite beyond one's comprehension.

She would get up suddenly from her seat and start running onto the street further and further. Nobody could hold her back, for nobody would ever venture to use force. Finally, there was no other way for her companions, except to break camp in a flurry and run after her. Sometimes she went to a station and got into any available train, and we would follow her. Then she would get down from the train at a station far away which nobody knew. We had then to look for accommodation." This was actually not difficult as Mā usually stayed in temples.

Gradually Mā's friends started getting worried; they feared that she would lose her power of speech and the faculty of communication with the world. They must have persistently tried to call her to "come back to the world" again. Above all, because they needed her advice and guidance. Finally, Mā agreed. When she began to speak after an initial struggle to articulate, she slipped again into a trance, and *mantras* gushed forth from her lips. In the beginning, she spoke only on Thursdays. This is the day of the week which is dedicated to the *guru*. Later she assumed normal habits.

I often heard that her behaviour became so normal after this period that she performed only a few miracles. Obviously, Mā took a deliberate decision to give up working miracles. I read about this: "We had gathered in relatively a large group around Mā and were talking about her earlier miracles, some of which we witnessed. Someone asked Mā whether she remembered this or that event. 'Of course', she answered laughing, 'I certainly remember that period. But later I had a *khayāl* not to perform any more miracles'."

Someone who knows Mā for a long time and lived near her for years told me further: "She is not like an ordinary Yogi. In his case, the ability of working miracles disappears at a certain stage of spiritual development. As for her, she continues to possess supernatural powers as before, but she makes use of them less often. She, at least, does not use them openly. Apparently, she no longer has the *khayāl* to cure patients or to help people with other problems, because she does not want them to come to her just to be cured or for other miraculous manifestations. If she were to fulfil all these wishes, the petitioners would crowd out those who come to her for religious reasons. We have experienced this before even from Westerners who made such demands on her: "Mā, I have a diseased spinal column. Cure me." One European lady once brought her sick dog to Mā and was annoyed when Mā told her to take it to a veterinary surgeon."

In 1937, Mā went on a pilgrimage with Bholānāth, her husband, and Bhaiji, one of her earlier disciples, to Mount Kailāsa in south-west Tibet, supposedly the seat of God Śiva, around which many myths have been woven. The pilgrims had to cross many dangerous passes in the Himalayas which were buried under permanent snow. On the way back, Bhaiji died on the south slope of the mountain in Almora. His delicate health was not up to the rigours of such a pilgrimage; but I heard that he wanted to die, for he had nothing more to lose. Bholānāth died of smallpox a few months later. Both men had obtained *saṃnyāsa,* one of the highest religious ranks that an ordinary Hindu can get.

Since then Mā led a perfectly ordinary life. You could say, she went on an uninterrupted pilgrimage during this third stage of her life. She did not have a house which she could call her "home", but she would say of every house, "I am at home here." In a narrower sense, this is true above all of the more than 30 odd *āśramas* which were built by her associates throughout north and central India during her life. She moved up and down to each one of them. The rooms in which she lived are now as simple – spartanly simple for Western tastes – as they were at that time, although the conditions in which Mā lived have changed. Earlier there were endless journeys in dirty third-class bogies of slow trains and in ox-driven carts. In the last years, Mā travelled in reserved first-class compartments of the fastest trains, and everywhere, the well-to-do of her disciples insisted on taking her to her destination by car.

She herself reacted to the luxury in her surroundings with the same indifference as to poverty, but when she was at home in our sense, i.e. in the *āśramas,* she did not tolerate any comfort. I always felt that she could have travelled by an ox-driven cart at any time and would have spent the night under a tree without being affected by the changed circumstances. There are affluent among her disciples who look after the maintenance of the *āśramas.* Mā was known as one of the wisest, saintly and venerable persons in the country.

Since the death of Śrī Aurobindo and Bhagavān Ramaṇa Maharṣi in the year 1950, many people regarded Mā as the most significant living spiritual power in the country. In India, a vast number of the population thinks that true value in life lies in spirituality. Many leading personalities from politics and intellectual life were among her followers, and they visited her frequently. Nehru's wife used to visit Mā for several years, and even Nehru used to meet her. His daughter Indira Gandhi was one of Mā's lifelong friends.

Mā was in Delhi on Nehru's last birthday. She disappeared in the early morning from the *āśrama* without telling anyone where she was going. The āśramites read the next day in the newspapers that Mā was the first to greet the Prime Minister on his birthday. Ministers, governors of the provinces, professors, great scholars and *mahārājās* used to meet Mā quite often. Many shared their family worries with her. Others came to seek guidance on their spiritual path, or to spend some time in silent meditation in the presence of her charismatic personality.

The cycle of religious festivals and functions, always repeated in the same manner, took place between Mā's birthday celebrations. It was her presence that lent importance to these festivals and functions. Her birthday was celebrated for nearly a month and it transformed the place (where it was celebrated) into a pilgrim-centre for many thousands. 14000 guests were invited for Mā's 60th birthday in 1956 which was celebrated in Banaras. The number of visitors who came without being invited was much higher. Special significance was attached to the annual week for fasting and meditation. *Durgā-pūjā* is the most popular of the remaining festivals and commemorative days. And there is an uninterrupted series of them. Sometimes, festivals outside the usual ones were celebrated like the beginning or the end of the great sacrificial fire which burnt between 1947 and 1950 in the *āśrama* at Banaras.

In the last years, Mā's followers changed. The constantly growing neo-rich middle class acquired an influence through their wealth which was not always good. A few among the *sādhus* who were not deeply enough rooted as monks were greedy for money and power.

It was clear that Mā suffered on account of this in the last two or three years, but she did not consider it her task to intervene with drastic measures, particularly because there was an organization set up in which such things were handled by experienced *sādhus*. Mā's sphere of work was concerned with the soul of her followers.

The result of large donations meant that new *āśramas* were established, temples were built and larger and larger functions organized. It meant a growing physical burden for Mā, without consideration of her age, and less opportunity for intense spiritual work with her individual followers. About two or three years before her last journey, Mā said to me: "Only a very few of these people, who come in such numbers, speak about God. Too many of them expect me to help them to get their worldly aspirations fulfilled." (People were convinced that Mā, thanks to her *śakti*, could work any kind of miracle.)

I can say from my personal experience that right up to the end of her life, Mā, regardless of the pressures of external obligations, continued her spiritual work. She left her body, after she had fasted for four months, on 27 August, 1982 during her stay in the *āśrama* in Kishenpur (Dehradun), her first *āśrama* outside Bengal.

Chapter 2

Prelude

It was the summer of 1962, when I came from Afghanistan and wanted to travel through India for a few weeks. Sheer coincidence brought me straightaway to Mā. I came to know in the meantime that Mā is regarded as the most significant saint in present–day India. She is known by the name Ānandamayī Mā. Its meaning is: "The mother who is imbued with bliss." I met her in her *āśrama* in Kankhal near Hardwar.

I have recorded the spontaneous impressions of my first meeting with Mā for my Indian friends. I am reproducing them here in excerpts.

". . . It was towards evening, when we - about fifteen people had gathered with me– were conducted to the roof garden of the *āśrama.* When Mā came, I had no choice to decide, whether it would be against my views to kneel before a human being. "It" forced me on my knees. It can hardly be expressed in words what I experienced in the next few minutes. I can explain it only in imageries. Say, something like this: imagine that a tree – a beautifully well-grown beech tree - is quietly approaching you. What would happen to you? 'Am I mad', you would ask yourself, 'or am I dreaming?' Finally you would have to know that you have entered here a dimension of reality that is completely unfamiliar to you. Well, that was exactly my situation.

As far as we know, it is in the nature of a tree that it is rooted to a particular spot. According to Western thought, man's nature is determined by the fact that he has an "ego". Here I suddenly saw a person in front of me, of whom I at once felt that she has no "ego", and just because of this, she was not less, but more than all other persons I have ever met in my life.

Later, I read some comments on the subject and learnt that absence of an ego is an essential characteristic of a *jīvanmukta*, of the one "who is redeemed in his lifetime". At that time, I did not know anything more about all this than what I saw with my own eyes. I tried to record in my diary what I had experienced. It is said there: ". . . This human being belongs to the category of *Mātā Gaṅgā* and *Pitā Himālaya*. Mā has the superpersonal personality that speaks to us, when we stand near an ocean or at the foot of a mountain. But what is talking to us there?"

For about ten minutes, Mā went slowly up and down on the opposite narrow side of the roof garden. Sometimes, she would stand still and observe the sky. It seemed that she was not aware of us. The evening clouds were reflected in her eyes. What I saw then, was beyond the sphere of rationality: the clouds, the woods, the peaks of the Himalayas entered this gaze, as if entering their abode. The moon which was reflected in a pool caused by the rains, was becoming tiny and pale. But Mā's eyes reflected the sky, as only an ocean reflects it; sisterly, of the same rank in the order of creation . . .

Later, she sat on the bed and talked to people. The alien, bewildering part of her existence faded, but it did not disappear completely even for a moment. One could try to forget it. Then, there sat between the pillows, a woman in a white *sārī* – I could have placed her in the midst of her fifties -, who carried a lively conversation, which was, at the same time, pleasant and forceful. Sometimes, she was engrossed in deep thought sometimes, she would suddenly burst into a laughter that had something of a storm sometimes, her eyes would sparkle with a friendly delight while bantering others.

How should I describe her face to you? There are millions of faces like that in India. Its contours correspond to a full, regular oval shape. Every individual feature is powerful, accurately marked out (there is no vagueness) and harmoniously fitted into the whole. The classical tripartition between the forehead, nose and the mouth/chin is well-balanced. The eyes below the strong, uncurved brows have a form which is called almond-shaped. The iris is presumably black, but often gives the impression that it is peculiarly bright. There is a shadow over the eye-lids which have a certain heaviness. The shadow is dark also under the eyes. The nose is straight, strong and "right" in its length. The mouth is curved and clearly marked. I found that a great clarity is expressed in it, and that it has the gift of knowing rightly when to talk and when to remain silent. There were moments, when Mā's face suddenly became the face of Buddha: narrow-eyed, full of equanimity, concealing the wisdom of the chiliads, representing an unfathomable Asia. But at the same moment, Mā was again a beautiful, motherly creature, who could be distinguished from many mothers of the West only by the colour of her skin.

You see that it is beyond me to give more than a couple of hints. I shall give perhaps the last one: while I was trying to portray Mā, I hesitated, when I wrote the word "strong". In a certain sense, her features are anything else but strong, when we understand by it something that is rude. Her features are rather delicate. Let me say: this face, like the whole personality, is simultaneously delicate and strong. She does not have that delicateness which results from a physical shortcoming or anemia, showing weakness. Her delicateness is rooted in the openness of the beautiful, strong body to the spirit: vitality, nimbleness and charm interwoven by the spirit and made transparent for the numinous.

I decided to cancel all my other plans of travelling and to go to Kishenpur where Mā was expected in the next few days. There she used to keep herself free in forenoons and evenings for a public *darśana,* mostly for about two hours. She was then constantly exposed to the onslaught of her worshippers. Several times, she took care that I could sit in her proximity in spite of the crowd. I felt like an enthusiastic music-lover: while he is open to the magic of the sound with all his heart and soul, he still follows the way the instruments are conducted. Mā's presence filled me with irresistible and mysterious fascination, as I have never experienced with any other person before.

And yet, I clearly saw the utter mundane in her. I saw, how her eyes lit up, when a friendly familiar face emerged from amongst those who threw themselves on their knees before her. I saw, how she was suffering because of the heat. I felt a gentle repulsion, when she withdrew her feet from an importunate devotee. I observed (informed by a woman staying in the *āśrama* about the situation), how she enjoyed making a pun. I saw, how she sent away a Parsi woman, who wanted a miraculous cure: "Take your husband to a good physician and pray for the peace of his and your soul." In this moment, she appeared sad and almost merciless. I saw also, how fatigue was expressed in her attitude and in the shadow of her face which was becoming deeper, before she got up and fought her way back through the crowd.

The Christian painters of the early Middle Ages had a simple and effective way of expressing saintliness, when they wanted to paint a scene from the life of Jesus or a saint: they painted the figures against the background of gold. This gold expressed the inexpressible mystery of saintliness. One who as a painter wanted to bring the news of a saint, was not allowed to let his brush become loquacious. He could only silently point out to the mystery of the shining background.

I am feeling like these painters. What can be described of Mā, is what is generally human, familiar. I do not have any medium of expression for the other, the numinous. But I could also use a similar cipher like the painters. Sometimes, I believed to have seen a beam of light coming from her eyes. But just at that time, I was also pained to feel that

I was blinded. I knew that, if only I were more able to see– I would recognise her whole being in this light. I felt it, however, albeit not seeing it, and I registered its effect in the complete peace which gradually gained power over me.

The mystery should remain untouched behind its veil, But I may perhaps try to come closer to it by a couple of steps. I felt that this light must have a connection with Mā's selflessness. It comes from the eternal fountain of all that exists, and it flows through Mā because it is not turned away in her by the opaque web of egoism, which we all carry – more or less closely – within us. Mā's secret power lies in her being, and not in her action. She is not what she is because she does good things. Her life happens as pure being, reposing in itself.

Probably, I should say: being resting in God. To that extent, Mā meets our highest idea of what is good. When I sat among people at her feet, and nothing happened except that we were looking at her, I felt the presence of the Holy, many times more powerfully than ever in a solemn ritual of a church. I believed, I understood that the divine presence is indispensable for all religious rite, as a gesture of wistful yearning for the one who cannot be compelled to come. But where the Holy *is*, even the prayers become silent. The religious ritual extinguishes in the mysterious presence of the divine reflection.

The filled void of this looking (at Mā) is a strange experience which cannot be shared: seeing with closed eyes, and yet also with eyes wide open. Many times, I become aware of something which can be hardly understood by an occidental brain, particularly when one is thinking: I do not know how Mā understands herself. Certainly not, as we would express it, like a man, in whom the divine spark shines particularly brightly, for she lives in union with *Brahman*. Thus, I believed to realize that Mā – in whom the Holy was incarnated right in front of us – agreed with us in a reverential contemplation of the Holy that she *is* herself.

There is a clumsy sentence in my diary: Sometimes one gets a feeling that Mā worships herself. But this attitude is something absolutely superpersonal!

This summer, I had Mā's *darśana* only three to four times. Thereby the numinous did not diminish, but, to my surprise, something changed basically: the initial feeling that one has got into a complete alien dimension of reality became reversed. I now felt that I actually discovered for the first time the true – man's very own – reality. I saw more and more clearly: what distinguishes me from Mā is what distinguishes the light of a candle from that of the sun. This was really an enormous discovery.

I remember Mā's last evening in Kishenpur. It was to me like a great festival. I saw her standing in the yard of the *āśrama* distributing *prasāda.* Not solemnly, but smiling like a mother whose greatest happiness lies in quenching the hunger of her children. It was, as if she was distributing herself, and she did it with hundred hands. Never have I seen the beauty of the immortal shining more purely in the mortal flesh.

This is, on the whole, my report of the year 1962.

I again started my journey in 1963 to live for several months in Mā's proximity.

The following notes in my diary beseech the reader to accompany me in this venture. It will be inundated by the same wealth of strange impressions which made me afraid at the beginning that I would never succeed in scenting even only an iota of the spiritual base of the world into which I have forced my way. I ask the reader to follow me patiently into the confusing, incomprehensible, not only stage, but at times disconcerting of that world, although this adventure will bring him very little "book learning" at the beginning, or perhaps no "book learning" at all. Hinduism has in its doctrine, in its paths of salvation and in the forms of its cult, a polymorphism, which a Westerner can hardly imagine. Only a very small aspect of it will come into picture here.

What I hope to communicate, by way of hints, is my encounter with the numinous in a non-Christian realm. Without my giving a special attention to it, it appears that my notes also offer a certain clue as to which phenomena appear, when an ancient great religion comes face to face with the conditions of the modern age.

The only form in which I can attempt such an account are diary-notes. Only in this way can also what is inchoate, tentative, erroneous and even the ill-feelings, in short, the inadequacy of the one who has ventured into this encounter, get a chance to speak and explain what he has experienced.

Thus I request my reader not to expect more than what such notes can offer. Notes of this type – if their diary-form is not distorted – can only gradually get their dimension in depth; at first one is completely preoccupied in finding one's way into the phenomena. Finally, I ask my reader not to get irritated by my notes which reflect the constant change of my opinion between an unquestionable openness with respect to the numinous and an attempt of an intellectual examination of what was experienced.

A last remark: it seldom emerges from the following account, and if at all, then only by way of a hint, how high are the demands which such an undertaking makes on the physical resistance and preparedness for a sacrifice. Besides, may everyone, who perhaps thinks that a religious tourism is enticing, know that the psychic pressures are enormous for the one who is "caste-less" and who is living together with orthodox Hindus.

Chapter 3

Alien World in the Āśrama

(*September 30, 1963*)

Starting from Bombay, I have traversed the subcontinent in the west-east direction – my train took more than forty hours for the journey –, then spent half a night on the railway station of Banaras, finally boarding a passenger train which took me to my destination for the present.

A young coolie put my luggage on his head at the rural station of Vindhyachal. "Are you going to the *āśrama?*", he asked me and scarcely waited for my nod.

It is early morning. Our path is hardly fit for walking on it. I go behind the boy; his wiry legs stride swiftly. After a while, we cross a highway. A caravan of camels is moving on it. Shapeless boxes are swinging on the backs of the beasts of burden; snootily, they are looking down upon us. Women are on their way to the next bazar. They are carrying flat baskets with cowpats on their heads. They are used for burning.

The way begins to climb gradually. Before it enters the wilderness, we come to a big tank, an artificial pond, near which several Brāhmaṇas, partially standing in water, are saying their morning prayers. The coolie stands still under a tree. Without putting down the luggage on his head, he takes out a thorn from the sole of his right foot, then he continues to walk laughing. I am finding it difficult to breathe, but he does not show even the slightest fatigue, albeit carrying a heavy burden on his head.

We go through a sparse jungle: old, mighty, projecting trees and low shrubs. Birds of different hues are chirping on the branches, monkeys are falling from a tree and jumping over the path, and a naked shepherd boy is driving his goats in front of him. The broad stream of the Ganges is flowing through the plains behind us: blue with yellow-grey sandy banks and many bays. Small fishermen's boats are drifting in the midst of the river.

The *āśrama* which was built in 1936 is on the other side of the mountain from where one can see the Ganges. The *āśrama* is small and two-storeyed and has almost no walls. There is a verandah of arcades around the ground floor, and on the first floor, there is only a lattice which encloses the verandah. There is a small garden behind the main building with a few simple bungalows for the accommodation of *svāmīs* and guests. The kitchen is between the first and the second bungalow: a shed with a roof and a cemented forecourt.

Even from a distance, I see Mā standing on the verandah in the upper storey. Without stirring, she is observing a family of monkeys which is searching for fruits on the top of a tree. When she notices me, she nods to me laughing. The modest ceremony is disturbed by two monkeys which are quarrelling and shrieking. Finally, the weaker one flees with a fruit, as big as an apple, in its paw. Mā follows it with her eyes and makes a gesture of eating. Then she looks at me and asks, "Are you hungry?"

I am not accommodated in the premises of the *āśrama*, but in a bungalow which can be reached in fifteen minutes by daylight. It is on the opposite side of the hill. There is a deep well midway between the two; several women draw water from it for the *āśrama*. They have to do this daily for many hours. They transport it in earthern pitchers on their heads.

Who knows how long my bungalow was not occupied? Hot and musty air greets me from it. There is a thick dust on the crumbling furniture. But I am happy, I have a cot. I do not need anything else.

There is a "bathroom" next to the bedroom, a cemented place in which there are a rusted brass bath-tub and two buckets. A woman comes in the morning and fetches water for me from the well. She lives in a village situated on the other side of the railway station. She squats patiently in front of the house till I come out. The water is yellow-grey and is full of "fish". I do not have an opportunity of boiling it; the cook in the *āśrama* has enough work, hence I don't want to ask him to do it. So I adjust myself to my thirst, because I don't like to drink such a dirty sludge. One gets a mug of tea in the *āśrama* every morning and evening. I shall see that I can manage with it.

I brave thirst for three days. The heat is unbearable and the food is hot. On my third evening in the *āśrama*, I find out by chance that there are two varieties of water in the *āśrama*: dirty water, which I also have in the bungalow for washing, and clear water which is brought from a well in the valley. My thirst is overcome. A typical small gaff: A guest coming from the West cannot imagine that there are in this country "two varieties of water", and the natives cannot imagine that they should make him aware of it.

My bungalow has one defect: I have to share it with a very prosperous family of rats. These companions in the house scarcely allowed me to sleep during my first night here. They romped about squeaking in a cupboard in which brass dishes were kept. When I forced it open in the morning, about twelve to fifteen rats jumped towards me. From now on, they were moving on the premises eating my soap and made penny-big holes in my tubes, cartons and clothes. Only after a few days, when I had a neighbour, an elderly army officer, who spends his holidays in Mā's vicinity, they emigrated for a while. My neighbour told me that they cheerfully nibbled at the hair on his head, probably because he is used to applying oil to it.

Mā's *āśramas* are run by the so-called "Shree Shree Anandamayee-Sangha", a Society founded in Banaras in

1950 in which her followers have joined together. Their task consists of extensive religious publicity, establishment and management of *āśrama*-schools and arranging for medical ambulances for the poor.

Everything in the *āśrama* is related to the presence of Mā. It gets its full significance only when Mā is physically present there. Then it is really transformed into a centre of radiation with a lightning speed and its influence reaches far into the land. In the first hour after her arrival, usually hundreds of people gather; they would like to see her. When she departs, everything becomes just as quickly silent again.

Āśramas have usually only a few constant occupants. Many of these houses furnished spartanly, as if, hibernating periodically, till Mā comes back; then they overflow with life and prove always to be too small. Mā has not established her own order in the narrower sense of the term. A few men and women who have renounced the world and live like monks and nuns have joined her. Many of them even decades ago. A few of them were *sādhus,* others got their monkhood only after their coming together with Mā. All of them are often on the move with Mā for a relatively long period, while they stay in the *āśramas* during the rest of the time. The distinction between these monks and laymen among Mā's associates is not so clear. One meets again and again men and women who are outwardly not different from *sādhus* and nuns and yet live only for a set period in the *āśrama.* Many for years, others for months or weeks or in the twilight of their life. Many of them have left behind them their full life in a family or in following some occupation (or both). Many girls are in the *āśrama* to be prepared by Mā for their duties, so that they will be a religious focal point of their future families.

The *āśrama* in which I am staying is considerably smaller than most of the others. Mā retires to this usually to rest here for a couple of days after tiresome participation in big public functions for several months. She protects the location of the house – which is not easily accessible – from the otherwise usual crush of her friends and devotees. Only about twenty people accompany her, mostly monks and *Brahmacāriṇīs,* for whom the peaceful atmosphere of the place is welcome, to become engrossed in reading holy books or in meditation. I see her sitting under the shadow of old trees often for hours together. "Mā's girls" (I would say: her nuns) assemble twice daily for a *kīrtana.*

Panuda, the elected secretary of the "Anandamayee Sangha", a former teacher of an *āśrama*-school in Almora, tells me the story of the *āśrama* here. He – in contrast to the monks – is not forbidden to speak to women: "A Brāhmaṇa acquainted with Mā had bought the land decades ago, to get a hut built so that he could withdraw here to meditate. Much before, the English had excavated here a small, insignificant temple and then did not bother very much about the place.

When Mā came here for the first time and there was nothing else except the hut in the midst of the sparse jungle, she went around like in dream. She was overcome by the mighty visions of the sacred past of the place. Mā recognized, what none had understood so far: that this mountain had drawn worshippers to itself for thousands of years. Like an invisible divining rod, she paced out the land and said, "Dig here and here and here."

We had no right to take up systematic excavations. But after digging at a few places, we came across the ruins of a piece of architecture, whose age we could not determine. It took quite a long time before we could convince the officials of the government, that it would be worthwhile to continue the excavation work here. A diviner, who fathoms the holiness of a place is also for the Indian archaeologists an unscientific phenomenon. Finally, the excavation work was started, and they discovered the ruins of several temples from many centuries lying over one another. The oldest must have been 2500 years old. Also many idols of deities were found. They are now in a museum in Lucknow. Mā had told us, where we would find them.

I sit in the forenoon for hours on the roof of the *āśrama* and look at the jungle which belongs to monkeys around this time. It rustles in the top of the trees before they appear. They must have slept, so quiet was it there. Suddenly I see that some branches start shaking, and the first one jumps down from the tree onto a bush, followed by the second, the third. They always come in big groups. Sometimes they are twenty, thirty. The old ones move solemnly. They are quite strong fellows with long tails which reach almost to their heads, if they bend them upwards over the back. Their face and the paws are black, the stomach is yellowish and the remaining body is grey. The revered progenitors and progenitrixes of mankind settle down, to muse, on the ruins of ancient temples which were scattered around. Those of the families which are in their best years must have been suffering from an unsatiable hunger. They squat in the bushes, and I see their paws moving to one or the other direction with the speed of wind, while they pluck the berries and put them into their mouths.

While the old ones are not putting in any effort to eat, the young ones are too playful for it. In any case, the youngest don't have to do it. They cling to the breasts of their mothers. But all the little ones, scarcely bigger than cats, do nothing but mischief: swing on the branches, chase one another, jump from one stone onto the other, balancing themselves on the ruins and playing with their own tails.

The *svāmīs* in Mā's surroundings are in different age groups. A couple of them are young, approximately in their mid-thirties. None of them appears to be one of those who choose God because they are afraid of the world. They are conspicuously tall, mostly strong, with intelligent faces; their movements are not hampered and their smile is unforced. I hear that Mā has guided them in religion from their childhood and has taken care of their general upbringing and education. At times, they are supposed to observe strict asceticism. It is a part of their statutes that they are allowed to talk to women only in emergency, and that too, without looking at them.

Svāmī Paramānanda impresses me the most from among the elderly monks. I have met a very few people in my life who were really free. He is one of them. He comes along cheerfully and calmly in his long, brownish shirt, which has no straps and which reaches up to his ankles. He has a swing in his shoulders that can be hardly noticed, showing that he is both mentally and physically relaxed. His face is more gentle than strong, wise and always ready to smile. He has an expression in his eyes which I don't see in any other man here. One gets a feeling that these eyes observe their object, no doubt, carefully, but perceive at the same time what exists deep within this object. It could be said in a figurative sense that Svāmījī, as he is called by all (the other *svāmīs* are called by their names), serves Mā like the prime minister his king. He conducts all her "business" for her.

C., an intelligent girl with a reserved expression particularly attracted my attention from among the *brahmacāriṇīs* who belong to Mā's regular retinue. The way she behaves with Mā has a combination of reverential love and a matter-of-factness which I like. P. is the name of the girl who is entrusted with the task of being the leading singer. She must be in her late twenties. She looks miserable, but her face is beautiful in a spiritual sense. She is all eyes.

Mā's mother Didimā is 90 years old. There is not even a gram of flesh on her face. Her head is clean-shaven. When I saw her for the first time, I could not know whether I had an old man or an old woman in front of me. But: what liveliness in her eyes; how much kindness, when someone asks for her advice; what determination, when she gives orders. I observe all this from a respectful distance. I am told that Didimā shies away from contact with the foreigners. This has to do with the concept of *Juta. Juta* means impure in a religious sense. If an orthodox Brāhmaṇa becomes *juta* by infringing the rule, he must subject himself to complicated procedures of purification. These ideas are also based on the rules which have to be observed before taking food. They also apply to the other realms of life. Women, e.g. are *juta* during their periods. Obviously, the danger of contamination is particularly great for the Brāhmaṇas, as soon as they come in contact with something that a caste-less person has taken to his mouth.

Keshavananda usually eats with me. He comes from a Parsi-family, and is, therefore, caste-less. While most of those who are present eat in the covered verandah in front of the guest bungalow, both of us are served food on a platform in the sparse shade of a thin small tree. Whenever the sun scorches unmercifully, I put an umbrella over my shoulder. Our table conversation consists of our nodding to each other, before we sit down, as far as possible away from each other. The *svāmī* is observing at the moment his period of silence. He sits there in his yellow-brown habit and cowl of the same material, bending down low over his leaf-plate and slowly clears away – eating with his hand like all of us – the gigantic mountain of rice which is his only daily food.

According to the precepts of orthodox Hinduism, those belonging to upper castes – which comprise most of Mā's associates – are not allowed to eat under the same roof with the caste-less like Keshavananda and myself. We have then to purify ritually, the place where we were sitting, with cowdung and water. It is important for me not to hurt anyone by disobeying these orders. Besides, we eat from leaves which, stitched together with twigs, serve as plates. Only the right hand is used while eating. We do not have cutlery. Water is brought to us in earthern tumblers which are thrown away after they are used once. The food consists mostly of rice, *dāl* (a liquid mush of lentil-like seeds) and different vegetables. It is generously spiced – I carefully sort out the chillies – but tasty and satisfying.

Cooks here are not cooks in our sense. The cook who prepares food for Mā is not allowed to eat anything before he has cooked for Mā and she has eaten. He follows the strict rules of ritualistic purification. Also the food for the other occupants of the *āśrama* has to be cooked only by a Brāhmaṇa. This activity belongs to the realm of a religious service.

When recently I said to one of Mā's girls, "It is a pity, I understand very little of what Mā says", she replied, "Mā once said to a French couple which had complained about this: 'Please do not worry. A sleeping infant drinks from the breast of its mother without understanding it. So you also pick up a great deal of what I say, without understanding my language. Truth is communicated to an open mind, without needing the power of understanding being switched on. As soon as it is expressed, it has a mysterious power which is continuously effective.' "This corresponds exactly to what I feel at times.

I was sitting this afternoon for an hour in the verandah in front of the door of Mā's room before she got up. When she came out – she had probably been sleeping –, she appeared to me to be terribly old and ill. Her face was pale, almost grey-green, her eyes were dull and quite without expression. Three minutes later, she appeared again in her door: firm, with a smiling face, sparkling with intensity, a dynamic centre of energy, discharging itself in lightning, emitting joy like fiery sparks. What a transformation!

For a while, she went up and down among us as she often does it here. I only wish, I could describe this "as". "With a spring in her steps" would be wrong, because it does not express the composure and dignity of her walking. I would like to call that element "royal" – but hesitatingly, for which of these epithets have not been worn out? –, or should I say "powerful"? But I must quickly hasten to add: the power that is displayed here, is, at the same time, graceful, not rigid and brutal, but elastic and lovely.

Later, Mā sits in the verandah on a lower wooden step, facing the door of her room. Three old men from the neighbourhood are waiting for her there; they have come to speak to her. The oldest is blind. We others sit down on her right and left. I am sitting about twenty centimetres away from Mā; there is nobody between us.

Mā sits there in the posture of meditation. I see her face only from one side. Her posture expresses a collected calmness. She does not stir for a long time. Suddenly, she turns her head towards me, and our eyes meet. Her eyes are focussed on me like the rays of a searchlight. The man seated diagonically behind me, tells me later, "I looked at my watch, because it seemed me endless. It must have lasted for about five minutes." What happens there is for me not to be understood in terms of time, but it has a quality that I have experienced again and again since my childhood: it is something that is beyond time. Without batting an eyelid, Mā's glance is focussed on me, penetratingly, shining like the great, serene light of the sun in the evening. Its peace is imparted to me. I feel, that doors have opened on their own. A powerful beam of pure light enters my heart.

Mā suddenly looks away, and at the same moment, jokes about one of the girls who with a grim face is knotting a bag. I have always observed that the transition from the highest spiritual intensity to the humdrum, indeed to something that is banal, passes with Mā in fleeting seconds. One has to be watchful, otherwise the precious moment melts away into what is triviality, without any transition. I think, I know, why this transition is without any break. For us the moments of illumination, of contact with the spirit, are precious and rare. Mā lives in the medium of spirit or of light. It is as natural to her as our day-to-day existence to us that she shares with us. But she does not live in two worlds, the one of light and the other of our materiality: for her the two are inseparably united.

There is something more to add: the sense of the

supranatural in Mā's glance this afternoon. What it conveyed to me, did not appear to have come from her human heart, but from a centre of power beyond it; it uses this heart only for a transit, as a transformer. It assumes there a quality for which our receivers are prepared.

Of course, the occurrence was extremely subtle. This transformation of the spirit into "a communicable spirit" as it takes place in Mā, is an achievement of love, like her life itself. The light she receives, she transmits to us, adapting it to our power of vision, because what she desires, is nothing but our "enlightenment": This is the goal of her life.

Exactly this was that my consciousness found observed when Mā looked at me today: the completely suprapersonal quality of what was conveyed to me in her look, and the loving gesture of giving. One of Mā's girls explained to me a similar situation thus: "Mā is the mother who says, 'God has given me a barn full of rice, and I have prepared food for you from it. Eat, so that you will become strong."

Later, when Mā had got up, I went after her and thanked her with a silent *praṇāma.* She almost ignored it. One who thanks lives in a world of duality in which something is given and something is received. This distinction is meaningless for the one who lives in unity. When I looked up, her eyes appeared to ask: Does one also thank oneself?

After a couple of rounds around the verandah, Mā goes and sits again on a low stool in front of her room-door. The three old men are still waiting for her to speak to them. She at once talks bubbling with enthusiasm and with great passion. In a pause, I succeed in asking someone what she has just said. And this is the answer: Mā had turned to the oldest among them and asked him, "How have you used your life, *Pitājī?* Every breath, in which we don't think of God, is wasted. It is an incredible chance that we are born as human beings. We can approach God because we are human beings." And to the others who are sitting around her: "Ask yourself, what are you doing with your time. We forget so easily that not a single day can be called back. They fade away without our noticing it. Suddenly, we are old and too tired to put in any effort. God is not the work of our old age, when we have nothing else to do; He is the work of our life, and we must use our full energy for it. Anyone who has not yet begun, must start today. Now at once.'' She looks around slowly in the circle. Suddenly she jumps up and disappears into her room.

October 13, 1963
Last night, I escaped from the rats to the roof of our bungalow. I wanted to sleep there on my blanket, but I could not think of sleeping: The sky is of such overwhelming beauty that one cannot shut one's eyes. As I was lying there, I thought: If you now stand on your toes and stretch out your arms, you will be able to touch the stars. Many of them are so near that one thinks that they are hanging from the tree-tops. Here it is evident that they are shining bodies and not just points of light.

There is constant movement in the jungle. I ask myself whether monkeys are moving about in the night; there is rustling in many trees, as if the monkeys are jumping about. The wind causes a gentler rustling. Perhaps, the goats are still there. I hear a cracking sound in the undergrowth. Or are there wild animals? Animals whose names I don't know. I only wish, I could see them. Sometimes I hear a strange wailing from afar, like crying of a child. Sometimes there is barking, loud and angry. Then at once a second barking in reply or a chorus. Probably jackals. It is quiet on the roof. Here, too there are creatures, but I do not see them; they are too tiny. I hear only the gentle scraping of infinitely small feet.

I like to stay awake here. It helps to form a mutual trust between the strange landscape and myself. I allow myself to be completely and fully taken up by it and dream that I am not any more different from the things which are at home here: trees, animals, stones and human beings.

People in the *āśrama* were talking this afternoon about a tiger which was prowling around in the vicinity. As I was returning around midnight on the narrow jungle-path from the *āśrama* to my hut, an animal suddenly roared close behind me; I had never heard its voice. I was terrified, and of course, I at once thought of the tiger. A young *brahmacārī* who was accompanying me said calmly, "You don't have to fear. One who is a friend of Mā is under her protection. Where we are with her, even a tiger sings a *kīrtana.*"

I have already mentioned above that events in Mā's life, as well as her utterances, have been recorded since many years (albeit with interruptions). I have found a report in these records today. It tells something interesting about Mā, in fact, about her being nestled into a cosmic understanding, perhaps I should say, into a cosmic love. I gather from many descriptions that Mā has a very sensible and lively connection with the work of cosmic powers – their play in nature. The endless turbulence of the sea, the unbridled raging of the storm, the burning sky in the evening – such phenomena must have often aroused in her ecstatic jubilation, also then, when all others were frightened by their power. Now everything that is emotional is withdrawn into a sheer quietude. But one feels the vibration of an intimate dialogue with the One which is revealed in the play of powers.

Except in the extremely rare moments of a mystic *union,* nature, for us, is always "the other life" that is opposed to our human existence. Nature is "the same life" for Mā. Everything is life "from the self". There is nothing except this self. The distinction between matter (*prakṛti*) and spirit (*puruṣa*) is dissolved in the self in which matter lives. The spiritual-corporeal gesture in which this *advaita* finds its concrete expression, can appear to us to be very strange, archaic, i.e. "primordial". But an enormous weight of power is felt in this primordialness. It is the basis of a spiritual superstructure which is striving for the highest subtilization.

Here, thus a report from the year 1959:

"... Mā was travelling in a car from Kanpur to Lucknow. Somewhere near Unnao, Mā suddenly pointed out from the window and said: 'See, Didi (D. is one of the oldest followers of Mā), what an enchanting little village. Are the trees not beautiful?' Didi had seen no trees and found nothing unusual about the village. Mā made the driver turn back. As soon as the village was reached, she got out and quickly went to a particular house. 'Where are then the trees', asked Didi. But instead of replying, Mā shouted over her shoulders, 'Bring all the garlands of flowers and the baskets with the fruits from the car'."

When Didi returned laden with them, she saw a small lake and two fresh trees growing side by side on the bank. One of them was a banyan-tree and the other was a margosa. Mā ran towards the trees and began to embrace and stroke them with such an affection that we stood there dumb-founded and extremely astonished staring at the unusual scene. While she was pressing her forehead and cheeks repeatedly against the stems of the trees, she said, 'It is good, you have called "this body" (Mā often talks in this fashion), so that it can see you.'

There was nothing conspicuous at all about the trees. Gradually, the villagers began to gather near the lake. The man who had planted the trees was not there, but his wife came, a shy thing with a veil, but she could not understand what was happening. Mā said to her, 'Take good care of the trees, and make this place, the place of your praying.' Then she decorated the trees affectionately with the garlands and distributed the fruits to the villagers. Besides, she said to the woman, 'I have made you my mother, and this here – pointing to herself – is your little daughter.' While taking leave of the trees once more almost affectionately, she gives the name *Hari* (name of Viṣṇu) to the margosa (*Azadirachta indica*) and *Hara* (name of Śiva) to the banyan (*Ficus bengalensis*).

She once more comes back to the episode after we continued to drive: 'How peculiar that these two trees drew this body to them like human beings. The car was driving fast, but it was as if they had grabbed me with their strong arms and drawn me to themselves.'

I found today the following in an *āśrama*-publication on the three most important paths of Hinduism on the way to salvation: "Mā says, it is true, that there are as many ways of enlightenment as there are people, but the devotees, who consider themselves to be her pupils, follow most commonly three ways of knowledge. They correspond to the three paths of Yoga, viz. *Bhakti-Yoga, Karma-Yoga* and *Jñāna-Yoga.*

Mā says the following on *Bhakti-Yoga,* which could also be called Yoga of God's love: 'The *sādhaka* (the believer who performs *sādhana,* i.e. takes a spiritual path which is supposed to lead him to enlightenment) chooses a deity, to whom he feels attracted and whom he makes his beloved (*iṣṭa*). When he begins to pray in front of an image (*vigraha*), which embodies for him the presence of his beloved, he reaches in the course of his exercises a condition in which he perceives the *iṣṭa* in whatever direction he looks.

He will know as the next: All other deities are in my *iṣṭa.* He not only sees that his *iṣṭa* is everyone's *iṣṭa,* but that everything that exists is in his *iṣṭa* and his *iṣṭa* resides in all deities and in everything. Then he says to himself: "Are not all the forms and ways of existence I perceive, the expression of my beloved God? For, there is nothing besides him. He is smaller than the smallest and greater that the greatest."

Trees, flowers, leaves, mountains, rivers and oceans: the universal form of the One pervades them all. He, who has many forms, constantly creates and destroys these forms. He is the One whom I worship. The *sādhaka* becomes aware of the constant transformation of all forms and ways of existence to the extent to which he has grown into the knowledge of truth which becomes more and more perfect and more and more extensive, and he will realize his oneness with all these changing forms. As ice is nothing else but water, the beloved God – although he was seen by the *sādhaka* in the form of a personal God (say, Kṛṣṇa), – is without form and attributes (i.e. he is the *Brahman*). Once I have known this, I do not then ask myself the question about a manifestation of my *iṣṭa.* I see him everywhere, and I see myself in him. For, finding the beloved is finding, discovering oneself, that God is my own, completely identical with myself, my innermost self, the self of my self . . .'

Karma-Yoga is the Yoga of sacrifices, rites and good works. It expects from a *sādhaka* that he, whatever he does, regards as his service, he renders to God. He has, therefore, to do his work punctually and faithfully and he should be completely disinterested in the success of his work. Mā says, 'If your *Guru* asks you to do something, and you have taken great pains in doing this work, but if you are called in the last moment before completing it, and someone else finishes the work and is praised and thanked for it, this situation must leave you completely unmoved. Then alone, you are really practising *Karma-Yoga.*' This Yoga is also a path to will power. It is true that good works as such are important, because they serve a fellow being, but this point of view scarcely plays any role for a *sādhaka.* They may have a significance for him only as a way of sacrificing the ego in the service of God.

The path of *Jñāna-Yoga* – it could perhaps be called, the Yoga of the highest knowledge of *Brahman* – is, comparatively, very rarely followed. It is a way which, in a narrower sense, is regarded as a "path of self-realization", and corresponds to *Advaita-Vedānta.* Whereas the ego of a *bhakta* burns in the fire of love of God, the ego of a *Jñānī* melts in the fire of self-knowledge. A *sādhaka* who wants to approach the highest reality (*Brahman,* the highest self) spiritually, can only encircle it on the *neti-neti* way. He examines every idea which emerges in his consciousness to find out an answer to the question: 'What is *Brahman*?', and finds again and again that the object of his analysis lacks the character of highest reality.

He must realize again and again: *neti, neti*! [This (is) not (the *Brahman*), this (is) not (the *Brahman*)]. This is the method of finding the highest *Brahman* by eliminating, one after the other, all that is ephemeral, also, and above all, one's own self. Finally, the highest self is seen in the enlightenment, as identical with one's own self.

Mrs. Khanna who had come on a visit with her husband and two sons tells me about miracles. She is certainly everything else but naive, but with respect to miracles, does not feel disquieted by scepticism. The cook of Mā's *āśrama* in Delhi, with whom they were acquainted, gave them the account of the first miracle. Once he had prepared food for 100 people, but actually 500 turned up and wanted to eat. Finally, he eked out his provisions, as well as he could, and provided food for 200 people. Then he went to Mā, not knowing what to do: "What should I do? There are still 300 people who have not eaten?" Mā asked him to get the pot with the last *chapattis*. She put a piece of cloth over it and said, "So, now distribute." All people were fed on this day.

Any Christian will immediately think of the account of the miraculous multiplication of bread in the New Testament.

I have quarrelled in this connection with a young Swiss who is here only for a day. He calls all these things "nonsense" and denies himself the possibility of knowing their "sense" by tackling them with the categories of his primitive rationalism.

Mrs. Khanna tells me about another miracle. She was sitting in the *āśrama* in Almora at Mā's feet, while her husband was travelling by his car in the Himalayas. He had an accident there in which his companion had died. The car had fallen into a deep abyss. At the moment of the accident, Mā suddenly asked Mrs. Khanna, "What sort of chain are you wearing? Give it to me." It was a gold-chain with black stones, the one usually worn in India by women whose husbands are alive. Mā moved the chain from one hand to the other for a couple of times and then returned it to her. "Continue to wear it", she said. A little later, she suddenly said, "I am thinking of your husband." A telegram was received in the evening informing them about the accident and that Mr. Khanna was not hurt.

Almost all the people here tell me the stories of miracles they have experienced with Mā.

I would not call many of these episodes "miracles" perhaps because I take the so-called laws of nature in a much broader sense. We understand only a partial sphere of their effectiveness, and even this sphere to whose appearance we are accustomed, is full of "miracles". Is it not wonderful that I wake up every morning refreshed from a condition, in which my consciousness moves on paths which I comprehend only incompletely? I find that countless "natural" things are not less miraculous than telepathy and the like. And even when I hear people saying that gravity can be overcome in levitation, I do not think at once: that can only be a deceit or a suggestion. It also does not urge me into thinking that a particular wonderful miracle has taken place; the laws of nature are not applicable here. It would be sufficient for me to say that if this phenomenon has taken place, it does not go along with the scheme of our concepts of what is, according to our common understanding, possible. It proves that this scheme is too limited. But these are only key words, tiny steps into a vast field, and I have almost no idea about its nature.

I read the following yesterday in the report of a conversation Mā had with a *Mahātmā* with whom she was acquainted: "He came on a visit without informing anyone, and someone advised him that he should write in advance about his visit in future. On hearing this, one of them who also came along said, 'Mā, you are omniscient, why should we then announce our arrival?' Mā replied smiling, 'One should not make any claims in this mundane world which cross the limits of a natural experience. Is omniscience a part of this world?''

This suggests a radical rejection of men who want to see her doing miracles. But there are other reports, and many people, highly educated even in the Western sense, have testified that Mā has performed miracles and has later spoken about them with a casualness, when she was asked.

October 16, 1963
Śrī Kaviraj, who was formerly the Principal of the "Government Sanskrit College" in Banaras, has come today. He has a title which has been conferred on only a few leading men in the country: *Mahāmahopādhyāya.* Obviously, he is suffering as he walks with great difficulty with the help of a stick. For the first time, a gesture "hits" me, which I have often seen and which I have found to be more exaggerated than impressive. With a great effort, G. K. Kneels in front of Mā's empty bed and touches the floor with his forehead. An obeisance in front of an absently present deity.

G. K. has a round, almost bald head with a few white hairs over the temples. His eyelids are heavy and they are often closed. His mouth is broad and fleshy. He has a small moustache. His face has the expression of suffering. Perhaps of the past? When he opens his eyelids, his look has a distant gaze. Sometimes he is in a trance. But sometimes, he is extremely vigilant so that not even a speck of dust escapes his attention. Then he is as cool and objective as a physicist.

In the afternoon, a big mat is laid upon the cement-plinth on which I usually eat. We gather there, and G.K. answers questions. He speaks in a Bengali which is interspersed with Sanskrit in which English expressions also appear. I understand very seldom what he is talking about. When he waits for the questions, he sits there with closed eyes. But hardly has a question been put, the heavy head is lifted and a stern voice replies with a great precision. Sometimes, a cautious laughter comes out of the breast of the old man; then the expression on his face becomes mild for a moment. But the strict matter-of-factness returns quickly.

Mā is lying on a mat behind the scholar. She keeps her eyes shut almost during the whole period. Her face is relaxed, as if in a deep sleep. But again and again, she suddenly interrupts the conversation with a remark. All become silent sometimes after that. Even G. K. closes his eyes and comes "back" to himself only after some minutes, to interpret what Mā has said.

The evenings here are beautiful. We sit in Mā's room or the verandah in front of it. Even when I sit outside, I find a place from where I can see Mā. There is only moon-light on the verandah. A feeble petromax-lamp is burning in the room. Twenty to twenty-five people sit distributed over the verandah which surrounds the house. We seldom here someone whispering, probably most of them are meditating or praying. Many of them have a rosary in their hands. For the first time, I get here a feeling of fellowship. I generally feel that the individualistic element among the Hindus is much more pronounced than among us, but this may, in any case, refer only to religious life. Something that corresponds to the concept of community does not exist in traditional Hinduism. Everyone has his individual relationship with his *Guru*, and he goes on his path. One hardly finds temples which are meeting places of the community.

Yet the feeling of fellowship appears to be developing here. It is too dark to recognize the faces. Thus, everyone remains unperturbed within his own self, and yet knows that everyone's mind and soul have been opened onto a common focal point, but really again, in a very individual manner. Many of those who are with me here will now pray to Mā, as in the West where people pray to the Christian saints. I am not praying. I am also not trying to meditate, and even when I begin to reflect on a question, I soon get stuck. I keep myself quiet and take in something which is as mysterious as the beauty of a landscape, the flashing of a great idea or the magic of one's favourite music.

Mā lies stretched out on her bed, keeping quiet for a long time, only sometimes, gently talking to someone. Her presence fills us all. When I look at her, I comprehend more and more clearly that what fills us, has less to do with the body in this bed, than we think. In any case, it is nothing more than an instrument which conveys the melody that is played on it or a mirror that reflects our own image that we see in it.

I forgot to mention that I go to the roof of my bungalow to meditate there every morning between 5 and 5.30. I sit down facing the east and see how the sun rises. It appears to be suddenly emerging from the Gaṅgā where it makes a loop. At first, I see only the upper edge of a pale disc which gradually becomes full. When the orb of the sun climbs higher, it moves into a layer of mist in which it shines fiery red. Then there is broad purple streak on the Gaṅgā, and higher in the sky, which is almost white, the clouds of mist reflect the red light. Gradually the eastern sky turns orange and starts becoming pale. The sun turns into a mighty radiant eye into which we cannot look without becoming blind.

There, where the Gaṅgā is nearest to me, in the north, it remains awhile before the veil of dimness vanishes into light. The river now plain in front of me has an eerie pale and yellowish grey hue. Gaṅgā at this hour is the river of the dead. Millions of people have made a pilgrimage to its banks for endless generations with an intention of dying there. Its holy water has taken in the ashes of the whole generations of the dead. Grey and leisurely, it follows the night which gradually retreats westwards.

I try to reflect in myself the transformation in nature of which I am a part: the slow climb of the light from the night and dimness. But is it meditation?

Chapter 4

Banaras—Among the Hindus

October 19, 1963

Banaras: after the quietude of Vindhyachal it is a hurly-burly. We were moving in cars, but almost only with the speed of a pedestrian, and I was, as if benumbed, when we finally reached the *āśrama.* What a turmoil of people, cars, rickshaws, cows, camels and once more people, people and more people. An elephant, before which a cycle-rickshaw looks like a toy, was walking leisurely in the midst of the crowd swinging its trunk. If it were to lose its good mood. . .

My eyes are full of dust; there is a layer of sweat and dirt on my skin, and everything is sticking to the body. Waves of musty stink come from the side-lanes; gulleys of poverty swarming with undernourished children and scabby dogs. . .

We have to get out in the main street. A windy lane leads to the *āśrama.* But one has to take a deep breath here: the Ganges is as vast as the sea, calmly flowing and promising peace. The *āśrama* is directly on the bank. It is the end of the city here. There are only isolated houses on this side of the bank and then lowlands.

The building is in the form of a rectangle, which is open to the river. The longish main building running along the bank is four-storeyed. In front of every storey, there is a verandah from where one can step into the rooms. When I stand in the yard with my back to the river, there is on the left the *Kanyāpīṭha,* a residential school for religious education of girls coming from poor Brāhmaṇa families. Below, there is a small hall in the right wing. Above it, on the first floor, there are two temple rooms with a large verandah which projects over the yard like a balcony.

The Hindu-temples are not meeting places of communities, but houses of gods. There are assembly halls only in big temples, in places where pilgrims gather. Priests, the so-called *pūjārīs*, perform *pūjā* in the temples several times daily.

The god to whom the temple is dedicated is received, bathed, dressed and fed by the priest in this *pūjā* as a welcome and revered guest through symbolic actions. The God is then offered flowers, fruit and fragrant essences. Thus, the ceremony signifies gratitude for the God's coming down, and at the same time, supplication for his beneficent stay. The priest has to purify himself by saying certain prayers and drinking holy water to become fit to receive the divine guest. Then he performs the rite which is developed in several phases. At first the god is invoked, a seat is offered to him. Then his feet are washed. He gets milk and honey for bathing. The *pūjārī* offers him clothes and ornaments in the next phase, applies fragrant essences, pastes and incenses to the idol. Finally, rice is offered to him and flowers are strewn on his feet.

One of the temples belonging to the *āśrama* is dedicated to Śiva. There is a low platform with five small *liṅgas* of black agate. They surround a big *liṅga*. Two artlessly chiselled Śiva busts and a *Nandi* (a Bull, Śiva's mount) are placed behind this platform. Almost a life-size photo of Mā's deceased husband Bholānāth adorns the wall to the right of the altar. A *yogī* looks at me with his intelligent, kind eyes, his beard hanging down over his chest. God's bed is placed between this wall and the altar. This is found in many temples. It meaningfully completes the ceremony of receiving the divine guest which is performed in the *pūjā*. A bed must also be kept ready for a guest. It is about one metre in length in our temple; it is an exact replica of a comfortable bed with three round pillows which have silk covers of yellow colour. Even the mosquito-net was not forgotten.

Today, I observed a priest performing *pūjā*. He was sitting in front of the altar with the *liṅgas.* Around him, there were several baskets with fragrant pastes, a small dish containing boiled rice, joss sticks, a bell and a conch. God's arrival is announced with ringing of the hand-bell. A long, muffled tone, which is blown on the conch, indicates the end of the rite. The significance of all these things cannot be easily known, but each one of these sacred objects is a symbol. For example, certain leaves that are offered to the deity symbolize the garments.

I cannot follow the spiritual sequence of the ritual, but is it so important? I see the hand of the priest – it is small and thin – carefully taking a white flower from the basket, dipping it in a container with Gaṅgā-water and putting it on a copper plate. I see both his hands solemnly grasping a big, red hibiscus-flower, see, how his hands are raised to his forehead in a reverential greeting and how they place the flower on the *liṅga.* Later I see it drawing a wave line on the black agate with the fragrant paste, see, how water is collected with a small spoon from a copper incense boat and poured on the symbol of the God. Again and again, the hand takes flowers and leaves from the baskets– they are carefully selected, only the most precious ones are beautiful enough to be offered to the God. Again and again, both the hands are raised against the forehead, and for the duration of a long prayer the place is filled with silence. Only the smoke smelling of sandalwood rises up in circles over the glowing stick.

All this takes place gently, with devotion and with cautious, solemn movements. The priest celebrates the mysterious presence of God: Peace wafts to me in the fragrance of the joss sticks.

During my earlier visit to India, I had serious difficulty in understanding Śiva's symbol *liṅga* which has the form of phallus. It is supposed to express the creative power of deity. Now I can look at the thing unembarrassed. The symbol is clear. Outside the Hindu horizon of understanding one might be disturbed by the outer appearance and only see a stone. Looking at the Śivaliṅga a Hindu experiences the presence of God, His creative power. It is a secondary thought for his mind that the stone has the form of phallus.

Liṅga is depicted in conjunction with *yoni*, the female principle. The *yoni* has the form of a dish. *Liṅga* and *yoni* stand for the combination of both the creative principles in nature. They stand for the positive and the negative pole of a creative activity, and they are worshipped in popular Hinduism as father and mother of the universe (Śiva and Śakti). Esoterically, *yoni* in which *liṅga* is encased, symbolizes the reflecting medium, while *liṅga* stands for the divine light–being reflected *yoni*. According to Hindu thought, the whole creation emerges from this light.

One of Mā's girls translated today the conversation Mā had with a Christian priest who asked her about her attitude to Christianity:

> Mā (rendered not literally): "One can find everything in Christ. Even this little child is in him. Many people worship him as an *avatāra* of the highest Lord of the world. In whatever form one may worship God, this little child[1] welcomes him with joy. But there are devotees of Christ, who look down upon all other religions, as if they alone are a testimony to the truth of God. This is wrong."

The priest: "How many people are there who have attained self-realization?"

Mā: "They are many who are close to it. But there is only one among the millions who has attained it."

Priest: "Does Mā think that she has attained it?"

Mā laughs.

Priest: "When did you attain it?"

Mā: "When was I not?"

Priest: "As a Christian, it is my first duty to seek God, but it is equally important that I love my neighbour

1. "Little Child" is a term, which Mā often uses to speak of herself.

as I love myself. It is my duty to serve the poor. There is so much poverty in India. What does Mā think about it?"

Mā: "Hinduism teaches the same thing. To serve God in every human being, and it is, without doubt, a way to the purification of the soul."

Priest: "You say *a* way. For us, it is the only one. Are there other ways to perfection?"

Mā: "There are many. Service is only one of them."

Our *āśrama*-family from Vindhyachal has, in no time, grown twentyfold. I rarely see a familiar face. Mā has disappeared into a well-guarded room to be away for some time from the throng of people who are constantly waiting for her.

Yesterday, I met Śrī Gopinath Kaviraj. His house is in a small garden. As soon as the gate is closed behind one, one enters the realm of quietude which engulfs this unusual man in concentric circles, becoming more and more quiet. There are a stocky, windspent palm tree and overgrown bushes, covered with white flowers; a little fire on the terrace, stoked by a servant who points to the direction of the house-door without uttering a word. A high, dark passage, a steep staircase, everything is unadorned and austere. The study-room of the wise man is rather a cell. Around the bed, where he sits, there are books, periodicals and manuscripts piled on the top of one another. He points to a stool. "Be seated." But I sit down on the floor. With ease: silence for a minute. At last, he starts speaking about the article in which I have described my first meeting with Mā. A great, gentle praise. Again silence. This time broken by me. I ask whether I may explain to him, where I now situate myself in my journey. He nods and listens to me with his eyes half closed. Sometimes he smiles to suggest that he agrees with what I say.

When I tell him that I have basically no special urge to talk to Mā, he opens his eyes in astonishment. "That is fine", he replies gently, "Don't talk to her, observe her and look for contact beyond words.'' Then I ask him whether I should meditate, although I seem to lack talent for it. ''It would help you very much.'' Again silence for a while; finally, he asks me to come after a few days. He would then give me practical guidance. He folds his hands without a word, a distant smile, a scarcely noticeable bowing of the head. I am allowed to leave. After getting up, I stay on for a moment. This room with bare walls and a mountain of books is more friendly to me than even my own room. I feel that the wise man with his sparse silvery hair and with the heavy eyelids must have been my father once or would be my brother some time.

I feel, when I travel in a rickshaw through the crowded lanes, that everything I see around me does not happen outside me, but within me. The skin enveloping my body has expanded infinitely. It includes everything. I am suddenly reminded of the peculiar physical feeling I had when I saw Mā for the first time. I felt, as if my heart– a physical muscle in my breast– had grown to double its size.

This town is teeming with mendicants, ascetics and members of different sects and orders. The difference and colourfulness of their style is superb. Today, a mendicant was sitting next to me and waiting for Mā. If I have not made a mistake in counting, the upper part of his body was covered with nothing else but 27 rosaries of different lengths and thickness of pearls. He had flung a yellow silk cloth around his hips, and it reached upto the middle of his calves. He was wearing nine red bracelets on his arm, three on the upper arm, three below the elbow and three over the wrist. Several broad white horizontal stripes ran from the shoulder to the hand. His hair was tied with a red string and fell down like a fountain. It was white, but had golden strands. His beard reaching to his navel and proliferating around his face was also golden-white. His face was powdered with a shining yellow powder and the sockets of his eyes were coloured in black. The forehead of the pious man was a real work of art: it was divided in the middle by a broad red stripe which continued on the ridge of the nose. On both sides, the name of his beloved god RĀMA was emblazoned in large, white *Devanāgarī* letters.

I got up early this morning to go to Sarnath, one of the most sacred centres of Buddhism. Buddha "set the wheel of his doctrine in motion" here. He preached there for the first time. I take a rickshaw. It is almost dark as we leave. We need about an hour to get there right across the city.

The ruins of several temples, *stūpas* and monasteries of the early days of Buddhism lie scattered over a vast grass land. The walls of the ruins rise – apart from a *stūpa* which has remained almost undestroyed – only to a height of about two to three metres above the ground. Many parts of the walls reveal the simple ground plan of the monasteries: a small, central yard, surrounded by the cells of the monks and a verandah in front of these cells. One side has the entrance portico, and opposite to it – the yard – the shrine.

Before the earliest monasteries were built during Aśoka's reign (3rd century B. C.), there was a big jungle here, where only ascetics and wild animals used to live. The first five disciples of Buddha who left their Master, when he himself gave up asceticism, returned to this region to continue their path of radical renunciation of the world. After years, the Master met them there again, Bodh-Gayā lay behind him, and he went into *Nirvāṇa* alive. His disciples recognized in him the Enlightened One, the Buddha, and they became the first monks of his Order.

This region which is awakened to a new dawn is full of prophesy. I hear its voices with the soles of my naked feet, as I wander slowly around the excavations. Everything testifies to the presence of the Enlightened One. He is in the shades of the old trees, in moss, covering the two thousand-year-old walls, in the sleep of the ruined temples and in the air, vibrating with the prayers of pilgrims.

Buddha, the Enlightened One, remained silent about God. But are silence and speech not the same in the heights he has climbed?

I stretched myself out under a tree. Like a violet silk-cloth, broad petals of flowering bougainvillea cover the branch above me. White, thick cobwebs are lying on the grass, widely scattered like the pages of a torn book. Buddha's doctrine, proclaimed here for the first time, is later taken into the world as a document. I am reminded of the vivid simile of the *Upaniṣads* which says that the cosmos has sprung from *Brahman* like the web from the body of a spider, *Brahman* from *Brahman*. The sun is shining on the bedewed cobwebs. What transcends words is reflected in the word of the doctrine. It is also reflected in me, here and now: as gratitude to all those innumerable nameless ones. Be with us, stay among us. Without you, it would be a never-ending night.

We have now a fixed programme: we meet during the forenoons on the plinth of a hall under construction, on the front side of which a big temple is about to be built. A carpet is laid upon the plinth which is covered by a paṇḍāla. A mattress is laid down in front of the temple for Mā to sit on it, and another mattress beside it, meant for the speakers, with a low desk in front of it. The right half of the space is reserved for women, and the left for men.

A number of functions in the forenoon start with a *kīrtana* for half an hour. Then silence is observed for ten minutes, so that we are mentally prepared for Svāmī Bhagavatāṇanda Giri's philosophical lecture in Hindi. He is a permanent inmate of the *āśrama,* a sturdy, elderly gentleman with a friendly face, a stubbly beard and clever eyes.

We assemble in the evening again on the platform. I guess, around 500 people crowd the place. We listen to a talk on *Rāmāyaṇa* by an emeritus historian of the University of Calcutta. The speaker is in brilliant form; I can know so much, although I do not understand his Bengali. He succeeds again and again in making the audience listen to him with rapt attention, and often, the tension is relieved by laughter. Sometimes, I see tears in his eyes and in the eyes of the audience; it hangs onto his words spellbound.

Professor Chakrawarti explained to me during an interval the word *khyāla* which is one of Mā's key words. In its popular sense, it means a sudden psychic impulse: a wish, an opinion which suddenly crops up. But Mā has given the word a new meaning. As she does not think any more that she has an ego, in which there could be such a sudden impulse, she opines that her "*khyāla*" is a spontaneous manifestation of *Brahman*'s will in her self. It is free from all conditionality; it is a divine "voice" speaking through her and guiding her steps. Mā knows that she has always to be ready for the directives of the *khyāla*. It intervenes apparently with a reckless spontaneity. Mā's steps, therefore, are only seldom predictable. One has always to be prepared for this *khyāla* suddenly altering all plans that are made for Mā.

Mā's complete surrender to the will of God is expressed in this constant readiness. "The divine truth speaks through her only because she does not have any ego." This is the explanation the Professor gave me for *khyāla*. He added, "It is also possible that *truth* sometimes uses us common people as its spokespersons. But Mā is in constant continuum with the divine truth or with *Brahman*. This distinguishes her from us. Even when she does not answer a question, her silence is the manifestation of the will of eternal truth."

When Mā sits in the verandah, a blind old woman in saffron-coloured vestments is often led to her. She gives the impression that she is frail. Sometimes, she says something, and it appears that it is in an imploring tone. At times, she touches Mā's feet. Mā remains then completely quiet with an expression on her face which makes me suddenly think of blood transfusion. I observed years ago how a man was letting the blood be taken from him which was to be given to an injured child. This feeling: take something from my vital energy. Here it is spiritual, there it was biological.

When the old lady let her hands fall down, she tilted her head backwards and fixed her eyes on Mā's face. Mā stood close in front of her. She appeared to be collected and earnest. A long, quiet look gazed at the blind eyes. Did it disperse the night? The face of the old woman became suddenly bright. Then she concealed it in her hands. Mā turned away quickly. When the blind woman was being led away, she was weeping.

Another bald-headed woman in ascetic vestments, who also appears to be old, often sits in the verandah at Mā's feet. Her face often gets an expression of ecstatic rapture. When I see it, I feel that she should have confined herself to the privacy of her closet, and not here in the gaze of the public eye. But these people do not have the painful feeling which the divulgence of inner happenings to the scrutiny of a stranger arouses in us. When I think about it, I also do not know why I should crow so much about our spiritual modesty. There are two styles – one as much "justified" as the other. This woman is a typical *bhakta*: a believer who has chosen the path of *bhakti* to attain enlightenment.

October 24, 1963

We have been celebrating *Durgā-pūjā* for days. It is one of the most important festivals of the Hindu calendar, above all, for the Bengalis. Durgā is said to be the most worshipped female deity. Her name is translated by the word "inaccessible". By asking people here, I have often tried to fathom, what they understand by her. Our Western urge to define phenomena clearly and differentiate them accurately is met with resistance here. Many people assure me that Durgā is only one name among many for the highest reality of *Brahman*. Others explain that each of these names indicates an individual deity.

God Śiva appears to be an example of contradiction that

cannot be easily understood. His name means "the good one" or "the merciful one". But in the threefold appearance (*trimūrti*) of the highest deities standing at the apex of the Pantheon, Brahmā-Viṣṇu-Śiva, he embodies (among other things) the destruction of the world. And yet, *liṅga* is his symbol, which expresses creative power. These deities do not do us a favour in incarnating clearly each time a restricted divine feature. Their nature is multi-layered. And particularly, Śiva's complexity, when we try to get to know his consorts. The most well-known are: Śakti, Pārvatī, Durgā and Kālī.

But we are concerned here with Durgā and even her nature is complex. People who have assembled here for the festival worship, see in her the "Highest Mother", "Mother of Pity" and the "One who is eternally loving". But so far as I remember, I have never yet really seen a graphic representation of Durgā in which she was shown differently from her representation in which she is fighting with her ten arms against an evil demon. The myths report on her nine bloody victories over mighty demons, but the demons whom the One "who is eternally loving" conquers in us are hatred, greed, vindictiveness . . . Recently, I found a quotation from one of the sacred books on Hinduism in which Durgā is invoked: "Only in you, O Divine One, who are sending forth blessing to all the three worlds, we see cruelty in the battle, combined with pity in the heart." Svāmī Bhagavatānanda explains to me: "The vanquished demon can attain *Nirvāṇa,* thanks only to his defeat in the battle with the goddess."

I saw in the city several Durgās, carried by coolies, on their way to temples in which they would be installed. It is a practice that Durgā-idols are made for the great *pūjā:* manufacturers prefabricate the complete structure at first from wire (it is approximately of half "life size"). Then the contours of the figure are formed from straw and finally modelled by clay and then painted.

Our Durgā-idol came today at noon, and it was installed in the temple room which is in the house of Mā's brother. I could see it only cursorily. The Goddess with ten arms: a powerful female figure in a red garment (*sārī*) and with a golden crown, and at her feet, an abominable, green grotesque demon (as much as I could see, in the form of a bullock), conquered by the valient Durgā. Two smaller goddesses stood on the right and the left of Durgā. Sarasvatī, the Goddess of Learning and Fine Arts, and Lakṣmī, the goddess of Family and Wealth. The whole, sculpture seems to me extremely glorious, colourful, emotional, naive and expressive.

The rite can be performed only by Brāhmaṇas who have subjected themselves to strict spiritual and physical cleansing: and the priests have to wear silk garments. I stand at the threshold leading to a small yard, opposite to the door of the temple, and see indistinctly that the Goddess has completely disappeared behind the garlands of flowers bedecking her. Mā's brother, helped by two young monks, performs the rite; I do not understand their individual phases. Mā herself sits in front of the temple, beside her, the three sons of her brother, two of them are still children. They are also clad like their father in *dhotī* of white wild silk.

The door of the temple is decorated with the garlands of flowers. Everywhere, there are branches of palm and wreaths of glowing colours. Today is the first day of the festival. The images of the deities will be consecrated today. Tomorrow is the day of "divine mother". On the third day, "Durgā's victory over the Demon" is celebrated, and "Durgā bids farewell", on the fourth day.

I stood almost the whole day at the threshold of the small yard of the house in which Mā's brother lives with his family. It is situated very close to the *āśrama.* One of the rooms in the ground floor is converted into a temple, and the actual rite is performed here. Mā had often allowed me to come into the yard and to sit at her feet to protect me from overwhelming crowds. But now, she makes me stand at the threshold. I feel that many of the orthodox Hindus who have gathered here are disturbed by the presence of a person who is not a Hindu. Many of them try quite openly to push me away from my place on the threshold which I take care not to cross.

I observe for hours the recitations of the priests and the mysterious game with the flowers, leaves, consecrated essences and an implement which looks like a feather duster– its handle is artistically engraved in silver – then joss sticks, fruits and a conch from which the priests sometimes entice a muffled horn-like sound. The believers give out at the same time a loud sound which sounds like the howling of a siren. Again and again, the implements, books, the threshold of the temple and those people who were present were sprinkled with the water of the Gaṅgā. It appears that Mā thinks that this is important. I often hear her saying "*gaṅgājala*". Purifying power is ascribed to the water of the holy river. The Goddess stays only in a temple from which all impurity is removed, and even the bodies of her devotees need a symbolic purification with the *gaṅgājala*. What I have described earlier (cf. Oct. 19, 1963) is, as it were an idea, at the root of every *pūjā*. Individual aspects of the ritual change, depending upon the deity for whom it is performed. For example, certain fruits or plants are offered to certain deities for whom they are sacred. During the *Durgā-pūjā*, hymns from the *śāstras* are also recited in which the "Inaccessible" and her deeds are glorified.

Many of those who have assembled here are simple people. At any cost, they look for an opportunity to touch Mā–may it be then her garment, one of her shoes or her mattress. They think that divine powers are transferred to them by this contact, and they expect concrete help from them: say, cure from an illness, employment in some job, peace in family dispute, a well-to-do son-in-law, etc.

It pains me when I see, how Mā is "encircled" by this

primitiveness and how she is also physically pestered by people. Sometimes, all this, I think, is a great misunderstanding. Is it sufficient to approach someone like Mā, only to take a little from his/her spiritual powers and carry it away like booty? By doing this, are not these people relinquishing the real present which Mā has kept ready for them?

Probably these are wrong questions. Mā says, "I am an instrument. What sort of music it gives, depends upon the manner in which it is played." Again and again, she emphasizes that there are innumerable levels of ignorance and degrees of knowledge. All that a man thinks or does, and with honest conviction, from the level, on which he is, is correct. One who is on the level of fetishism, acts thus correctly, if he is satisfied by touching Mā's garment. One who plays primitive music, hears primitive music. But what is astonishing is: nothing lets one know that the instrument would prefer that it is played rather by an artist than by an amateur. Mā meets simple people with the same cheerful warmth with which she meets the educated and the intellectual people. It is, thus, nonsense that I indulge in sentimental contemplations and expatiate on the tragic fate of a saint in this world of badly brought up children. Probably, such thoughts crop up in my mind, because I feel that I am exceptionally "grown up" and accordingly not properly respected.

When I "meditated" on it loudly a little while ago that many of Mā's devotees paved their way to her with brutal disregard, Vasu, one of the youngest of Mā's girls said laughing, "What do you want? She loves her bad children, as much as the good ones. And she knows that the bad ones need her more than the others, who have any way learnt to rein their desires and not to be pushy everywhere."

Kumārī-pūjā, a part of *Durgā-pūjā*, is performed in the yard in front of the temple. I find the following explanation for the word *kumārī* in a book of Śrī Gopinath Kaviraj: ". . . the eternal undefiled virgin who has divine nature. The divine power assumed her form before the creation of the world. Kumārī is the Mother of the whole creation."

Three small girls (they should not be older than ten years) are elevated in this rite as the symbols – Mā often speaks of "focal points" – for the worship of the divine *kumārī*. The three little ones (they are the pupils of the *āśrama* school) clad in shining red *sārīs* sit next to one another in the yard. They have pulled their knees towards their bodies, and their feet are resting on silver-plates. The soles of their feet are painted in red. All the three have covered their heads with the *pallā* of the *sārī*, and they are bedecked with garlands of flowers. In front of them are the implements, which are kept ready in front of the idols of the deities in the temples, before a priest performs the *pūjā*.

A Bengali advocate, who has been in the *āśrama* for quite some time, to give meaning and purpose to his retired life by devoting himself to a religious activity, takes over the role of a *pūjārī*. He is a kind old gentleman, wrapped in a yellow shawl, and sits down leisurely on the ground in front of the girls. As in all *pūjās*, the deity is greeted by symbolic actions, feasted, given a drink, bathed, anointed with noble essences. The priest reads the text of the ritual from a book and sprinkles the purifying *gaṅgājala* on the girls, puts flowers on their heads and feet, feeds them sweets and gives them water to drink from a consecrated container. All these things take place in such unforced simplicity that it could be said that here a kind grandfather is feeding his granddaughters. One of the girls obviously does not like the sweets, she is supposed to eat. For a long time, she stubbornly compresses her lips, but she does not reckon with the patience of "her grandfather" who holds again and again a morsel of food to her mouth. Finally, she opens the lips and gulps it bravely.

The idol of the Goddess was immersed in the Ganges this evening. It was taken down to the bank around 5 p.m. in a big procession and carried in a broad boat which was rowed by two men. About a dozen people climbed into the boat, and I along with them.

The idol of the Goddess was placed on the broad side so that there was a broad, empty space in front of it, and the people accompanying it stood at the bow and the stern-side of the boat.

We crossed the Gaṅgā in big boats for about two hours. The *ghāṭs* (steps on the banks) filled up gradually with thousands of people who accompanied the idols. Here and there, boats pushed off from the bank, like ours, loaded with Durgā-idols. In many, people were singing and playing music.

A young Bengali was dancing in our boat all the time without any break in front of the idol of the Goddess. While dancing, he held in his hand a clay dish which was full of burning coals and incense. He was wearing a long brownish shirt which reached to his naked feet. I had noticed his face very often: He had a dark skin and close-cropped hair. On his back head, there was a thin, small plait, as small as a finger. The shape of the eyes and the prominent cheek-bones gave an impression that he was a Mongolian. His mouth was powerful, but not thick. His body had tiger-like elegance and suppleness. At the beginning, he danced slowly and almost clumsily. He moved the container with incense first over the head, then under his right hand, while he moved partly striding and partly dancing in circles. But the musicians (drums, conches, gongs) did not allow him to rest for a long time. Swiftly they increased the tempo and compelled him to do quicker and quicker jumps. With the swaying of his hips, he swung round in circles between the bow and the stern. Sometimes, he jumped with his feet close together or sometimes with his outstretched knees. Again and again, he jumped into the air and cried out the name of the Goddess: "Durgā-Mātā" (Mother Durgā)– "*jai*" (hail to you), answered the chorus. "Ānandamayī Mātā" – "*jai*". Gradually, the drums drove him to a mad frenzy: with his head thrown back, rolling eyes and gaping mouth, he danced in ecstasy. Then the musicians showed him mercy and they reduced their tempo. His movements twitched only for a while like an extinguishing fire. He came back to senses, smiled at us and fell back into a quiet circling.

In the mean time, the Sun had set behind the city. The eastern bank with its broad strand had become rosy, and the water near the bank was shining blue. The water in the middle of the river was violet. Gradually the shadows of the city grew onto us. The first stars emerged dimly in the milky blue sky.

The dancer once more took leave of the Goddess by jumping up into the air crying our: "Durgā Mātā" – "jai' – then it was immersed in the river along with many idols from other boats The moment Durgā-Mātā went down in the Gaṅgā, her dancer also disappeared with her. But he again came up laughing, let himself be pulled into the boat and again began to dance at once. When we returned to the *āśrama,* he showed no fatigue even after dancing for more than two hours. He lept up the hundred steps easily, ran in front of Mā's room and began to dance there again hailing her name. Later, his ecstasy threatened to devour him. He was no more in a state of consciousness to end his own dance. Several people had to compel him to do so.

Chapter 5

Philosophical Discussions on the Ganges

Mā's girls told me today that she had fever and was not feeling well. The forenoon *darśana* was brief. She appeared tired and seldom said anything. Her room was closed for hours in the early afternoon. Probably she had flu.

I was standing near her door as Mā appeared. Her face was pallid. It could be seen that she was still sleepy. She stumbled a little as she was on her way to her palace between the temples. A man stood with a big garland of lotus-buds which were almost closed. He was standing at one corner of the passage, almost invisible to Mā. These buds are hard and heavy. The moment Mā turned round the corner, the man put the garland around her neck with such a force, as if he wanted to throw her onto the ground. Mā was not prepared for this "attack", particularly because she was still not fully awake. She was startled. An expression of pain came on her face; at the same time, I heard her gentle moaning: "Hari, Hari, Hari!" But at the same moment, her smile scared away the expression of pain. It appeared to say: "What sort of children you are! But you do not know any better. I love you!" She stood quiet for a moment and then went back into her room.

I have now been observing Mā for exactly six weeks. I do not know, how many thousand people I saw her greeting in this period. For almost four decades, they throng to her, day after day, those who are in need of consolation, her devotees, those who are simply curious and those who are hungry for knowledge. She receives them always with a smile and its charm is irresistible. This smile has many nuances, only its charm is constant.

It became clear to me that I occasionally "spy" on Mā with an unconscious intention of catching her, at least once, while smiling which is only a mask and not a loving gesture really felt at the moment. So far, I have not succeeded, and I am happy about it, although it would, perhaps give me a questionable satisfaction to see her once smiling like the great men of the world. It would perhaps give me satisfaction, because what I observe here in Mā is hardly humanly possible. And because it "disturbs" to experience something which cannot reasonably exist: an expression of kindness which has lost nothing of its freshness, originality, genuineness and power in spite of its "wear and tear" in the last forty years.

Take for example, the inconspicuous episode today, when Mā was carelessly "attacked" by that man: she felt sick, she was still sleepy; the scare, the darting flame of physical pain– which was clearly written on her face – and then the imperceptible, charming smile. After she had disappeared into her room, she had asked one of the attendants, whether people were waiting for her in the verandah. When she got an affirmative answer, she was immediately on her way. She walked with great difficulty, as I have never seen her before. Probably, she is really ill. When she then silently sat on her place – she left it again in ten minutes – she had a touching and an eloquent expression which defies description: it said, "Look at me dear fellows. Sometimes, our flesh is very miserable. As mine today. But God is infinite splendour and power. Look at him, through my miserable face."

"Charm" and "charisma" are derived from the same root word. One understands this the moment one looks at Mā. Her charm is a religious gift. This is also valid for her indiscriminating kindness. It can be understood only correctly, when it is explained within the concept of unity of *Brahman* which forms the scope of Mā's conception of herself: her kindness is an expression of love, with which God loves himself.

When I was drinking a cup of tea yesterday evening in a small restaurant, I got into conversation with a gentleman, a youngish physician from Madras, whom I have often met in the *āśrama*. He has just completed his specialist training in America. He sat next to me and said, "Are you not surely of the opinion that, in any case, rites are a matter of primitive minds? And before I could answer: "Are you a Catholic or a Protestant?"

"I was born in a Protestant family, but now I do not belong to any church. Many things of Catholicism interest me."

"And what do you have to say to my question on rites?"

"It is not that simple. Many Protestants despise the abundance of rites among the Catholics. They think that it is primitive. A spiritual religion needs these props in the world of the visible, audible, and what is perceptible to the senses of touch and smell. They like to say so. But are they right? The longing for God or the joy in him is expressed in the inner – the so-called spiritual – and in the outer gesture. Why not? Neither the one, nor the other, has to be primitive. The Protestants' attitude, which is hostile to rites, can signify impoverishment, desiccation, and the Catholic attitude, which takes pleasure in rites, can signify externalisation."

My opponent listened to me, nodding vigorously: "Do you know that your attitude corresponds exactly to that of Hinduism? We approve both the ways and leave the choice to the individual. You have seen, with what joy and intensity Mā celebrates the ritual, but it is certain that she does not depend upon external props for that purpose."

We remain silent for a while, then the young doctor continues. "And what do you have to say to idolatry of which the West very much likes to accuse us? Do you find that our idolatry is essentially different from that of the Christians?"

"I have tried to think about it, but I would need a more peaceful atmosphere for it than one can find here in this city. First: What do you understand by idolatry?"

"In a strict sense, that someone believes that the idol of God is God himself, or it is godly. But I doubt, whether this is stated anywhere in Hinduism."

"It also does not exist in Christianity."

"I have often seen Catholics kneeling with devotion in front of the images of their saints, as we bow to the images of our deities."

"Of course: one worships Virgin Mary in front of her image. But the image itself is not worshipped. It only helps the believer, to be prepared, while praying, for the spiritual presence of the one who is represented in the image."

"I would have said exactly the same thing about the idols of our gods. The idol is only a representation of the deity. The crudest is in three dimensions, which is refined in the two dimensions of painting. In a symbol, say in *Śiva-liṅga* which is considerably more sublime, and in a *yantra*, in concretization of a *mantra* by a diagram in which it is totally abstract."

"But only in *pūjā* – the Goddess was called over on the first day. Divine life was breathed into the image of wire, straw and clay. Farewell was made to the Goddess on the last day. How can the God be made to come and go? Does it not smack of primitive magic practices?"

My partner in conversation laughed heartily: "I was waiting for this question. When I saw you recently standing on the threshold, I thought, I read in your face that you were grappling with such questions. I decided to speak to you about them, if there were some occasion. See, it is possible that primitive men believe that a priest has power over a deity, and he may make it appear or disappear. But that is only a misunderstanding. God is omnipresent in all his aspects – even in Durgā. When a worshipper calls him, i.e. as if calling the clay image, then he does not give the command to the deity, but only to his own mind. He orders himself to know the presence of God, to make it real. We forget it so easily, and that is why we need such rites for clarification and exhortation."

"Fine. But how can the believer send the God away again at the end of the *pūjā,* as it were, drive him out of the image?"

"How little the image itself means to us, is eloquently expressed by throwing it into the water. Once the God has left it, it is only clay and straw. Unfortunately, we cannot – in fact, most of us – be in a constant state of worship. *Pūjā* must have an end in time. But we destroy the image so that it does not exist and perhaps we forget that it is only of clay and ascribe to it a divine power. When we - through our human condition– finish the *pūjā* and destroy the image, we bid farewell to God. Not because he has gone away from us. He is omnipresent and always with us –, but because we have to turn our attention to other things, to our family, to our occupation, whatever it may be. You know for sure that every *pūjā* celebrates a symbolic reception of God as a welcome and respected guest. It does not mean that he is with us only for a short duration of the rite. It means that we think of His holy presence at this time."

"Have you come to Banaras only for *Durgā-pūjā?*"

"No. I care very little for the rites, whatever they are. I came here to see Mā and to get her blessing for my plans."

"May I know, what sort of plans?"

"Why not? I got acquainted with a young Israeli lady doctor in America. I would like to marry her."

Professor Chakrawarti continues, evening after evening, to narrate the story of *Rāmāyaṇa* and give his commentary. Yesterday, A Rāma-*bhakta* visited us; he is a young monk who has chosen the path of love to God Rāma to find enlightenment. He was wearing a long, saffron-coloured overall and a small turban of the same material. His hair was braided in twenty or more thin pigtails which reached down up to his chest. He had a small moustache and a small fluffy beard. After the Professor had left the speaker's seat, the *bhakta* sat there. Before doing so, he had reverently touched

Mā's mattress with his forehead and was garlanded by her. When the programme was interrupted, the 300 to 400 people, who had gathered there, as on every evening, began to make noise, as usual, without caring for others.

The *bhakta* sat there for about fifteen minutes with his eyes closed and his head bent amid this noise. His moving lips indicated that he was praying. Suddenly, he began to pray in a low voice: "*Rām, Rām, Rām* . . .". When he opened his eyes, tears were rolling down his cheeks. Continuing to pray, he was looking, blinded by ecstasy, beyond the heads of his audience. Did Rāma appear before his eyes?

Then he began to sing softly. The quieter the audience became, the more vigourously he sang. Nothing in his voice corresponded to the sound of a human organ. Extremely strange sounds for my ears, his was an artistic achievement: nasal, squeezed out, wailing, suddenly crying out brashly, full of boldest dissonances like the vibration of steel strings, gurgling and strident. His slender, dark face was profusely sweating, and his eyelids were half-closed.

Suddenly he stopped. He sat there for a moment with his head tilted backwards, with closed eyes and trembling lips. Then it appeared that he had recovered. He looked around in the circle in a friendly manner and began at once with the explanation of his song. He spoke rapidly, in a high-pitched voice and in a monotonous rhythm. His words were supplemented by *mudrās*. The long, nimble hands easily and elegantly formed those signs which in Asia is a secret spiritual language. When the monk began to sing again, even the faintest noise from the crowd of his audience did not disturb him at all. Half sobbing, half jubilant, he raised his voice with the name of his God on his lips - he was a dreamer, a man in love, no more living in this world.

Mā listened to the young monk in the ecstatic state with an almost tender, motherly expression. She knows the ways on which his soul is approaching the peak of enlightenments. When he bows to her at the end, she puts her hand on his head and speaks to him, as if speaking to a son.

A young Indian in European dress put a couple of questions to Mā; he translated them himself to me. "Is it true that you are a deity?

Mā: "There is nothing except God. You are also an incarnation of God."

"What is the goal of your life in this world?"

"In this world? I am not here or there or in this world. I Myself rest in my Self."

"But for whom are you here?'

"For whom could I be here; ... there exists only the One!"

The Agfa-thermometer in a photo shop showed this afternoon – today, it is October 30-37°C. in the shade. The old nun, who was almost blind, had come again for *darśana* in the morning. She appeared to be in a particularly sad condition. She was weeping, when she touched Mā's feet. Obviously, she has now completely lost her eyesight.

Mā spoke to her extremely cheerfully, laughing several times inbetween. She said, "It is now time that you open your inner eye. God has helped you by making your external eyes blind. Tell yourself: "what is really important, I have not been able to see with my eyes all my life-long." Believe me: what you will see with your inner eye, is infinitely more beautiful than what you have seen so far with your external eyes. But as long as you are not ready to close the external eyes, the inner one will not open."

The nun is quiet for a moment, then she begins once more to wail. Mā's face shows that she is stunned: "How is it possible that you go against the will of God?," she appears to ask. Mā looks down silently on the face of the old woman. Around the mouth and the eyes, there is a brief flaring up of pity, but again, it quickly makes room for clear cheerfulness. "You would not be the first of my friends", she says laughing, "who has begun to see by becoming blind."

I have again and again observed that Mā answers the lamentations and wailings with a smile, although not in all cases when someone weeps at her feet. Sometimes, she silently strokes those who are in despair; sometimes, she speaks gently to them; but mostly, she appears to answer the tears with a laugh. She said several times: "You should weep to make God come to you. You should shed tears only for his sake." She sees, what we do not see: the transitory behind the mundane process of decay, and the light, in which our human darkness is only like the shadow of a fly on a white wall. She would have to disown her knowledge and come down to our level of ignorance in order to lament with us.

Mā was invited today by one of her devotees to visit his industrial firm. We all went to the main street. Cars were waiting for us there. When the last car had driven off, I was the only one left out. Occasionally, there are such situations. People think, first of all, of the monks and Mā's maidens; all other people have to look after themselves. If one is not accustomed to forcing one's way forward, one is left in the lurch. It happens sometimes too that the car door is shut on your face because the occupants are afraid of the physical contact with the castess.

It was difficult for me at the beginning not to get upset in such situations. But I judged them wrongly. I took them personally. These things are not aimed at me personally. Perhaps, mercilessness is the law of a land, whose population grows enormously fast, without growing enough food for all. Misery and cramping in the cities lead almost compulsively to egoism. It is not an accident that I notice these characteristics more among the poor than among well-to-do people. The ruthlessness is not aimed particularly at the foreigners. Often, the natives are ruthless with one another (All sorts of events happen like these in public places!) They baffle with the mercilessness of their servants or those from still "lower strata", say the coolies. It is true, but I have also experienced the opposite.

The animals appear to share the lot of the coolies. Right

here in Banaras, the streets are teeming with dirty, half-hungry dogs, bony donkeys and old and sick cows. What I call mercilessness is also shown against one's own person. One meets at every step men and women who possess nothing except their begging bowl, and this creates havoc with the normal needs of their bodies.

Surely, nature itself colludes with this human dilemma. The mercilessness of the sun, immensity of the rains, catastrophes caused by floods inundating the whole stretches of land. Famine which brings devastating starvation, epidemics and raging whirlwinds . . .

As long as the inhabitants of this land can recall, generation after generation was confronted with this terrible mindlessness of these destructive powers. Every man, down the ages, has been a contemporary of thousands, often of millions, who starved, drowned or miserably perished on account of disease. This experience is a part and parcel of their life.

When I tried to explain to Mā, how abominable the bombing was during the war, in which ten thousand men were killed just in fifteen minutes, I thought that she did not understand me. She did not comprehend, why the memory of these nights of bomb-attacks frightens us even today. Ten thousand people, who starve after one failed crop, and three thousand, whom a typhoon kills in an hour, are the dangers which threaten the inhabitants of this land almost constantly. Who talks of such catastrophes after a couple of years? A tree, the blossom of which is destroyed by a night-frost, blossoms again, when it is the right season. An individual life is of little importance in an infinite cycle of birth and death. Every *ātman* goes through aeons of rebirths. A life to which the preciousness of "only once" is not ascribed, has negligible claim to mercy. Perhaps, one of the causes for what I have called ruthlessness is in this attitude.

I should learn first to refer all phenomena only to what

is Indian and to observe them calmly. It leads to misunderstanding and misinterpretation, when one goes on constantly comparing the East with the West and what is Christian with what is Hinduistic.

As soon as one ventures to make a comment on what is Indian, one must clearly know, that its opposite is also true. I have never come in any direction to a conclusion, the opposite of which was not equally correct. This appears to me to be really typical for India.

"Collecting" contradictions, about which I do not know, whether these are real contradictions, has begun to give me great time; for example: What do feet signify for a Hindu? Mā often talks of the lotus-feet of God. I have heard that the wisdom of those who are enlightened is transmitted by touching their feet. And I have constantly observed, how people long for touching Mā's feet. On the other hand, it is particularly outrageous, when someone touches someone else with his feet, it may be then by mistake or intentionally. (Only after a few months, a monk explained to me that in many respects the exact opposite of what is valid for an average man is valid for a saint. For example, food touched by an ordinary man with his mouth, cannot be enjoyed by anyone else, because it is impure in a ritualistic sense. But by touching it similarly, Mā transforms it into a beneficent *prasāda.*

Concerning physical contact: I observe that all residents of the *āśrama* take meticulous troubles not to touch one another physically. For some of the āśramites, it would mean in addition almost a misfortune, if they were to come in physical contact with me. But often (for example, while taking *darśana*), fifty people sit on a place on the ground, which would be, according to our understanding, to some extent sufficient for ten. On the one hand, over-sensitiveness, on the other hand, complete insensitiveness.

Or take the attitude with respect to animals: one should do nothing to harm them, because God is embodied also in an animal. According to metempsychosis, a man can become an animal in his next birth. There are also animal-deities like Hanumān, the Monkey-God, or Gaṇeśa, the God with the elephant-head. But how many miserable, sick, half-starved and neglected animals do we not see here everywhere!

Or the explicit rationality of the *karma*-doctrine. What is logical, almost arithmetical in it: Every action is precisely repaid, the good one, as well as the bad one. And on the other hand, the strongly irrational element: Nobody is earnestly surprised at a "miracle". Or the wonderful spiritual tolerance: Pictures of Buddha, Christ and Mary in Hindu-*āśramas.* On the other hand, the very common orthodox exclusiveness in practice : say, when a non-Hindu would like to enter certain temples.

And the same element of contradiction in the nature of the deities themselves: Kālī is the Great Mother– but she wears a garland of bloody skulls of the dead. This can be continued *endlessly.* But what I have learnt from it is: Caution. We make distinctions and categorize too quickly. This leads to endless misunderstanding. Let the whole range of phenomena roll on. A wave full of apparent counter-currents, but *one* wave. Like the Ganges: full of countless flashing whirlpools, and it is one river.

Mā narrated today, how the *āśrama* got the beautiful Gopāl-idol that was in a shrine of sandalwood in one of the temples. Gopāl was to be presented to the *āśrama,* but the day of his arrival was delayed several times. "I went to Vrindavan at that time, before the thing could be settled", tells Mā. "On the way I said to Gopāl: 'Look here, what is all this? It appears that you want to come to us, then it appears again that you don't want to come. Decide. If you really want to come, come soon, don't be so indecisive.' The day, I returned from Vrindavan, I sent the car which had fetched me at the station and brought me to the *āśrama,* immediately back to the people with whom Gopāl stayed. And what do you think? He really came at once to us in the same car. Now I even knew, why he was delayed so long. He had not come earlier, because he did not want that I take him with me to Vrindavan (Gopāl's birthplace). He wanted to stay on in Banaras. Incidentally, the day he came to us, was his birthday. We adorned him, put him into the cradle and rocked him." (As there are beds in many temples for deities, the devotees of Kṛṣṇa have a cradle for the divine Child whose name is Gopāl. Śrī Kṛṣṇa is called Gopāl when he is worshipped in his form as a child.)

Mā narrates all this in a matter-of-fact manner, without any trivialization or as a fairy-tale. One could think that she was talking about a son of a friendly family and not about the Kṛṣṇa. She really spoke with the divine child and reminded him, not without a gentle reproach, to come at once, if at all he wanted to come. God is as real to her as a man. This is not fiction, it is a reality that is experienced many times by me.

Something else is also expressed in Mā's behaviour: the hierarchial order. I suppose, a simple believer would not venture to scold the divine child for his apparent indecisiveness. But Mā talks to the gods, as if they are her equals. I read it in many of the records of her conversations maintained throughout her life: Mā sees suddenly a deity under a tree, in her room, at the threshold of a house – and she speaks with this deity. Sometimes, she describes the clothes or the posture or the movements of her divine guest.

The question about which I am again and again pondering: What are these gods? Who are they? A room next to mine in the guest house is occupied by a family of four since a few days. Early morning, I hear the wife singing, and while going past their room, I saw the husband sitting on his bed with a rosary in his hand. He told me today that he was teaching mathematics in a college. Obviously, he is thus a believer in an "oriental" and an educated man in an "occidental" sense. As we were sitting on a bench in front of the guest house, I brought the conversation round to Hindu deities. He explained to me a theory of their "origin". Some time in the misty past, one of the men, whom the Hindus call by the name *ṛṣis,* must have had an overpowering meeting with the numinous. He must have translated this self-experienced revelation into words and signs, giving it form and name.

I interrupt him here with a question, whether this meeting was to be thought of as inner-psychic one, or whether that *ṛṣi* had perceived the numinous with his senses or had heard or seen it in an outwardly world?

"For us, inside is outside and outside inside", answered the teacher and laughed. "You will meet many people, who would tell you that Mā suddenly appeared to them on certain occasions to help them. My wife recently had such an experience with her *Guru.* She could clearly see that he had a yellow mango in his hand and he was wearing a rosary of glass beads, what she had never seen before. His voice sounded harsh and low, as it always sounds. But she will not be able to give any answer to your question, whether she met him within her psyche or in the outward world.

Something similar is also true of the experience with the numinous which that *ṛṣi* of the past had. The news has been handed down to us through many generations. Perhaps, because the experience was overwhelmingly powerful and had an effect, perhaps, because the *ṛṣi* had an exceptional faculty to translate it into an image. Whole hierarchies of seers/priest-poets contributed further to the image of the deity. The great epics were produced in which the revelations of many *ṛṣis* handed down by tradition were woven into a gigantic tapestry. What was originally seen, mingled with all the elements of human fantasy, pure and impure, sprung from love, fear and lust for power."

After keeping quiet for a while, I said, "You are a believing Hindu, aren't you? I am surprised at your rationalistic attempts at interpretation. While doing so, do not the deities lose their reality?"

"I speak to you in a language you understand", answered the teacher smiling. "My own religious goal is self-realization, i.e. the identity with *Brahman.* But my wife is a Kṛṣṇa-*bhakta,* and I think that on account of it she is not farther than I am from the truth about the unfathomable mystery of *Brahman.* Why should not the numinous germ in the image of the deities, which stems from the original revelations of our *ṛṣis,* represent really a power, which exists far above the human sphere? Not only exists, but also influences the life of human beings? When thus, a Kṛṣṇa-*bhakta* says the name of his God, why should not his call be heard by that numinous power, we call Kṛṣṇa, and why should it not be answered?"

The disturbing question since I haye met Mā for the first time: who are you? I ask this myself everyday. Who is she, when she talks to those transcendental powers, as if talking to her equals?

It appears to me to be significant that she speaks only seldom or only in quite special contexts– say, when she wants to tell the story of the Gopāl-idol that was presented to the *āśrama* – about one of the deities, say, about Kṛṣṇa, Śiva, Durgā, etc. She talks about God as *Bhagavān* in her religious discourses, and she uses this name in the sense in which we talk about God in the West. Sometimes, she also uses the word "Lord" or the "highest Lord of the world" or simply "He". Then the whole pantheon of the deities appears to be receding into the background. Occasionally, she speaks to him thus: "You are Mother, you are Father, you are Beloved, and you are Lord. Really, you are all in all."

When she talks to sceptics or to those who have knowledge of philosophy, it appears that she prefers to use the language of *Vedānta.* Then she talks about "*tat*", that, about the impersonal highest reality, *Brahman.* But whereas we, always and everywhere, try to differentiate and define precisely, everything is seen here in one, and one in everything. *Bhagavān* is only a personified aspect of *tat.* As ice is only solidified water. And this process of giving form (and shape) continues in the individual deities: Sarasvatī is, thus, the Goddess of Learning and Fine Arts. This special aspect of God is personified in her.

Mā is often directly asked: "Who are you?" – It appears that most often she gives the following answer: "I am, whom you want to see in me."

To the question, "What is the meaning of your life", she recently answered: "I myself rest in my Self." This appeared to be an evasive answer.

Her answer to the question of a Catholic priest appeared to be similarly "evasive". The priest had asked, "When have you experienced self-realization?" And her answer was: "When was I not?"

To the question, where she feels at home, she has occasionally answered: "This whole universe is my home. I am always in my house, although it appears that I move from place to place."

On some other occasion she explained, "I am both dependent and independent. I am neither infinite nor finite, and yet I am both at the same time." Or: "My will would be irresistible, if I were to explain it." Or: "I am with everyone, whether a child, a youth, an adult or an old man. I existed before the creation of the world and I shall exist after its annihilation."

All these statements express the same thing: identity with the highest *Brahman* realized in Mā's soul. They are a variation of "*ahaṃ brahmāsmi*". – I am *Brahman.* Countless utterances appear to prove that Mā had experienced (and she understands) that she is one with the highest reality or with *Bhagavān,* in fact, in an unlimited identification. I notice that I have never asked myself so far, whether Mā is arrogant or humble. I must have taken for granted, particularly after all that I have heard her saying, that she could be hybrid to a shocking extent. But the fact is that one who has seen Mā does not ask oneself this question at all. When one looks at her, one understands immediately: the question about arrogance or humbleness works with categories which are here altogether out of place. He who has no ego cannot be "smaller than the smallest". How much less could he cross the limits of legitimate claims!

Mā used to identify herself, occasionally also explicitly, with individual deities, with Kṛṣṇa, Ḍurgā, Kālī, Nārāyaṇa, etc. in her earlier years, when she used to perform *pūjā* herself. It must have been completely concrete for her devotees. I hear and read often that Mā had become at that time Śrī Kṛṣṇa, Durgā, etc. before the very eyes of her devotees. Probably, an extremely superficial explanation with which I try to approach these phenomena would be: she had seen the idols of these deities so many times in the temples and she became so fervently engrossed in them that her body suddenly and spontaneously represented certain postures (*āsanas, mudrās*) and the physiognomical expression in which the nature of the deity in question was revealed: a happening which should not be considered as conscious.

In the meanwhile I hear that Mā does not identify herself any more with individual deities. She no longer comes out of her unity with *Brahman.* I do not know why she has given up all this. But she does not perform *pūjā* any more and she usually does no more pray. Perhaps, her oneness with *Brahman* has reached such a degree of absoluteness that she cannot play any more "the game of duality" for the benefit of her followers; an expression which I have heard repeatedly. It suggests that she considers her past life in which she had identified herself with the deities, performed the rites and prayed, was only "a game". I hope to get more information in due course of time.

When people ask Mā about the condition of enlightenment, she repeatedly says that questions of this type are an attempt to cross the sphere of what can be expressed with words. There are only allusions in paradoxes: "He (enlightened) walks without feet, speaks without mouth, hears without ears . . ."

I have found the following utterance of Mā in the records. I think, it says, somewhat "cryptically", something about her spiritual condition: "The realization of ignorance and the realization of knowledge is absolutely revealed to the one who has seen the *tat.* He does not consider any more that they are two separate things which must be distinguished. His actions, whether he walks, speaks or eats become non-acting actions. Whether he performs religious rites in this condition or not, makes no difference at all."

It is easy to understand the path of a man who is striving for enlightenment. But it is difficult to understand what is happening here. It is no mere question of attaining or not attaining something for the one in whom knowledge and ignorance are contained as a whole. And therefore, not attaching does not mean a loss to him . . .

Mā welcomes the people coming to her with a greeting with which *svāmīs* welcome one another: "*Namo Nārāyaṇa*", or mostly: "*Nārāyaṇa, Nārāyaṇa*".

Namo Nārāyaṇa means: I welcome in you the highest embodiment of God. Nārāyaṇa is another name of Viṣṇu. I saw Mā today folding her hands in salutation to a one-year old boy who was brought to her in the arms of father. Bowing down slightly, she said thrice earnestly: "*Nārāyaṇa, Nārāyaṇa, Nārāyaṇa*". She salutes to the highest embodiment of God in the child.

Mā does not assume the responsibility of becoming someone's *Guru,* at least, not in a formal sense. She does not give *dīkṣā* and thus, in the strict sense of the term, has no pupils. But if someone tells her, "I see in you my *Guru,*" she does not contradict him. Many of her followers have got the *dīkṣā* (initiation) from Didimā, Mā's mother. At times,

I see Didimā early in the morning sitting with a pupil in a corner of the *āśrama*-temple and teaching him. It is the temple in which *Gopāl,* who was presented to the *āśrama,* lives in his carved shrine of sandalwood. The pupils are young boys. They sit at Didimā's feet and listen to the hardly audible whispering of their ninety-year-old teacher.

Recently I asked someone why Mā does not initiate the pupils herself. "No distinction is made between *Guru* and pupil, where Mā is in *unio* with *Brahman.* The pupil/teacher relationship belongs to our dualistic realm."

I find the following words of Mā in the records: "Since this body has no personal will and no pre-conceived notions, there cannot be for it something like accepting the responsibility of giving *dīkṣā. Mantras* come suddenly out of this mouth on many occasions. It can then happen that somebody hears them and uses them. That is, he hears the *mantra* and goes away believing that everything has been prepared here for his initiation. What objection one could have against it? What has to happen, happens."

"In the beginning was the word" – this has an equivalent phrase in Hindu-philosophy: *śabda brahman*; Śrī Gopinath Kaviraj explains it as under: "*Śabda brahman* is the term used for the eternal sound which is the very first creative manifestation of the highest reality; it preceded all Becoming." (It is not accidently "is" instead of "was", because creation, preservation and annihilation for Hindus is a process without any beginning and end running concurrently and merging into one another.)

The deity is realized in the word. The *mantra* means the presence of God in the word. The divine power can be transferred from the teacher to the pupil with the help of the word. Not wisdom, which may determine the intellectual purport, but the spiritual power present in the word; the mystic tonal embodiment of the highest reality in the syllable "*OM*" is a part of this. It is also considered as the tonal expression of *śabda brahman.*

After the meditation-silence on all evenings, one of the monks or *brahmacāriṇīs,* who are present, sings always the following *mantra* from the *Upaniṣads*:

> Truth, knowledge, infinity – all that is *Brahman.*
> Peace, kindness, beauty – all that is *Brahman.*
> Embodiment of joy, unity –all that is *Brahman.*
> One without a second – that is *Brahman.*

Something that I can mark only with three crosses in my diary (with the three crosses, which an illiterate person makes, instead of his name, because he has not learnt to write it): I am now and then overwhelmed with joy – in the street, or when I sit in the *āśrama,* or in the midst of the night –, I wake up suddenly, and it is there. A joy that shines on its own accord, without cause, without an object, without a name. Dissolving all wishes, wiping out all questions. In the focus of the moment: eternity.

Chapter 6

The East and the West: The Two Points of View

November 10,1963

Mā's *darśana* this afternoon: crossing the limits of all that can be said or described with words. She made us wait for over an hour in the verandah in front of the temple. When she came, she was, as if in a cocoon of invisible light. I can express this only in such a paradox. We had an impression that her body was enveloped in an aura which was very different from ours. It was no doubt transparent like the other, but at the same time, it appeared to be an impervious protective coat, not glassy, but pulsating with surging liveliness.

Mā sat down on a low stool between the two temples. Generally, immediately a lively conversation starts with the visitors who ask her questions. Today, she had such an aura of quietude that nobody ventured to talk. She gave a hint to P., and the girls began to sing. I have often observed that Mā makes her girls sing, when she has a particularly powerful aura. Perhaps, she prevents a general conversation in this way, when it cannot be foreseen what spiritual value it may have.

I have never heard P. singing before as today. She is different from many Indian singers in that she abstains strictly from any external means of expression. Even the subjective expression of emotion in the voice, which is cultivated by many singers here, recedes into the background when she sings. P. closes her eyes and lets her head tilt backwards. Her narrow face is marked by ascetic self-renunciation, and yet it is a youthful face. It is lovely in the rare moments of smiling. Sometimes, she sits there for a moment with a slightly open mouth. She waits till singing emerges out of her. Mostly, it begins softly; it never becomes loud; but it acquires at times an electrifying spiritual intensity.

Mā is sitting in a relaxed mood, leaning against a wall. She is listening with her eyes half-closed. P. sings first a long series of variations of the shout of joy, "Jai Mā". Then follows a song which begins with "*Mahārāṇī, Mahādevī*" (Great Queen, Great Goddess). These hymns are also sung to express adoration to Durgā and Kālī. Here, they are addressed to Mā.

Mā is slightly restless in the beginning. Her shoulders and hands are moving. Is it possible that her body expresses repulsion against such an adoration in these gestures which hardly imply much? But this is thinking from a Western point of view. The restlessness has completely gone. Mā's eyes are now completely closed. Her head is slightly bent sidewards. Suddenly, she has the same expression which had bewildered me, when I met Mā for the first time. I did not understand then what it was. Now I know what it means. It means that she, in whom the holy is embodied for the eyes of her worshippers, agrees with them in reverential observation of this holy, that she is herself: "*aham brahmāsmi* (I am *Brahman*), *Mahārāṇī, Mahādevī.*" I am whatever you see in me, for I am *Brahman*, the One that is all in all.

Later Mā opens her eyes. She is looking at something behind us in the far distance. It captures her attention. What begins to reflect in her face, defies all description. Here and there, a head turns, a pair of eyes follows the direction in which Mā is looking to see what she is seeing. Even I cannot easily resist the temptation of looking back, although I know that I would not see it. She alone sees it, and nobody else. Probably its reflection on Mā's face goes beyond what we can perceive – without obscuring it on account of our greed.

I was talking in the city today to an elderly American who has been training Indian technicians. He told me that his students, who mostly come from upper castes, have a good grasp of the theoretical; but they find it extremely difficult, when it comes to converting into practice what they have learnt in theory.

"Most of them can easily tell how a machine works. Under circumstances, they also find out fairly easily where the fault lies, when something does not function, because they understand the causal connections, but when they themselves have to correct the fault, they become helpless. American youth has a sort of sixth sense for technology. Which young person does not take passionate pleasure in disassembling his motor cycle and assembling it again. They have simply the right hands for it. The hands of the young Indians seldom cope up with it, although their thoughts can cope up with a motor."

I think, that this observation is connected with the basic difference in understanding the world. The universe is an emanation of *Brahman* for the East. The course of events in the world proceeds from the divine centre into the periphery. From the absolute real of the One *Brahman* to the unreal of the phenomenal diversity, which we perceive, because we do not look behind the veil of *māyā*. One who thus wants to meet the absolutely real, *Brahman*, God, has to turn his back to the periphery, release himself from the diverse world and his ego caught up in it and strive for pre-cosmic reality, which he can approach only in total spiritualization.

Western thinking is based on the concept that the world is a real creation of God. Man subjugates the world "in thc mission of God". This attitude causes quite a different promise to deal with the things in the world. When they are to be understood as reality, that has to be mastered, they must be comprehended. There arises a bond of trust, grown in countless generations, between human hands and material things. But when the worldly things are reflected only on the veil of *māyā*, when one has practised for chiliads to turn one's back to it, how should the hands understand them, as if dealing with a reality? This may apply, above all, to those belonging to the upper classes.

When I was contemplating about the "profound alienness", which differentiates between the East's and the West's experience with the ways of the world, my eye fell on the following entry I made yesterday in my diary: ''One knows from the basic religious behaviour that one finds more and more common things (in different religions), when the horizon of one's own experience becomes wider and wider. What frightens us in Hinduism, as long as we have not got to its bottom, is an element of cruelty that is added to the idea of what is divine. Do we think any time that it could be exactly the same the other way round?'' A woman who had grown up in a convent school told me recently:

"The horrible cruelty in your idea of God disturbs me. Not only that he allows his Son to be crucified by men, but he also condemns the sinner to the eternal perdition, which is more so cruel. Every Hindu believes that he – albeit only after many rebirths – merges with *Brahman* in spite of all his sins. Your God gives you only one insignificant chance of one life on the earth, and the one who fails is threatened with a perpetual torment of hell. Is this not horrible? Could a Father of human beings be so unkind as to treat his children so inhumanly?

The *pūjā* this afternoon came to an end with the usual sacrificial fire. Mā and her mother Didimā were invited in the night for *Durgā-pūjā* at the house of one of her devotees. Sixty to seventy people joined her. We drove at first in cars up to a street-crossing, at which we had to turn into a lane which was not fit for driving vehicles. Two sedans were waiting for Mā and Didimā. One was covered with a gold-embroidered purple velvet; the other was orange and silver-embroidered. They appeared like diminutive domed temples.

The poles with which they rested on the shoulders of their carriers had an artistic silver mounting. The procession meandered slowly through dark lanes, stopped only once by a camel.

Unexpectedly, a larger square opens up, and we are in front of a stately house. Musicians with conches, flutes and drums greet us on the flight of outdoor stairs. There are shouts of "*Jai Mā, jai Mā, jai* Mā" from many throats. The owner of the house leads his distinguished guest to a hall with a low stage on the front side. It is bordered by arcades. In its midst is an extremely artistic shrine of the Goddess; on the left of it, an armchair for Mā. I see its silver-embossed feet under silk sheets, the arm-rests are cushions of fresh roses. The hostess, after bowing to Mā, puts a white silk shawl around her and a garland of red roses around her neck. An equally comfortable seat is kept ready for Didimā. C. and U. (one of Mā's girls who has not uttered a single word for nearly twenty years), stand behind the chairs, to be of service any time. The youngest son of the house, clad only in a *dhotī* of raw silk, is swinging a huge fan of peacock feathers. Among all the men, only Gopi nath Kaviraj is honoured with a raised seat. He is sitting on a simple chair and wears, as always, his brown, faded shirt. His hands are resting on a walking stick and his head is tilted. He does not move even once during the *pūjā*, but the cause of the silence emanating from him is not to be found in his physical disposition.

A few dignified men are seated on a carpet on the left side of the shrine of the Goddess. Those men of the family, whose hair has not yet become grey, are standing. It can be seen that they do not usually wear these silk togas, but tailor-made suits. The children greet Mā one after the other and disappear quickly again. Women in white *sārīs* are making the last preparations.

The offerings are collected in the middle of the stage; they are to be offered to the Goddess so that she can enjoy them and transform the profane meal into a consecrated, blessed one. Precious silver boxes are lying on purple cushions. Plates with the choicest sweets are kept on red carpets. Flower-wreaths are resplendent between all sorts of silverware.

Two *pūjārīs* are performing the rite: men whose faces, voices and gestures reveal a great culture. While they are chanting the *mantras*, drums, horns and bells are making a loud and ecstatic sound. The atmosphere is filled with fragrant clouds; precious incense is burning in a container with glowing coal. *Āratī* is performed at the end: The priests wave the receptacles containing the burning wicks, suggesting dance-movements, before the Goddess in the shrine and before Mā, the guest in whom the incarnation of the deity is worshipped. The moment the music stops the men fall flat on their faces for a great *praṇāma*. Then the mistress of the house gives Mā a little water in a silver container, and the men of the family distribute sweets in a small leaf-bowl to several hundred guests as Mā's *prasāda*.

The rite comes to an end. It was not only its perfect formal offering, the aesthetic beauty of its setting, but also the extreme collective, joyful atmosphere of devotion, which permitted even an "unbeliever" to feel that he is also a part of the whole atmosphere. As if in a focal point, the devotion of all was concentrated on Mā.

There was an element of buoyancy (floating) in Mā's attitude, in which again there was something that can hardly be described; and in the pervasive and altogether suprapersonal joy of her face. When I write this, it is in my memory as something that is brightly shining.

Sometimes I see people pulling the bloody hide of small dogs with a string. What could it mean? In any case, it is a nauseating sight. In this city, the aesthetic feeling is brutally tested in many ways. And yet, it has a strong aura of holiness. And it is noticed – not because there are countless mendicants, the turmoil for ritualistic bathing or eternally burning pyres, but in spite of all this.

I find the religious activity here as repulsive as that in some catholic places of pilgrimage, although for other reasons. Therefore, it is all the more remarkable that this place breathes, nonetheless, intense holiness. The spirit of devotion has been impregnating this bank for centuries, perhaps for chiliads. It has created an aura which remains untarnished by all concrete disgusting things, over which one stumbles in the present-day Banaras. One who does not see here anything else except dirt, misery, religious hysteria, superstition and the priests' greed for money, can be compared to a man who had met St. Francis of Assisi and saw in him a tramp who was infested with ulcers and persecuted by crazy notions about religion.

I observed today a young monk in a silent conversation with the idol of Gaṇeśa, the god with an elephant-head. His lips and hands were moving, and his face revealed a lively changing expression. For these men, the spiritual reality must have been as important as the material reality. Ideas are as real as things. They are different from them, as it were, only on account of other physical conditions. Like vapour being different from water. And that is why, importance is given to blessings, and people fear a curse: that is why also, their belief in miracles. The direct influence of mind on matter must have been much greater for these people than we are inclined to accept.

According to Mā, only that person prays correctly, who has become *one* with the object of his devotion. A Kṛṣṇa-*bhakta* becomes himself Śrī Kṛṣṇa. This is strange for our notions. We are inclined to think that this identification would be the end of all praying. If the *vis-á-vis* between the one who is praying the object of his prayer is not kept up, then the prayer appears to become impossible. If I myself become God, how can I then speak to him?

On the other hand: when I pray so that I do not "do" it myself, when *it* prays in me, then that is also the end of all words and thoughts. What then remains is only the name of God. I think in such moments that all praying should be the invocation of his name. Is *japa* thus the real prayer? Perhaps, but only, as it is not "done". But it is done by all the Hindus I see around me. They sit in a corner doing *japa* at all times during the day. And many do it also while listening to talks. Their lips murmur uninterruptedly, often terribly fast, the name of their *iṣṭa*. While doing it, their fingers count the rosary beads, a thousand times and more during the day. It appears to be happening quite automatically. At the same time, the thoughts can be concentrated on the talk. Mā recently said to a young man doing *japa* in front of a temple, "Don't forget to dedicate the fruit of your prayer to your god." – Whenever a believer says the name of his *iṣṭa,* he should offer the blessing which this prayer "brings" to him, to his beloved god. It is, as it were, stored with him. It is common among the Hindus to count the *japa,* but they should detach themselves from the blessing, so that they are not tempted to "hoard" these prayers to take pride in their religious fervour. "We put it down before the god", I read recently. "It is not ours. It is his work, and it will come back to us as his blessing at the right time."

As I was reflecting about all this, I also understood what it means, when the Hindus say: 'The worshipper and the one who is worshipped become one in a perfect prayer.' St. Paul: "I do not live, but Christ lives in me." Or Meister Eckhart, a German mystic (1260-1328): "God and I are one in knowledge."

The owners of the boats have gradually got used to me. When one approaches bathing-*ghāṭs* as a non-Indian, one is virtually attacked simultaneously by at least a dozen Indians. They earn their livelihood by ferrying the foreigners on the Ganges. It takes an eternity till one can shake them off. Now they know that I often come to the bank, but I do not hire a boat. More pestilent are the hordes of begging children.

If one is unlucky, one cannot get rid of them at all. Only during the night and very early in the morning, one is free from the menace. I have a trick to shake them off at least for a few minutes. Occasionally, I throw a small change to a far – off place. They run after it. But they always find their victim again.

The most famous temple of Banaras is dedicated to Śiva, the divine Patron of the city. It has one of his "thousand names": Viśvanātha temple. Non-Hindus are not allowed to enter it. One can look only at its roof from the upper storey of a house situated opposite to it. It is of copper with a gold leaf coating and has many ornamented towers. The lane in front of it is about one and half metre wide, dark and dirty. There are countless shrines with plump idols of deities in the houses on the ground level to its right and left. Begging priests, among them also women, are sitting in front of them. When they are given a few paise, they pour a murky liquid with a small spoon into your hand. But there are also countless beggars who do not suppress their misery by this pious business: one next to the other– men and women of all age- groups – are sitting near the walls of the houses. They have a plate or a bowl in their hand. Most of them staring indifferently in front of themselves, some stepping in the way of the foreigners demanding alms. There are already a few paise and a little rice in their begging bowls.

People sit in the proximity of cremation-*ghāṭs* beside the corpses of their relatives, whisking the flies from them only with a casual nonchalance. I also saw people lying there; by looking at them, I did not know, whether their agony was already over. They have dragged themselves from some far-away places to Banaras to die here. Someone has carried them to the bank of the Gaṅgā who will pick up their ashes, as a mother picks up her tired child. This thought may give them peace. The western bank of this river, from the confluence of the Assi in the south to the mouth of the Varuṇā in the north is considered by Hindus as "the most

Holy of the Holies". Here are the famous *ghāṭs,* the earth of which is consecrated by the feet of gods: Durgākuṇḍa, a place, where the Goddess threw down her sword after killing the demons Śumbha and Niśumbha; Hanumānghāṭ, Aśvamedhaghāṭ, where Goddess Pārvatī's earring fell into a well; the marble stone which has the footprints of God Viṣṇu . . . a myth, which is even today a living reality for many of the pilgrims, who come to this bank, year after year, to get themselves purified by the water of the holy river.

Pilgrims and inquisitive people throng the bathing-*ghāṭs.* Priests look for believers who may ask them to perform *pūjā* on their behalf. They have to support their family from the money they coax out of the pilgrims. After bathing, women hold their *sārīs,* like sails in the wind, to dry them. Young men do acrobatic Yoga exercises. Barbers, whose customers are squatting in front of them. Everywhere bathers: women do not remove their *sārīs* while bathing; men enter the water half-naked.

Monks sit in meditation-postures, rigid like statues, on the upper steps of the *ghāṭs,* above the crowds. When I walk around here early in the morning, they pray to the rising sun with raised hands. Many of them sit praying all night, completely wrapped in clothes.

Here and there, wire-frames of the Durgā-idols from the last *pūjā,* enveloped in straw. The colourful painted clay-painting is washed away by the river. Ęven water-rats are not interested in what remains of them.

Black smoke rises over the cremation-places. The earth is soiled by charred wood and cow-dung. Five or six burning fires. There is a tired flickrring under a half-burnt corpse; another pile of wood has been almost completely burnt; the third one is waiting to be set on fire. On one side, the dead are lying, covered in white cloth, some of them in violet silk. Ragged men bring the next corpse. Four of them carry the dead with stretched out hands over their heads. They sing in a harsh voice – almost crying out loudly – in an edgy rhythm, "*Rāma nāma satya hai*!" Children in rags, a man who is drying his shirt over the fire of a burning pyre, corpses with flies buzzing around them, hungry cows, dirt.

Śiva triumphs! Death is neither aesthetically nor ritualistically euphemized. It is seen in its naked form. But I see nobody weeping. One who has many rebirths, has also many deaths; an individual is not important. And there is no other dying that is craved for than dying on the bank of the holy river.

Yesterday I discovered a young bearded *sādhu* in the last row of the people who had come for Mā's *darśana*. I have talked to him very often. When he was leaving the *āśrama*, I followed him on the steps down to the Ganges, and asked him, whether he had time for me. Instead of an answer, he sat down on a step and showed me a place on the side plinth.

With me I had a letter from Germany. A Catholic friend of mine had made some points in it, and I wanted to give her an apt reply from the viewpoint of Hinduism.

The first principle of Hinduism, so it was written in this letter, is monistic pantheism, whereas Jewish-Christian thinking considers that God and creation are two entities. "This difference appears to me to be absolute. Whether besides the existence of God, there is another existence, created by him, but a real existence of a different sort, or whether everything beside the deity is only illusion." It could not be said that the monistic pantheism *and* the Christian viewpoint are (both) correct.

My conversation partner listened to me, as I was translating the letter, with an expression of a patient teacher on his face. "We distinguish two aspects of *Brahman*", he said, "The Highest *Brahman* – we call it transcendent and acosmic - is doubtlessly without any characteristics and is above time, space and causality. Thus the question about a creation of the universe cannot arise from this aspect, because all that exists is *Brahman*. But this Highest *Brahman* is perceived only by the eye of the one who is enlightened. It is enshrouded and it appears to us, thanks to the illusion of *māyā*, as a phenomenal cosmic *Brahman* of infinitely diverse forms and figures. An unenlightened eye perceives this second aspect of *Brahman*. And what it sees is reality from the level of its knowledge. The relative *Brahman* is manifested also as a personal god. Water remains essentially water, even if it takes the form of ice. God does not cease to be *Brahman*, He is *Brahman* that has become a person. You know that we speak about God, in this realm of the "second level", as the Creator, Preserver and Destroyer of the world. To this extent, our thinking combines the strict monism that is expressed in the doctrine of the duality-less Highest *Brahman* with the concept of a creation which can be differentiated from its creator. There are Vedic myths of creation as there are Biblical myths of creation."

My second question was about *samādhi*. It read: "What happens in the soul of a person, when he succeeds, thanks to his religious nature and his acquired technique, in bringing about this condition? Is it correct, if I say that it is a perception of God's image in oneself? This would be an explanation that can be understood by a Christian. But he usually doubts that there is a direct or even an absolute perception of God Himself in *samādhi*. A man, according to Scholastic theology, must experience first an intense metamorphosis in eternal life, to be able to endure the eternal divine light."

My Conversation partner: "Allow me to preface my remark: among the prerequisites necessary for attaining *samādhi*, you have forgotten the most important one to which Mā has again and again pointed out: the Grace of God. All efforts are meaningless without it. And now I must repeat, what I have already told you. Again here, both dualistic and non-dualistic explanations are possible in Hinduism. You know the phrase. 'How does it help me to become sugar? I want to taste sugar!' That is the viewpoint of a dualist. He experiences himself as a servant of God, whom he approaches endlessly, but without the distance being completely reduced. There is always duality in the blissful unity with the Lord. A non-dualist "*becomes* sugar". He believers that there is only one *Brahman,* and he penetrates all the veils of *māyā,* over all the stages of *samādhi,* to reach the mysterious border, at which God's grace receives him into an absolute unity with *Brahman.* You see, one does not believe here only that a man can see the eternal divine light, but that he can become one with it. The purifying transformation which the Church-doctrine transfers to the other world, has prepared the soul of man for the *union* with God on the earth itself during the period of his countless rebirths."

"But only one could be right. Either the one who says, 'Man can *see* God in enlightenment', or one who says, 'He can become God!'"

"How do you know it? Religion is not mathematics. You start from the premise that a certain conception is correct and conclude that everything else is wrong. Where it concerns God, you must be cautious. Everything is possible for him."

"My third question ensues from the second. To be more exact: it is the question of the letter writer. Let me translate it: Revelation of God bestowed upon a Hindu – say in *samādhi,* is within man's natural feasibility of knowledge. It is to me (she writes) the manner of experiencing God 'from below', that is from man's position, within his given world of experience, in a direction in which he advances towards God and God lets him find him. But God has done, on his own, still something beyond this. He has moved towards man. Besides creation, he has taken other initiatives. He came into Christ and spoke to the world through him. I would call it a supernatural revelation, in contrast to the natural, archaic one of Hinduism. What can you say about it?"

"In this context, natural and supernatural are categories of man's contemplation about the mystery of transcendence.

We use them also, but only on the level from which we observe the relative aspect of the highest reality of *Brahman*. On this level of knowledge, *Brahman* is revealed as a personal god, as the highest Lord of the world, as *Bhagavān*. We also believe that he is evident not only in creation, but has taken, even several times, initiatives beyond it, by coming to us and teaching us, for example, in the form of Śrī Kṛṣṇa, or of Śrī Rāma, or of Christ or Buddha. Where is the difference?

I have read recently that the Christians 'accuse' our *avatāras* that they are not real men, but only Gods in disguise - Gods who have disguised themselves in human flesh. This is clear, they say, from the fact that our *avatāras* have not really suffered. I ask you: Who will decide it, and by which criteria?

And if the matter of suffering is really so important, read the *Rāmāyaṇa*. Śrī Rāma's life was a chain of suffering. What is so unique about Christ? That he was crucified? Sacrificial death of God is a glorious and horrible truth. It is also found in our myths, in what your scientists call myths. I would say, in traditions, in which an eternal truth is revealed, although it is covertly done. Or is it the resurrection of Christ that gives him special position? Even today, you will find in India people who will confirm to you that they have spoken to the dead, over whom Death has no power. They come to us in a spiritual body. My father's *Guru* lived more than three centuries ago, and yet he is seen several times by my father, and he touches him, as if touching him with a hand of flesh."

My opposite speaks so fast that I have a problem of understanding him. We have, in the meantime, attracted a few urchins who are observing us with astonishment. Our conversation has got an apologetic element. It is disturbing me. In fact, I find the young monk so kind in his openness and his taking such a passionate interest in the conversation. I must tell him once more that he should not see in me an equal partner. My knowledge is only deficient. I am at the same time reminded of a remark by a protestant theologian, who told me about his experiences with the Asians and he had already found out years ago, that a generation of young Buddhists and Hindus is growing, which has been influenced by religious ideologization of the West, and has been increasingly making apologetic arguments.

The monk perhaps reads from my face, what is going though my head. He tries to make a compromise:

"Do we want to fight like children to decide who has, among us, a more powerful father? See, you find that our belief is archaic or cosmic, and it got stuck in the realm of natural revelation of God. If I should answer in the spirit of this statement, I must say that we feel that your dualistic thinking, together with the claim of absoluteness which you make for Christ's divine incarnation, is childish. We would think that this position corresponds to the level on which only the second aspect of *Brahman* is perceived; it is called by us dualistic and relative, and it is said about it, that it corresponds to the intellectual capacity of the one who is not enlightened. But such a reply will not take us further. I, therefore say: You are right, as we are also right. Both truths are 'nullified' in the Highest *Brahman*; preserved and merged into the last truth."

Obviously, the young monk was suddenly in a great hurry. In a couple of strides, he was at the bank of the river and scooped water in his hollow hand to power it over his head. Then he removed his spectacles, shook himself laughing and nodded to me. When he suddenly returned, he had already moved a dozen steps along the bank towards the city.

"Listen", he said, "forget all labels: transcendent, cosmic, acosmic, archaic, etc. That is the sophistry of the people who are in love with their wisdom. I will tell you what Śrī Kṛṣṇa said to his friend Arjuna: 'Let others go. You alone take refuge in me. I shall release you from your sins because I like you.'"

The short-sighted eyes of the young man are suddenly focussed with a radiant cheerfulness on me; it is simply infectious. So we stand facing each other and laugh. I would have liked to know, whether I could resist the temptation of arguing with him, if only my knowledge would permit a genuine discussion. Besides, how much more authentic he is now in the moment, when he has shaken off all ideological "I-know-all" manner. I suddenly understand that one of the most profound mysteries of Mā's credibility is not in her knowing something better, but in her knowing something.

We are now counting our hours in Banaras. It is a pity that I got acquainted with the young *sādhu* only in the last few days. I would like to discuss so many more things with him. But he comes for the *darśana* only when Mā has already come, sits only in the last row and disappears before she leaves. I ventured once more, nevertheless, to talk to him. He made a hasty gesture, then he laughed, and we went and sat under the bushes in the yard of the *āśrama*.

Every time, he cuts short the pleasantries with a sweep of his hand. "What is it today?"

"The problem of good and bad. I often hear and read that an enlightened one is beyond good and bad."

"It is true, because morality is a part of the imperfect world. You are moral. You say for example, 'As a matter of fact, I should go as a nurse to a lepers' colony', isn't it? Should! This 'should' shows that you are imperfect. Only the enlightened one, as Mā often says, whose ego is burnt in the fire of self-awareness or is melted in the love of God, has absolute freedom. He does not fight any more on the side of good against bad, for, virtue has become his nature. Hence, the laws of morality do not apply to him. He does not say, 'I should do good', he is good."

"I understand it. But does he not really fight any more against what is bad."

"No, he releases it. Did Christ improve the sinner by his sermon or punishment? He released her by showing her love and grace. That has nothing to do with morality. What does Śrī Kṛṣṇa say? 'Love me, and I shall release you from your sins.'"

"Mā answered, when I complained about the bad in me, 'I do not see anything of it, I see only your divine self. ' Has, thus, what is bad, no factual reality? Shall we make it more concrete, say a murder on account of greed or envy."

"It has a reality on the level where you are standing now and which I called the level of phenomenal *Brahman*, and you have to fight it in this reality. Good and bad in absolute *Brahman* is nothing else but waves in an infinite ocean. I know, it confuses you that we think in the categories of different levels of knowledge, and yet see the one in the diversity. Every level has its correct aspect of reality. A ten-year-old boy is a good pupil if he masters the fundamentals of arithmetic. Nobody expects him to have the knowledge of higher mathematics. You are accessible only to the mathematical thinking on a different level."

"My second question: Where is the origin of evil?"

"Have I not already told you that we call the world-happening or the cosmic process *līlā*? The game of *Brahman* with himself. This *līlā* is infinite with respect to both the dimensions of time; it consists of an infinite chain of spontaneous manifestations of *Brahman*. There is no plan at its basis like the one of the Biblical creation of the world. There is, thus, also no origin of evil as a power, which could be created once; some time or could be made to emerge in a different way from non-existence. There is no evil or satanic power whatever. Everything is Brahman."

"But that does not alter the fact that we see and do evil, for example, a murder on account of greed. If it does not have a cosmic and historical origin, it must have a cause."

"Of course, in *karma*. Whether and how you faced light and darkness in your earlier life determines whether the bright or the dark forces are powerful in your soul. On the level of the ethical, you can replace bright and dark by good and bad or evil."

"Here functions thus this pedantic mechanism: for a kilo of evil a kilo of *karma,* for a kilo of *karma* a kilo of suffering . . ."

"If you want it that way." The young *sādhu* is diligently busy "counting" the pearls of his rosary, while talking to me; or was he possibly doing *japa* with a sort of his second consciousness? My audacious wording has startled him. He lets the rosary disappear in his robe.

"We would say that an immanent retributive justice of world happening rules here. What spontaneously comes from *Brahman,* can appear to us as law. We could just as well say: divine justice rules here. But did we not speak about grace and love that alone can release us from the evil? Since we identify ourselves with our body and with the wishes of our mind, we say: That here am I, that there are you. Our 'I' wants to possess, to acquire 'you'; if it is resisted, it becomes bad and acts bad. Our self feels the holy attraction of the eternal self. God's Grace cures it from ignorance which is the cause of all evil and all suffering; it comes from the error that this 'I' thinks that it has (an isolated) self. The one who is enlightened by the Grace of *Bhagavān,* is brought to a path at the end of which he sees only *Brahman.*

"But how can he see nothing except light in all that darkness, or, expressed differently, what can I do to see less darkness?"

"If you were to be sagacious enough to understand a reply to this question, you would not ask further. A tree does not ask either: 'What can I do to bear the fruit?' When it has become ripe enough, it bears the fruit."

"But it must be possible . . ."

A crafty brown hand interrupts me almost angrily. "Keep quiet now. Words will not help you here any further!"

November 19, 1963

Many people come to bid farewell to Mā. We have a first class compartment which is almost exclusively reserved for us. Mā usually travels in a coupé. The upper berth is fully packed with the luggage, and she rests on the lower one. P. stays with her during the journey to look after her. When I some time expressed my surprise that the upper berths in Mā's or her mother's compartment were not used by the persons accompanying them, but are always packed with luggage, someone said to me: That is obvious; one cannot lie over a being that is worshipped as a deity. Would anyone be allowed to sleep over a king of a European country? And Mā is, after all, more than a king.

Mā's retinue gives emphasis to a conservative style of travelling. Suitcases are not welcome. But there are gigantic hold alls, buckets, baskets, bundles, big earthen jugs with drinking water and smaller ones, often beautifully embellished jugs with the holy Ganges water, of which everyone has a precious stock. Rail journey for Mā is the only opportunity to rest a little, often in months. She lies in bed almost the whole time, sleeps a great deal, talks to those who travel with her, who come from other compartments or from the third class in which most of the *sādhus* and the girls travel. Or she dictates her replies to the letters she has received. Unfortunately, she does not have sufficient peace in the train. Often groups of her followers come on big stations and storm the compartment or call her to the door. Some of them travel for a while in the train, so that they can speak to Mā. How often I have been woken up – even during later journeys – in the the night by impatient throng of people, who were waiting at midnight, at 1, at 2, at 3 a.m., for the train on some bigger stations to see Mā.

P. sleeps on the floor in front of Mā's bed half sitting and half leaning against the luggage. When I said to her, "I admire you that you can sleep like this", she replied and smiled, "Wherever I am with Mā, I get excellent sleep. When I am not with her, I can't sleep well." Mā's compartment is not locked during night journeys, quite contrary to the usual practice of travelling in India.

A stranger travels only in my compartment, a teacher, hidden behind his newspaper for hours. I am asked not to enter the other compartments of our bogie. Many of my travel companions adhere strictly to orthodox rules. They eat and drink only what comes from the *āśrama.* The moment I would come under the "roof" of their compartments, their stock of food, would become impure in a ritualistic sense. Then the āśramites would have to fast during the remaining part of their journey.

In the afternoon, the train is travelling for a long time through an afforested hilly land. It is November end. Trees are getting autumal hues. Many dead trunks look peculiar in faded white-grey; they have bizarre forms. There is still a reddish blossom in the underwood, and the sky is very bright blue. Transparent aquarelle-shades, a fine web of lines. A profile of rocky slopes, fallen trees, a path that is lost, flight pathway of a white bird. Everywhere a silent withering. Śiva triumphing without violence.

I have an interesting conversation with the teacher. He is working in a Dutch Missionary School, but comes from a – as he says – " very orthodox brāhmaṇa family". His father is now 85 years old, and his mother is 79. He has nine siblings, 7 sisters, who are all married, and two brothers, who are educated like him. His father was an official in the Ministry of Education. When all his children had settled and his services were not required by the State, he retired finally, together with his wife, from his civil and family life. He had thereby fulfilled his traditional religious obligations.

"Now he lives with my mother in a mud-hut, he has himself built on the bank of the Ganges in the vicinity of Haridwar", said the teacher. "The hut has two rooms. The assets consist of a fireplace, two sleeping mats of my parents, a bag with books and the writing material of my father. And besides, of course, a small *pūjā*-altar.

My parents get up at 2 a.m. Then my father reads out from holy books till 4 a.m. Then they go out for a walk for two hours. They take the morning bath at 6 a.m. in the Ganges. They don't give it up even in winter, when the water is ice cold. In the course of the forenoon, my father teaches pupils in a nearby Sanskrit-school. Only at noon time, he eats a little for the first time during the day. My mother takes tea in the morning. They take as much or as little lunch as small children. Each one eats three *chapātis* and some vegetable. Then they take rest. Later, my father alone studies the Vedas. Sometimes, has discussions with the teachers of the Sanskrit-school. My mother meets wives of other men who have also settled down in the surroundings like my father. Women sing *kīrtana* and pray; they also gossip sometimes. Of course, my parents perform *pūjā* together. There is a *Śiva-liṅga* on their small altar, but they do not pray to a particular deity. They sing and recite verses from the Vedas, and they meditate. They go to bed at 8 in the evening. Incidentally, no physician has touched them so far. My father says: 'God must help us.' Since the time my parents have started living in a hermitage, we see them seldom. We visit them sometimes, and the teachers from the Sanskrit-school tell us that they are always cheerful and kind. I also think that they are happy."

"Is it exactly in the same way true for your mother as for your father?"

"Our mother would not utter a word about it, but I think, she does it for our father's sake. She would not like to part from him, and she will also not leave him alone. If my father were to die first, she would come to one of us. If she dies first, my father will stay to his end in the hut; it may be that he ends his life as a mendicant, although he has a pension, from which he would live in a city?"

"May I ask: will you also do what your father is doing now, when you become old? Will your wife go with you?"

The teacher has a face of an old race which has a long culture. He is fair-skinned; he has fine features; he is serious and betrays the signs of secret knowledge and restrained suffering. He speaks softly and hesitantly. He does not reply to my question for a long time. Then he says smiling:

"It appears to me now almost impossible, to detach myself so completely from all that, what makes our life comfortable. But who knows, how I shall l think about it when I become old. My wife would go with me, wherever I go. There, I have no worries."

I utilize the long railway journey for reading. For quite some time now, I have been engrossed in reading an interpretation of the *Bhagavad Gītā* written by an Indian scholar. He has made a reference to Christian and Western philosophical thinking in it. But what I have found in it, provokes me: The author, who appears to be a famous man, has made serious mistakes while using occidental terminologies.

When I read Western interpretations of the books on Indian heritage, I am often worried, that the German or English translations of the Indian terminologies may miss what is actually meant. That begins with the translation of very "common" concepts like *Brahman* as "an objective mind" and *Ātman* as "a subjective mind". I am always happy, when the Sanskrit-terminologies are used. There may not be direct translation in the languages of the West for many of them. One has to try to describe them, although it is cumbersome.

I found out earlier in my conversation with the teacher who works in a Christian school and who also masters, incompletely like me: the Western tradition of education, that it was not possible to come to an understanding of the concept of forgiveness. We had talked about a murder announced in the news. This experience should keep me from showing over-hasty optimism to say that Hindus and Christians (including myself, although I cannot count myself among them in an orthodox sense) should only talk together to understand one another. Conversations with the young *sādhu* in Banaras were so peculiarly "flat". Later I had asked myself the question: Did I not feel then: caution, we are going around so generously with concepts? Besides, he was scarcely typical. He knew so much of Christianity. The teacher, who is now lying on his berth and reading *The Plays of Oscar Wilde,* had little idea about Christian concepts. And yet, I would not say that he was a stranger to me. I can share so many things in terms of what is purely human, below the level of concepts: his worries about his kin, his own health, his professional success and the peace in the world . . .

When I stretched myself out in the night on my well-upholstered berth to sleep, a precious contentment flowed through me from top to bottom: at home with myself, in this railway bogie, in this country, in this world . . .

At daybreak, I had the fill of my sleep. I heard the gentle sound of the rosary pearls from the bed of the teacher. I go out to the passage. It is just only 4.30 a.m. The doors of the compartments are open. Narayana-Svami is praying with his rasping voice: "Nārāyaṇa, Nārāyaṇa, Nārāyaṇa. . ." Even Gopinath Kaviraj is sitting on his bed, motionless. Is he meditating? They are talking in whisper in Didimā's compartment. P. is squatting in front of Mā's bed. Mā's is still sleeping.

Chapter 7

Fasting and Meditation in Ahmedabad

November 23, 1963

A great *Saṃyama Mahāvrata,* a week of fasting and meditation is observed in Ahmedabad. It is organized by Mā's followers every year, now for the fourteenth time, usually in place which is famous as a pilgrim centre. This time they deviated from the rule while choosing the place to fulfil the last wish of Mā's old follower, who had prayed to Mā to hold the meditation-week at his place, before he died.

From the very first moment, one has the impression that the programme is well-organized. We were received at the station and taken in cars to the house of the organizer. He had erected a beautiful small house of compressed sheets for Mā on his estate; a big elegant paṇḍāla was built next to it. These paṇḍālas have a solid construction. Their columns go deep into the ground, and their roof-structure takes the load of gigantic fans – in this instance sixteen— and lamps and loudspeakers.

The residential building of the organizer is modern, spacious and practical. People who are close to Mā are accommodated here. I was shown a verandah for my accommodation; I also eat there. I do not go into other rooms to avoid unnecessary complications. I can sleep in the house of a tile-manufacturer, who has kept three comfortable rooms at the disposal of the participants of the conference and has shown that he is a very pleasant host.

We can choose, whether we want to register our names in the class A or class B of fasting diet. All participants fast completely on the first day. Several tanks of *gaṅgājala* are kept on the premises, and we are encouraged to drink as much as possible from it. It is particularly necessary for spiritual and physical purification. The water was brought from Rishikesh where the holy river leaves the Himalayas and flows into the plains.

The diet-class "A" drinks only Ganges water on the seventh day and has only a *pot-au-feu* (one-pot-cooked-dish) on other days. Of course, smoking and other stimulants are prohibited. The diet-class "B" to which I belong, has a *pot-au-feu* (one-pot-cooked-dish) and a glass of milk in the evening.

The proper programme of the conference begins at 8 a.m. with one hour's meditation, and this applies also to the afternoon session. Apart from rather a long break at noon, the day is filled up to about 10 p.m., sometimes even longer without a break, with recitations from holy scriptures of Hinduism, lectures and *kīrtanas* or with question hours. It makes great demands, not only on mental receptivity, but also on physical stamina, particularly of those who fast strictly. I have the impression from the first day that the élite have gathered here people who are serious about their spiritual goal. Many of the participants have been attending these weeks for years, and they are obviously no beginners in meditation. Probably, even their average level of education too is fairly high. I see faces—among men and women of all age-groups—on which spiritual heritage and self-discipline are stamped. And they are not few. It is noticeable as well in the general social atmosphere.

All these functions are deliberately "open", i.e. anyone from the local inhabitants of Ahmedabad is welcome to participate. These people who have not registered their names occupy the back portion of the paṇḍāla.

It is a part and parcel of the traditional upbringing of people of this land that they learn from their childhood to concentrate on spiritual matters, even in noisy surroundings. And so, such a function can be a happy synthesis between the demands of the élite, the *vratīs*, and the masses. The *vratīs* are seldom disturbed, so that at the periphery, things go on as cheerfully as in a public festival. Hundreds of people from Ahmedabad come in the afternoons, often whole families with children of all age-groups. They camp on the lawns. The children play, and the elders listen with one ear to lectures and discussions. Probably most of them come, because they hope to see Mā.

The organization of the proper programme of the conference is in the hands of a young *Brahmacārin*, who had come to Mā in his adolescence. He discharges his difficult job with great charm. A giant: broad shoulders, a round head with thick growth of hair, his hair reaching down to his waist, bushy eyebrows, a small beard and beautiful teeth. Day after day, his face disappears further into the jungle of his black hair, because the *vratīs* are not allowed to cut the hair. The young giant holds the reins with almost girlish gentleness. His voice never becomes harsh or even loud, when he gives instructions on the microphone. Sometimes, he raises his hands, half smiling and half beseeching to make people understand a necessary action. In his saffron-coloured sleeveless overall, he looks like a young athlete in a classical toga, and he gathers up the folds of his robe with the charm of a youthful princess. It is indeed strange that he manages to keep order without the use of any force.

Only in one point he has an ongoing problem. Most of the speakers exceed the time given to them and mess up the whole programme. Finally, the gentle giant brings a large alarm clock and holds it before the nose of the speaker. But many take little notice of this.

There are couches for the speakers, puṇḍits and other *svāmīs* on the dais. As usual I do not understand very much of what is said, but I notice a few general things. And all speakers talk freely. One feels that they follow the train of their thought completely spontaneously, and at the same time, ignore the heckling and interruption with skill and wit. Occasionally, they interrupt themselves to ask Mā or the *puṇḍits* who are present there for their opinion, and there follows an improvised discussion. Often there are incidental remarks from the dais or from the auditorium. Sometimes a speaker lets someone else speak in between, even lengthily. As a result everything is lively, unlike in the West where often speeches are a monologue. Here, dialogue is always maintained.

The general oratory skill of men is surprisingly high. Their liveliness, ability to modulate the voice, forcefulness of changing expressions, eloquent gestures, all these prevent the audience from wandering to its own thoughts and even falling asleep. I think the most striking difference in style of such religious functions between the West and the East is the way we conduct them in a serious, dignified manner, with a stiff neck, and the people in the East "waste" one third of their precious time in laughing. All these lectures have serious themes. They deal with interpretations of holy scriptures, with questions about religious education, religious life in a family or in a village, with problems of meditation or contemplation and other such themes, and yet sometimes, gales of laughter follow one another. And these speakers do not go on talking rubbish in a nonchalant way. Well-known people who are respected on account of their wisdom sit on the dais.

A *svāmī* often speaks in the evening session. His lecture is different from the others. It is very popular–and probably not only for its contents. After the tense mental concentration of a long day, he appears casual and refreshing. Although the other speakers sit there stripped to the waist and the fans are whirring, he wears a thick, woollen ski cap. He has a deep, harsh voice, and he gives the impression that he is spinning a yarn. But this feeling may be wrong. It is true, he makes simple jokes, and Mā shakes with laughter, the whole paṇḍāla is booming, the *vratīs* are full of merriment. I do not see anyone who stands aloof and does not laugh at the harmless jokes.

A Man who is in his fifties was for me the most impressive speaker. He is an elected Director of an Organization of Indian mendicants which was established a few years ago. The aim of this Organization is to separate the sheep from the goats, i.e. to separate genuine monks from vagabonds disguised as religious men, and thereby enable the State to take action against anti-social people. Śrī Akhandanandaji himself does not look like a mendicant. If he were not sitting there stripped to the waist, he would have looked like a diplomat from a Western country. This is probably too on account of his neat exterior, his social manners and keen intelligence. Possibly also because of the matter-of-fact quiet and forceful manner of his speech. One sees from his eyes behind his horn-rimmed glasses that he is not only clever, but also wise, not only an organizer of monks, but himself also a monk in the real sense of the word.

One evening, he speaks on *Rāsalīlā* of youthful Śrī Kṛṣṇa with the *gopīs,* the cowherdesses. This cycle of myths has given rise to the most profound and the most beautiful mystic interpretations in the *bhakti*–philosophy of the Hindus. Unfortunately, I do not understand anything he says, but the atmosphere which is permeated by objectivity, sensibility and religious ecstasy arouses me in participation. Mā takes leave of the speaker by pressing both her hands to his face.

A professor from Calcutta makes a touching, but alas an unsuccessful effort to solve my language problem. His mother tongue is Bengali, and he has reasonable mastery over Hindi. The State language in Ahmedabad is Gujarati, but many of those who have come understand English. The speaker, therefore, talks in a mixture of Bengali, Hindi, English and Sanskrit in the hope that most in the audience would understand at least something. Finally, he is interrupted by an impatient clapping of hands. The audience reminds him that he has exceeded his time limit. Basically, most wait the whole day for the moment in the evening, when the speakers withdraw, and the microphone is placed before Mā.

Mā answers the questions with astonishing rapidity. A question is barely put, and her answer is already there. Sometimes in a word, sometimes in a number of sentences. Mā herself says that she does not think before giving a reply. She opens her mouth, and it is not her understanding, but her *khyāla* that replies through her. At times, one has the impression that she herself is surprised later by her answer. Occasionally she tries to interpret it for herself. Often the answers are such that the whole paṇḍāla booms with laughter. Mā herself laughs at her answer, as if someone else has given it. And really, they are indeed not "her" answers.

Once in a while she is suddenly startled after listening to a question. One feels that she is awaiting an answer. But: "My *khyā*la says nothing. Ask another question." Occasionally, she makes *svāmīs* answer the questions. "*Puṇḍit bolo*" (Answer, learned gentleman). Perhaps, she wants to make a friendly gesture to the learned men who assemble there in great numbers and occupy their seats on the dais. But sometimes, a member of the audience demands: "We want to know your answer, Mā."

Very seldom does anyone translate the question and her answer to me. For example: "Isn't sleep a type of meditation too?" – "If you want it that way, yes." – "Why shouldn't we then sleep during meditation?" – "Sleep a little." – "And on what do you meditate, Mā?" – "Who tells you that I meditate? Perhaps, I also sleep?" – This is accompanied by uninterrupted laughter.

But there are also long, serious discussions. Say, on the question, "What happens to a pupil, whose *Guru* dies? Or on, what is *vairāgya* (detachment, aversion)." Mā's reply is: "When real meditation happens within you, worldly pleasures become boring and empty. There is *vairāgya,* when every contact with the worldly stirs the fire of renunciation in you. That does not mean that you deny or despise the world. The worldly things are no longer acceptable to you. Your body refuses them. Everything belonging to the world appears to you to be too hot; you can't touch it. In other words: the Death dies.

When you come out of meditation, and if you are still able to behave in a worldly manner, then you have not as yet experienced inner metamorphosis. After real meditation, you will begin to seek the divine with passion. Your hunger for it will make you recognize that nothing that is ephemeral can give you any more satisfaction. How can I make it any clearer, *Pitājī*?

Many times people come to me and tell me that their sons and daughters have got into a vehicle and have gone away without looking back ignoring the distress of their fathers and mothers. [In another context, Mā repeatedly and forcefully warned her friends: "Serve your father and mother with love and reverence, as you love God."] They are completely untouched by the suffering of their parents. See, it is exactly like this at a certain place on your spiritual path. One suddenly feels: 'Those whom I thought were near and dear to me in the world, are related to me only according to my flesh and blood. What does that matter to me?'

Nobody puts his hand in the fire on his free will or steps on a serpent. So you must view worldly things and turn away from them. Then you swim in a current that carries you in the opposite direction; and later, when you have detached yourself even from the detachments, you will see that there is nothing left for you: detachment or non-detachment. All that is, is *tat.*

Many people say that one attains enlightenment by an uninterrupted effort in *sādhana.* But is it true that effort can bring enlightenment ? The veil of ignorance is destroyed, and once this has happened, then *tat,* that which is, is revealed. He is unveiled light–Self the Eternal. . . ."

Mā advises again and again those who want her to lead them on the path of enlightenment that they must totally turn away from the world. More precisely: not from their duties on this earth, but from mundane diversions. One who runs after them, "goes on the path of Death", but the "Death dies" for him, who turns his back on them.

Someone asked during one of the last evenings: "What about the people who leave their families in the lurch to live as mendicants or to go to an *āśrama*? Is their action right?" Mā's answer was:

"I would advise the one who is uncertain, whether he should stay with his family or dedicate himself to spiritual life: 'Stay with your family.' One may leave one's family, only when there is no question whether one is doing right or wrong. One who is called by God, does not ask, he follows the call without looking back. God will look after his family."

November 27, 1963

Mā sang today. "Singing" is hardly the expression for it. It is like asking a tightrope walker, if he is going for an afternoon stroll. It was melodious; the girls say, she has a cold. Her voice was peculiarly husky,, low and almost flat. She tilted her head a little backwards and closed her eyes. Her lips were half open. I saw that this complete detachment from the world was reflected in her features. There was silence in the paṇḍāla. The silence flowed from her and filled everywhere. Suddenly: "*He Bhagavān*! –a gentle, blissful cry. *Heo Bhagavān* – O God – *preo Bhagavān* – beloved god – *jeo Bhagavān* – Victorious God – *ānandamayī, he Bhagavān* – O God, imbued with bliss – *maṅgalamayī, he Bhagavān* – fountain of goodness, O god – and again: *he Bhagavān* . . .

"Supreme bliss of the drop, which, returning homeward, falls from the cloud into the ocean–becomes ocean." A phrasing I have come across several times while reading Hindu Scriptures. Of Johannes Tauler: ". . . For, the Soul is fallen from its own self into the Beloved (God), in whom it is lost like a drop of water in the deep ocean."

One of the questions addressed to Mā today was: "Should a married woman practise *sādhana* first or look after her husband and the family?"

Mā answered, "Women, your *sādhana* is in your serving your husbands and your families. But you should try to find time and strength for your prayers and meditations too."

I have heard Mā say: "Women are basically happier than men. It is their normal task to subjugate themselves with love to their men, in whom they should worship the incarnation of God and serve them. Thus, their natural life is already an effective *sādhana*, which can lead them to enlightenment. It is more difficult for men who are masters in their family and in society to practise in their life the spirit of living devotion to God."

I tried to ask Mā today about the difference between *mokṣa* and our Christian concept of salvation. She answered, "*Mokṣa* is not release from sin and suffering, but the knowledge of the true nature of our own self in its identity with the Highest Self, *Brahman*." It is true, it is not a general Hinduistic view, but the view of the *Vedānta*. We have been *Brahman* since time immemorial, but we realize our own real nature which was hidden before by *māyā*, only when there is *mokṣa*. One who is awakened to unity with *Brahman* does not need salvation in the Christian sense.

And once more coming back to the question of detachment from the world which is so often discussed: it is generally imagined that an apostle who renounces the world is a gloomy type of ascetic. I am sure that there is such a type even among Śivite monks. Surprisingly I frequently find that those who break their ties with the world are the most cheerful and happy men I have ever met. Almost all *puṇḍits* who speak here and who are monks have a serenity that is so enchanting in Mā. They are already beyond the need to practise detachment. There is only *Brahman* and *Brahman* alone for a *saṃnyāsin* who has realized the highest reality. So there is nothing more from which he has to detach himself. Mā says, 'Everything is *Brahman*. Thus everything reflects the bliss of *Brahman*. Even my diseases bring nothing else but joy.'"

There was a climatic change yesterday in the morning session. It was only the third day of our week. Who could have anticipated it at this time of the season? A few minutes after we had assembled for meditation, we heard a distant thunder which suddenly burst over our heads. Squalls started tearing at the poles of the paṇḍāla; it had become so dark, as if night had come. Finally, there was a downpour of tropical rain. It beat on the roof of the paṇḍāla, as if with gigantic hammers.

The canvas roof split directly over the place where Mā was sitting. A huge torrent poured down into the paṇḍāla. Young *svāmīs* protected Mā with umbrellas and cloths to the best of their ability. I did not take my eyes off her even for a single moment. Mā had leant back on her pillow at the start of the meditation and closed her eyes. After that, there was no change whatsoever either in her posture or in the expression on her face. One could see that she was alert and knew exactly what was going on around her, but there was no nervousness on her face when water poured down around her, and the timberwork of the paṇḍāla began to crash everywhere.

Soon there was no dry place in the remaining area of the paṇḍāla. Time and again, the canvas of the roof started tearing at a new place under the pressure of water. Most of the women stood to avoid the torrent. A few stalwarts on the men's side remained sitting upright in the midst of water. It appeared that they were not at all disturbed in their meditation.

About twenty minutes later, the raging of the storm diminished for a while, but nobody seized the opportunity to leave the dangerously unsteady paṇḍāla. There was a pause only for a moment, and the storm erupted again with double force. Everyone was soaking wet in the paṇḍāla. There is fear of epidemic if sudden cold damp takes over. Will the paṇḍāla collapse? The heavy fans above our heads were shaking, as if they were made of straw.

I often imagined during my first days here in the paṇḍāla that it was a ship. I imagined like this, because the pictures framed in glass on front side of the paṇḍāla used to swing gently in the wind causing a peculiar reflection of the broad blue stripes of the canvas that formed a part of the paṇḍāla wall.

But now our ship is in distress, but although there is lightning and thunder crashing around us, nobody seems to be in a grip of fear. There is some whispering here and there among some women. Nobody is speaking loudly. Whenever one looks at Mā, one feels the presence of protective power. Her eyes are closed as before. Her face has an expression of complete detachment and complete attention. Her mouth is opened a little. Sometimes, there is a barely perceptible smile on her face.

Soon after meditation, one of the *svāmīs* sings a song that is always sung on this occasion, in a soft voice, so that one imagines more than one hears it, but this time loudly into the raging hurricane: "*He hitā, he pitā, he brahmasvarūpa* . . . " (O merciful One, O Father, O eternal *Brahman* ...). It is one of the songs which "resounded one day in Mā" and ever since sung by her friends. Mā opens her eyes and looks around quietly and kindly, as if everything is as always. In the meanwhile, young *svāmīs* are telling us to leave. "Run as fast as you can into the house", the voice comes from the loudspeaker, "Mā will stay here till the last person leaves this paṇḍāla."

I read in the periodical of the Association of Mā's friends, what happened next. I had very quickly run into the house, and did not see it myself. "As soon as the last *vratī* had left the paṇḍāla and Mā had come out, the whole construction collapsed 'in the twinkling of an eye'. It was a miracle that nobody was injured. It was like the legend of Śrī Kṛṣṇa in which it is said that he held the mountain Govardhana over the heads of his friends, the cowherds, to protect them from raging downpour."

I guess that around 400 to 500 people sought shelter in the house of the organizer after the collapse of the paṇḍāla. One would have expected the meditation week to come to an abrupt end. But nobody mentions it. Groups are formed here and there, where *kīrtanas* are sung. I see many people doing *japa.* The guest speakers come without much delay and hold their lectures sitting at the threshold of the large living room. Their voices can reach the few hundred people filling the surrounding passages and spaces. It is one of Mā's basic principles not to enter a house of a person who has a family. So, she stays for hours outside the house at the entrance, and an icy, wet wind is blowing there.

It stopped raining in the afternoon. The programme is interrupted for a short time and continues in the evening according to plan. The speaker sits on the steps leading to the house of the organizer. The audience is partly in the house and partly on wooden frames on the sodden ground in front of the house. Ox-driven carts loaded with stones come into the premises during the lectures. Are they erecting a paṇḍāla once more? Yes. When I enter the estate around 7.30 a.m. next day, there is a brand-new paṇḍāla in some other place. I am not imagining this. The ruins of the old one can still be seen.

Gujaratis are more friendly to strangers like me than the people in Banaras. Many speak English. Someone always draws me into a conversation. They ask me again and again, "What does Mā mean to you?" Those who ask this question appear to be fascinated by Mā, without being able to say why. Some of them make disparaging remarks about the orthodox practices of the āśramites. A physician tells me, "I am not interested in religion. I think, it is outdated. But I am here to observe people. One can make very useful psychological studies, especially in the field of religion." He is disappointed that I–an "intellectual" from the West–love Mā very much.

An elderly man supported by a younger one makes critical remarks. He claims that major part of the people here are happy with *bhakti* and neglect Yoga; this leads to sentimentality. "Most of them think that their work is idolizing Mā; one's *sādhana* is not taken seriously.

I can say with conviction that my impression is different. It could be true in some cases, but I see many who are serious in their *sādhana*. People really are fasting, and how many people do I see praying even in brief intervals.

A man asks me about the monks and nuns who are constantly with Mā. "They do not capture one's attention even when meeting them. Are there no bright souls?"

I defend my friends – I consider these people who belong to Mā as such: "Look at Svāmījī", "he is brilliant. And even Mā's mother is certainly brilliant."

"But what about the others?"

"I think, we should not be critical. How much do we really know? Besides they are people who are drawn to Mā like you and me. Do we shine? When I think about the girls: it must be difficult for them. Do they ever have peace? They constantly move from place to place; probably, they don't have enough sleep as they need; besides, everyone of them has so many spiritual and practical duties. If one is constantly overworked, although they would not admit it, it is hardly surprising, one might look downcast at times. In such a hurly-burly as here, they can never have a quiet minute with Mā."

When I see in the evening shadows under the eyes of the girls and the dreadful fatigue in the faces of many of the monks, I am reminded of what Nietzsche said about the Christians: "They should appear 'more released'".

Usually fifty or more people wait in front of Mā's hamlet for an opportunity to talk to her personally. Cars drive in constantly with the "prominent personalities" of the country, like a minister, a scholar, a respected person from the Industry or a *Mahātmā*. Although Mā tries frequently to leave the paṇḍāla without being noticed, she never succeeds in moving without hundreds of people running after her.

Classes from schools, village communities from the locality, various Associations, come to see her.

I am surprised that Śrī Gopinath Kaviraj is never in the paṇḍāla. When I ask for him, they say that he stays in a room in the upper storey of the organizer's house. There he can hear all speeches relayed from the loudspeaker. When he wants peace, he shuts his window.

"I find it strange that he travels such a long way and then hardly ever participates in the function", I say.

I get the answer: "What is so strange about it? He participates more intensely than any of us. Who knows how much we owe to his presence without seeing him? The sheer presence of this enlightened man, even if not seen or heard, contributes to the success of the week."

Yesterday Mā told a couple respected for various welfare activities: "The most important thing is to use all your energy in realizing God. Practise *sādhana* diligently. Those who cannot in spite of their effort, should try to serve humanity and consider that it is the service of God."

It is becoming clearer to me that greater significance is given to the love of God than to practical love of man (*caritas*). One who sits in a cave in the Himalayas seeking God or reality and attains self-realization, achieves, according to the views of the Hindus and his contemporaries, more than the one who practises charity. Suspicion that such an existence in a cave is religious egoism, even though very spiritual and testing, does not arise. The main reason is the concept of one single Self, *Brahman*, and all people have their share in this with me. When I realize this Self in me, I serve its realization in all souls, it is only separate from me as long as I am misled by *māyā*.

The religious support of charitable service is not regarded as so important, partly because poverty and disease are regarded as the fruit of the *karma*-seed that was sown in earlier life. A sick man has to "work out" his bad *karma* through suffering. His illness, therefore, is not an evil, but a beneficial atonement.

A conversation during the question hour of the last evening: A *vratī* asked one of the *puṇḍits* what he should do to free himself from his moral defects. The *puṇḍit* answered: "Put them at Mā's feet; she will release you from them." Then the man asked Mā: "Is it true, Mā?" "Can you release us from our sins?" "Have you noticed what a cow does with her calf? Does she not lick it till it is completely clean? It is exactly what God will do to you. You have only to go to him and keep quiet. He is truly your father and your mother."

The meditation week concludes with a ceremony of sacrificial fire that is performed by several priests. All *vratīs* have a black sign drawn on their foreheads. Then Mā stands on a pedestal and distributes *prasāda.* Sweets fly in all directions right across the forecourt. At noon there is a feast with numerous choice vegetables of all kinds and fancy sweets. Gujaratis must have the best Indian cuisine. What is served here is delicious. There are people watching, how well the Memsahib likes the food. A couple of times a voice over the loudspeaker warns: "Take care *vratīs.* Your belly is accustomed to frugal eating for a week; do not take much rich food. It may not agree with you. One of the hosts says, "The feast is a fancy end to a week of fasting. A good *vratī* can be seen from his observing moderation in spite of hunger and tempting offers."
All monks appear in the afternoon with their beards and heads completely shaved, and the *vratīs* are suddenly clean-shaven too. A sobering sight. Most of the men look marvellous in beards. The gentle giant with·out his thatch of hair looks like a shy young man.

December 1, 1963
We stay a couple of days more in Ahmedabad. Many of Mā's followers had invited her to visit them. As she does not enter family homes, she is received each time either in a garden or in a verandah. First, she visits a number of schools in the

early morning; at sunrise, a higher secondary school for 400 boys and girls. A flight of steps is the centre for the fire place in the school-premises. There are four old trees forming a square above the steps. A red canopy. is put between them. It shields the couch on which Mā is sitting. The teachers sit on the carpets to her left and right' and the pupils in two blocks below the flight of steps.

I admire the discipline of the children. They have to listen to the talks of three adults and their senior school-mate for about one and half hours. They sit absolutely quietly and don't appear bored. Finally, a young teacher sings a song accompanied by harmonium and *tablā*. Then Mā sings "*Heo Bhagavān*". I am amazed how young she looks. If I did not know her age, I would think she was in her early thirties. She has such freshness, directness and cheerfulness that I can understand those who claim that she can become supernaturally transformed.

All pupils of this school which is non-denominational– assemble every morning (even on Sundays!) at 5.30 a.m. for prayers. They sing, do yoga-exercises and sit with closed eyes for fifteen minutes "to meditate to the sound of gentle instrumental music." Then they return home. The classes begin at 11 a.m.

Mā visits an owner of a mill this morning. He is worth a few millions. A large, bright, very modern home with ultra modern furnishing and huge expanse of English lawns, a few trees and bushes in fancy order, splendid flowers. Everything ambitious, testifying to good taste, but not at all "Indian". Millionaires live like this in California, in Ticino and near Tokyo. Only the prayer hut of the lady of the house in the back region of the garden is Indian. A simple mud hut with a popular, colourful little altar. The only place on the large plot without elegance.

One of the daughters brings me the "opinion book", i.e. the visitors' book and proudly shows me entries made by

Nehru, Mrs. Kennedy and other prominent personalities. Later, the lady of the house gives the book and a pen to Mā. Mā takes it smiling and makes a small point in the middle of an empty page.

A "throne" is placed for her in the garden, and pillows and carpets are kept ready for her "retinue". The family performs an *āratī*; there is a very refreshing *prasāda*.

I find it difficult to understand the spiritual and emotional attitude of the hosts. Outwardly, they live in a completely "Western style". Perhaps, this "Westernization" is the reason why they feel a certain, may be sceptical, distance with respect to their religious tradition. I think, I feel something of it. The whole "reception" here is social. Mā goes to many people in the neighbourhood; is it perhaps a question of social prestige inviting her to their house too? "The prayerhut"? Even this could be a mere ornamental addition. I am only asking myself this question. I may be wrong.

Then Mā visits a middle-class family. Mā's girls and some of the monks are already there. They sit in a rather narrow, dark yard, where thrones are kept for Mā and her mother, and sing a *kīrtana*. There is turmoil in the yard which is more like a room. Neighbours and friends of the host have come with their children in their Sunday best. Even a couple of neglected street-urchins have come along.

Mā's throne has "style"; it has the gaudy colours of a fair. The hostess adorns her revered guest with a silk-shawl in shocking violet and a crown of colourful glass-beads which are stitched to a carton. It is lined inside with red velvet. Finally, Mā is given a garland of roses. The *āratī* lasts for a long time and is full of gesticulation. Mā sits there like a child allowing itself to be dressed up by its playmates. An old woman prays to her standing with raised hands. Mā focusses her calm, attentive eyes on the face of the enthusiastic old woman.

There is an open space of about three-fourths of a square metre between Mā's throne and the wall. She withdraws now inside there with the hostess – a sheet is put up in front of the "entrance" of the niche–for her to take lunch. Both the hostess and Mā sit on the ground. The woman has cooked the food herself and feeds Mā. She eats with an expression of a patient child who has no appetite.

Mā spends most of her time in this house. The happiness she gives to the whole neighbourhood by doing so is strongly felt. Basically it is good and much more appropriate in the situation for one feels that these people do not know how to treat Mā. They run helter-skelter like frightened and happy children. These people cannot usually cope with organizing such a visit, say, as one would with a displomatic reception.

I meet Mā only after ten hours. She is surrounded by a couple of hundred people in a shabby block of rented flats. Mā is on her legs all day and appears to be dead tired. I sometimes wonder why nobody who is close to her intervenes, when she urgently needs peace. But it seems she does not want to be spared. She would be impatient only if anyone tried.

My companions laugh when I say in the car, "Poor Mā! She must be terribly tired." I have noticed very often that people do not seem to realize how exhausted Mā must be feeling. Someone says to me, "It is unnecessary to talk of suffering here. Mā lives on a level where there is no suffering." I consider, this is wrong! According to the Indian view, enlightened souls live in "another body". When I looked at Mā today, I doubted it. But also I do not understand what it means and how someone has "another body".

Two years ago, I saw a *fakir* pierce a dagger through both his cheeks without shedding a single drop of blood without the slightest physical pain. It was not a trick. I held the dagger and looked very carefully in the mouth of the fellow. I also saw how the (dry) wound closed again in the muscle so that it could hardly be seen. The dagger was as thick as a pencil. Probably, such things are a misuse of spiritual powers. Mā insists on warning her friends against them.

I think the insensitiveness to pain shown by *fakirs* cannot be the result of a spiritual effort. It is different for an ascetic who becomes insensitive to heat and cold, hunger and thirst, as he strives for unity with the Highest Reality, concentrating all his spiritual powers. Where does the path fork on which a religious ascetic and a "magician" go? Is theirs a similar path, as it is often claimed?

I asked myself the question whether Mā feels physical pain. Would many of her followers think that it is disparaging, if it could be conceded that she is physically as frail as we are?

When I see how quickly she changes from over-exertion to such dynamism, then I feel, she has other means than we have for the regeneration of her spiritual condition. "The spirit helps her in her weakness", and not the mind or any physical training.

The question is: Does she really have this power? Or does the spirit take possession, where it wants to? She has herself told me that her *khyāla* comes spontaneously. She is open for its presence. If it happens, she obeys. Does the spirit transform her physical weakness as well?

Chapter 8

Hindu and Parsi Attitudes to Life and Faith

We are again in Bombay for a few days. I had a long discussion with Mā today. Her reply to a question really struck me: I asked Mā, "Why are you so particular that in your presence the laws of Hindu orthodoxy must be strictly observed? You maintain, there is no other reality except *Brahman*. These laws divide not only the castes from one another, but also Hindus from non-Hindus!"

Mā laughed at my question. She had obviously expected it. She sat on the front edge of her bed and spoke with great enthusiasm.

"I shall tell you. You probably know that I come from an orthodox brāhmaṇa family. In the years I was practising *sādhana,* i.e. during the period of repeated fasting and silence, in which Mā (Mā many times used to addressed herself in the third person) experienced different forms of religious ecstasy, I did not observe all these rules. This behaviour had a serious outcome. My friends' opinions were divided about what would result from such behaviour. One day I asked a well-known scholar who was a liberal man: 'Is it correct for me not to follow old rules?' He thought about it and then answered, 'I advise you to respect the laws. The existence of religions will be in danger, if more and more people think that traditional observances which demand personal sacrifice for their preservation are superfluous. Even more important: many orthodox Hindus who would like to come to you would not venture to do so, because they fear that your disrespect for the laws would cause them conflicts (say, on account of ritualistic impurification). Your attitude is a constant worry and burden for them. There are also many *sādhus* and heads of religious communities who will not be able to visit you, for such contact would undoubtedly endanger the orthodox among their followers. The dispute raging among your followers is threatening to spread. It must be avoided.'

I obeyed the scholar. From that day onwards I saw to it that traditional rules were observed by my friends. I personally don't care to which caste or faith a person coming to me belongs. You know that I touch all, but I arrange my life in such a way that I don't cause danger to my orthodox friends or hurt their feelings. That's what matters to me.

Most people live on this level. Traditional laws are still important for them. As long as this is so, they must observe the laws. It is like fruit. You cannot artificially accelerate its process of maturing. It takes time to grow. As long as one is unsure, whether to keep to the laws or not, one must keep to them for one's welfare. A moment comes, when they can be dispensed with. When there are no more doubts, one just does it, and it is right.

I am sure, it is burdensome for the non-Hindus who come to me; but I cannot change the life in the *āśrama* to spare them and thereby cause conflict to my Hindu friends. They are after all a minority. One who loves this little child, does not complain about the rules. He accepts the inconvenience. One day they will no longer be a burden."

On December 12, we went to Poona for a week. It is to the south of Bombay and in a rural setting where Mā has an *āśrama.* A paṇḍāla was erected in its garden for our meetings.

Svāmījī had asked the N. family to accommodate me. Mr. N. is a "constructor"; he constructs roads for the State. The family and three children live here in a simple, beautifully furnished bungalow on the outskirts of the city. A hearty and natural atmosphere makes me feel at home at once.

Mr. and Mrs. N. get up at 4.30 a.m. They devote the first two hours to prayer and meditation. They have made a *pūjā*-room in the cellar. Its long wall is covered with pictures of deities. Mā is the centre of worship. Her pictures occupy the central place. A pair of sandals worn by her are placed on the small altar.

Mr. N. and Mrs. N. perform their *pūjā* here in the morning. I hear them singing a *kīrtana* lustily. Mrs. N. has to begin her daily chores, while Mr. N. is still in the prayer room; she prays while working. The children are only occasionally included. Mrs. N. explains that they have to sleep longer and even the fourteen-year-old Gugu is spared on account of his delicate health. He had polio and he limps a little. The family is not wealthy, but it has done everything to cure him. As Mrs. N. tells me this, she throws light on her religious devotion and her attitude to Mā.

"It is difficult for us. We know that Mā could cure him, and yet we cannot ask her: 'Cure him.' We have again and again forced ourselves not to. We do for Gugu what we can, and we pray: 'O God, do with him whatever you want.'"

When I ask Mrs. N. on one occasion, "What does Mā mean to you?", she answers beaming, "She is the mother of the universe." We are standing in the garden. Mrs. N. is picking flowers which she will give to Mā. "Look at this bush", she ways, "how beautifully it is blossoming. Whenever Mā comes, she takes care that our garden is full of flowers so that we have enough for her. When she is not here, the bushes are often without flowers."

I watch with interest my hosts: surprisingly smooth amalgamation of traditional Indian religious attitude and a modern way of life. This enables them to make efficient use of present-day technology. I do not know how typical this is. I have noticed it elsewhere, but then I am mostly in contact with religiously minded families. It is possible, say among the intellectual élite in the cities there are circles, where there is conflict between conservative and modern attitudes and where a unilateral decision is made in favour or the latter.

The N. family leads a simple life, but it has all technical gadgets of a well-to-do Western family – even an automatic toaster. Mr. N. needs lorries for his work; some of them are kept near the house. He himself drives a jeep, and his wife a big Chevrolet and she knows to deal with the technical faults in the car like an expert mechanic. Modern technology is obviously a part and parcel of these people, who at the same time, are rooted and grounded in a deeply religious world.

The focal point of this world is Mā. She determines everything and knows everything in advance. When decisions have to be made, for example, about the school attendance of the children, or a journey, they pray to Mā and seek her advice in prayer. It is always beneficial for them. And however difficult it may be, they act accordingly.

Mrs. N. firmly believes it was Mā, the Mother of the universe, who saved her family and other people in Poona from the floods which engulfed the city in July 1961. I find the description of the events in the reports to which I often refer. Not a single follower of Mā suffered any damage at that time. Mā said in this report to a circle of her followers:

> "When we got the news that the water was rising with terrible speed, this body had the *khyāla* to tell the water: 'Now start to recede gradually.' And really, the floods began to recede slowly from this moment."

I feel, Mā is left alone much more in Poona, although many people throng her here too. Because she really answers those who seek. Where she comes across an honest search for the truth or a longing for God, she suddenly lights up, however tired she is. But when there is no call on her, then she withdraws into herself oblivious of everything.

I am reminded of an early morning train journey. She was sitting on her bed and had a terrifying expression of inaccessibility. I have only once experienced this here. Her beautiful, sensitive face was chiselled as if from a stone. Her features were angular and inscrutable with an indecipherable expression. This revealed neither anger nor pain, impatience or antipathy, only an unfathomable distance, an inaccessibility and a feeling that she was unmoved by anything around her.

I have often wondered: Does Mā experience what the Christian mystics call "the dark night of the soul?" I have tried cautiously to find out, whether people who have long known Mā, have perceived such a phase of darkness and despair, or if she herself mentioned such experiences. All replied in the negative.

Many people tell me that between her age of 25 and 30, Mā went several times through a long phase of "petrification" in which she not only remained completely silent, but did not also communicate by gesture or facial expression. Could this long "petrification" correspond to what I noticed in the train? And what was going on inside her then? The classical Hindu interpretation would be: her soul had so completely merged with *Brahman* that her body became lifeless like an empty shell.

May be so, or perhaps behind this apparently impenetrable shield, she was undergoing the annihilation of the ego, the final precondition for the total merging with *Brahman,* thus also "the dark night of the soul?"

One thing is certainly true: What happens in Mā, is more removed from us than we think, when we are with her daily. Although she appears to us to be "open", we are in touch with her essential being only rarely.

I wonder too: Is there anything in Mā that corresponds to fighting the forces of darkness – sometimes a lifelong encounter with demons – as testified by Christian saints? I cannot find any reference to this, and from the impression she makes on me, I cannot find any chink within her soul where demons can enter. Peace and harmony appear so closely woven in every cell of her being that the spirits of darkness would search in vain for a loophole.

But if Mā were not protected from them for other reasons, her philosophical stance would have to be such to give her a total immunity. Many Christian saints feel that they are tortured by an anti-god, a satanic principle and the whole arsenal of devilish or demonic spirits. Her non-dualistic thinking prevents all this.

One who has realized *aham brahmāsmi* must be so completely invulnerable. This invulnerability does not come from a mere philosophical idea. Mā lives in this consciousness, i.e. from the existential experience of unity with *Brahman.* It says, "There is only one *Brahman,* without a second". In other words: everything is *Brahman.* Then those unearthly creatures which are so clearly eliminated from the Western conception of the world (psychologists admit them still, all the same, as projections) must also be *Brahman.*

December 18, 1963

Mā stayed for a few days in Bombay after our return from Poona. On one of these days, I met Kamubaba, the Muslim Guru of my Parsi friends.

The old man comes from the garden, when I am about to ring the bell. He is of medium height, delicately built, has a white beard and a fine, slender face. I think, he looks inquisitive and a little worried. But the moment he begins to speak, one sees only cheerfulness and goodness in his clever eyes. Kamubaba holds me by the hand and leads me into the house. He asks me to sit in his waiting room. Unfortunately, he has to go for an opening ceremony of a factory, but he will return in an hour and then have time for me. He embraces me before going away.

The waiting room begins to fill up gradually. Provided with comfortable chairs, donated by the rich followers of the sage, it reminds one of a doctor's waiting room.

Kamubaba's wife, a plump motherly creature, is amiable and I enjoy this. She brings me a cup of tea and lets me know that I can wander around in the house and garden without any inhibition. I sit for a while in Kamubaba's tiny room and try to attune myself to his personality as a spiritual adviser and a leader of many people who belong to different religions. Kamubaba's voice suddenly startles me from my reverie. I go to the corridor. But where is he?

A young Muslim follower of the sage (a student) who is cleaning the house points to a big bird's cage. Only now I see a parrot who imitates the voice of the master perfectly. Later I see a number of cages hanging everywhere in the house. Someone tells me, "Kamubaba prays sometimes in the garden. When someone comes from the street, he thinks, Baba is in the house. But actually, it is the parrots repeating his prayers."

It is good to move so freely as a stranger in the house. It has retained the character of a private house. Although the whole estate is situated in the suburb of the city, it appears rural. Kamubaba appears to be financing part of the cost of living by selling vegetables and fruits grown by him. The house which is spotlessly clean is set in a large, carefully cultivated vegetable garden.

Kamubaba has been ailing for some time, so the gate of his garden which is normally open throughout the year, is now open to the public only on Sundays. Then thousands come within a few hours to seek the blessings of the sage. Only his friends come on the other days of the week.

When Kamubaba returns after an hour, people in the waiting room run towards him like children, and he embraces everyone with paternal warmth. He laughs and pats the younger men on their back, pulls the nose of the children and strokes the cheek of a young lady.

People are called one after the other into his room. When most of them have gone, Kamubaba comes into the waiting room and sits next to me on the sofa. When I talk about myself, he holds my right hand, puts his arm around my shoulder. When I mention Mā, he bows his head down reverently and says smiling, "Mā, very nice!" His English vocabulary is limited to these words.

Finally, he wants to know whether I am "a good Christian". I try to explain to him that it is very improbable. Frowning a little, he observes the back of the fingers of my right hand (I have met several Indians who claim that one can get a better clue to a man there than from the lines on the palm). Suddenly he breaks out laughing, kisses my hand and leaves it. What he saw there must have consoled and amused him. Then he clasps my right hand again, puts his left hand on my head and murmurs a long prayer. His eyes have an expression which I know from Mā. Then he embraces me again and lets me go.

During our days in Bombay, Mā was invited by a *Mahārānī*, a member of Parliament. She lives in a temple on the premises of her palace and crowns a function by her presence; it is supposed to benefit the salvation of the soul of the deceased *Mahārājā*. I go to the lectures only by the hour. Most of the time, I stay with my Parsi friends Meher and Behman. They are to me like my brother and sister.

My relationship with Meher is so valuable to me, because she has the religious attitude of Mā on the level of a "normal human being". Without this experience, I would have probably thought that such an attitude could be attained only in the life of a monk in strict withdrawal from the world.

Meher recently counted the number of prayers she says several times daily. At first a Parsi prayer composed in Old Persian, then a Sanskrit prayer. As the third, the Lord's prayer and finally an Islamic prayer in Urdu followed by two prayers in English which are close to Hinduism.

Her syncretism is not artificial. It is an expression of a profound religious conviction which strives for expansion and inclusiveness. When I asked Meher why she was praying syncretically, she said beaming, "Because it gives me happiness. I like to pray so much with all people in all their languages." On some other occasion, she confessed to me that her wish to intercede has brought her into a difficult situation; the number of people who seek her prayers is now more than hundred.

"It is good that I get up so early in the morning. This gives me time for praying." Sometimes, she begins at 3 a.m. But she also prays during the course of the day whenever she can. While doing work in the kitchen, which does not need her full attention, while stitching, or in a bus. I am convinced that she belongs to those in the Eastern Church who practise "unceasing prayer". I can see, she lets the prayer "continue" in her while listening to a conversation or talking part in it. While her mouth answers questions, her eyes show that she is praying.

Meher presides over housekeeping which is demanding complicated by the constant presence of many guests from all parts of the world and she undertakes a thousand things in which she helps other people. So she assists in decisions of a welfare organization which she helps to propagate, arduously, in spirit of genuine social responsibility. She instructs people in different disciplines who cannot pay. She always has a couple of people from the huge slums of the city in tow to protect them from extremes by doing all she can for them. She also does what not everyone likes to do: she regularly looks after extremely "difficult" people for days together, and nearly always, has one or several sick or old relatives in the house, and she looks after them.

And yet she is never in bad temper. On the contrary, she has a marked sense of fun and an affable humour. Small, affectionate and nimble, she runs around between the people and quietly brings about peace and joy. When I wandered with her for hours through the scorching city, God knows, to get something and for someone, I finally declared, "If I don't get a cup of tea now, I shall drop from exhaustion." We went into a restaurant. I ordered tea. "And what do you want to drink, Meher?" "Nothing, thanks." "But you must be terribly tired" "Yes, but I shall soon be fresh, you will see." "How do you do it?" "I think of God. This refreshes me better than your tea does for you."

I am occasionally impatient with her, because of her blindness for the bad qualities in some people. She simply does not see the evil and realizes exactly what Mā advises, "Abide alone to what is good in human being." When I recently said with reference to an acquaintance, "I am sorry Meher, but I think, he is a scoundrel", she shook her head and explained to me that she could not find, with the best will in the world, anything bad in him, but if it is not the case with me, I should feel free to find what is bad in him. "What is important is that you forgive him and try to love him in spite of it."

Meher's behaviour has never a tinge of sentimentality. She is a very loving human being, but she always exudes a great clarity. Anyone who imagines sentimentality there, will find she is rather cool.

I asked Meher one day whether she clashed with her usual and unusual duties. "No", she answered, "God makes me live people. I like children as if they were my own. I know, it is not a passionate love, but a mild one. I pray to learn to love better. But I do not search for people to help them. I am not bothered to know whether they are poor or rich. Many people think that one should help only the poor. But I cannot. It is my fate to love the person who crosses my path. It is not an achievement. I have to act like that because I cannot make a distinction between me and other people. I don't feel any difference."

This is an existential statement which must be taken quite literally; it clearly distinguishes Meher's experience of existence from that of the Christians. She does not love her neighbour "like herself ", but she perceives only one Self in the other and in herself; the Self that loves itself in all. She participates in this love with her experience. She is this love. When she says something, urged by my questions, about this manner of experiencing existence, she sometimes makes use of Western dualistic terms and conceptions, because nothing that we understand about this *union* can be drawn from the *union* that is already accomplished.

She lives her religion, and therefore, the religious focal point of her life is her conviction that man is potentially a divine being. She knows that her attitude is very close to Hinduism. She gives sometimes the impression that she is closer to it than to her own religion.

One of her prayers is: "O my Father, because you and I are one, help me to reveal more of your perfection in my body and in my soul, so that I may be what I am in reality: the essence of blissfulness and love."

Meher told me, "I try to live in accordance with this prayer." She said, "I try to live this prayer. I began to live it the moment I accepted that God and I are one. It was horrible before. I hated myself, and I suffered terribly on account of my deficiency. One day, I understood with my whole existence that God and I are one. I have been happy even since."

Two things become clear in touching manner in Meher's quiet and clever face: the original suffering which comes from inborn weakness and insufficiency, suddenly darkening her features, and its "natural darkness" is absorbed, almost for a moment, by a "supernatural light", in which the experience is expressed that God and I are one! Probably a very Indian way into the life of real fulfilment.

An Englishwoman who has been in contact with Meher for years told me, "She is the best Christian, I have ever met." But Meher lives, as she lives, because she realizes in her own way "*aham brahmāsmi*" – oneness with God, rather she is an authentic example of Indian piety. One who calls her Christian, gives her a wrong label.

One of the girls has translated a *mantra* that is often chanted. It is addressed to a *Guru*; one should not perceive him in a living man. Mā often speaks about an "inner *Guru*" in the soul of a man. ". . . the One, eternal, pure, that is in all: as an inner light and an eyewitness; beyond our pious emotions and not made of what is earthly – I bow to the *Guru* who is all this. *Guru* is Brahmā, *Guru* is Viṣṇu, *Guru* is Śiva, *Guru* is the highest *Brahman.* I pray to this *Guru* who is above the creation. I bow to the *Guru* who is the mother. I bow to the mother who is the *Guru* . . ."

Chapter 9

Calcutta—Bloody Sacrifices for Kālī, "The Goddess of Mercy"

December 22, 1963

The journey from Bombay to Calcutta, including delays, takes 28 hours. Mā is invited to stay by a cigarette-baron on her arrival in this city. His estate is in a quite street. He has put up a small paṇḍāla at the back of his house. Mā receives her followers for private talks in a kind of garden-house which has a thatched roof.

Colourful bulbs are attached to bushes and trees in the garden and the paṇḍāla is splendidly decorated with flowers. 200 to 300 people have gathered on the first evening, and everyone wants to welcome Mā with fervent adoration. Gradually the enthusiasm grows to such a pitch that Mā is almost swallowed up. People try to embrace her, at the same time, from behind and in the front. I have never before seen Mā allow her followers to come so close to her. She sits smiling in the midst of the crowd and dispenses blessings by allowing people to touch her. Sometimes, she clasps a head which is pressing on her knees with both hands. She strokes the face of an old woman. She tousles the mop of hair of a young boy kneeling before her in a boisterous manner – and all this, while she is continually answering jovial calls.

Later, the hostess performs an *āratī* paying homage to the revered guest on behalf of us all. Mā tilts her head to the side. She is momentarily engrossed in profound contemplation. It is strange how clearly she remembers the scenes from her youth. One feels the agelessness of spiritual power which streams through her, and her physical appearance is transformed. It is clothed in gentleness, elasticity and the charm of unscathed youthfulness.

Today Mā made an interesting observation on Yoga, which is often seen as a kind of gymnastic feat in the West. Every single body-posture – the Sanskrit term for it is *āsana* – corresponds to a spiritual objective, and one who is serious about it, needs a lifetime to attain mastery in the extremely differentiated system of these body-postures. Every single *āsana* bears its fruit, "when a particular divine mood is awakened in the soul; this particular *āsana* is its physical expression."

Mā made a distinction between this Yoga which is mastery of mind and body by a long and tough training and the Yoga which happens spontaneously as a grace and is a development of deep psychic contacts transferred into the physical. This was the Yoga she practised in the third span of her life. The following quotation shows what an extremely spiritual significance Mā attaches to this Yoga:

"Here (when the Yoga happens) man is quite pure, shining, free, eternal, and all the innumerable names, forms and attributes of God are an eternal reality for him. He sees the nature of names and forms and he is overwhelmed by the mystery of divine ardour, enlightenment and ecstasy. He is completely lost in God. Divested of all, he merges with him. Then he knows that the whole world is merely an outer expression of inner reality, the One himself, the field of His creative action. He alone, He and nobody else, is elevated for ever onto the throne in the *āsana* of *Mahā-Yoga,* in the Highest Yoga. To realize Him in the world and beyond the world–that is the death of the Death. The Death is conquered in this *āsana* and time is overcome."

This time I am a guest in the family of a 94-year-old man, an early acquaintance of Mā. His house is in a busy street. It has a small front garden. My revered host, his loving wife and two sons live there. One of them is a chemist – I become friendly with his wife Gauri quickly – and the other son is a doctor. The doctor combines his worldly and monastic life. He practises his profession, but lives as a *Brahmacārī,* in a close spiritual contact with Mā and in strict *sādhana.*

The house has a pleasant atmosphere of peace and simplicity. It is rather dark and cool. The spiritual stamp of the housefather who is nearly a hundred years old is noticeable in everything. Misery of the countless poor people of his country has always been gnawing at his heart. Luxury gives him pain.

The second day of my stay in his house is Sunday. He sits in his verandah in the forenoon and distributes rice to beggars who come every week around this time. Most of them are women; many drag their children along. Everyone gets a handful of raw rice in their bowl. Around fifty women have already been there, when I leave the house. There is utter misery in the city. This morning I saw a man in a torn *dhotī* kneel down on the ground and carefully lick a few drops of spilled milk from the road. When I return home in the evening, I see thousands of homeless people sleeping on the streets. Although it is very cold in the night, many of them have nothing to cover themselves. Others build a sort of cave: a very small "house" from stones which they steal from construction sites. Planks or a piece of corrugated iron form the roof. Many of these poor cave-dwellers maintain a tiny fire in their shelter to keep themselves warm.

My host was head of a college of education. He is surprisingly alert in spite of his old age. His ideas seem to hover around two main wishes: how to give effective help to the poor and how the spiritual world can be protected from the onslaught of materialism.

He is imbued with the idea that all human beings are children of God, and as such, are brothers and sisters, and therefore, should live as brothers and sisters. He loathes outer "class differences". A few years ago, he wrote a hymn to Mā. I am translating a verse from it:

"Mother, break to pieces the chains with which men are oppressed by men; all distinctions of class, caste, race, faith and culture, of riches and power. Break the chains to pieces by your touch that gives freedom. Help all men and women to live from the foundation of the divine, of the *ātman,* by offering their transitory personal interests before the holy altar of your feet."

Gauri, wife of the chemist-son, keeps the house hold. She is a quiet, a little shy person. Her clever, but at times, sad eyes reveal more than the mouth. She looks after me with great care. I seldom see her husband..He must be too much busy with his occupation. Even he is friendly, quiet and reserved. His brother, who is a doctor, does not seem to do his practice as long as Mā is in Calcutta.

Gauri tells me that Mā suddenly asked her one day a few years ago: "Stay with me." Mā gave the impression that she had to rely on Gauri's help for her personal care. "There are many women who would serve Mā only too willingly. It was a great privilege that I was allowed to do so. It was the most decisive phase of my development. She has educated me for life and completely changed me. I have never trusted any other person so completely as her, and what I own to her is priceless." I try to find out cautiously about the fundamental change Mā's influence has brought in her. Her sensible face makes me realize that Mā's influence was necessary and had far-reaching consequences. Gauri's answer is: "Since then, I have no fear." Besides, Mā enabled her to know and fulfil her life's work. "When I went away, Mā gave me a Gopāl, a small statue of the divine Kṛṣṇa-boy. From then on, I perform *pūjā* everyday."

Mā has prepared many young girls and women for their "job" in the course of her life, so that they could become the human and religious focal point of their families. Gauri cannot think of her life without this guidance. Also, she is now called in sometimes to do special services.

Svāmījī asked her on one of the last days to cook a special preparation for Mā. Gauri works alone for six hours in the kitchen, which nobody else is allowed to enter. She does not talk to anyone, when she has to leave the room, and I am sure, she must have undergone a spiritual and physical ritual of purification beforehand. There are certain restrictions, as a part of the rules, with respect to ingredients. She has to observe them when she cooks for Mā. As she is not a brāhmaṇa, she is not allowed, for example, to prepare eatables that are cooked with salt.

One day I emitted a deep heartfelt sigh because of the huge crowd Mā has to constantly face here. Babaji, my host, recounted a conversation Mā had with several friends on this topic.

"We said, 'Mā, why do you allow crowds of people to come close to you?' – 'Perhaps, this body irresistibly attracts them. It is not their fault!' – 'But don't you feel very uncomfortable?' – Mā answered, beaming with a counter-question, 'What is the weight of your head?'– 'I don't know', I answered in surprise. Then she looked at the man next to me. 'What is the weight of your right hand?' She asked the next the weight of his left foot, and the next to him, the weight of his right foot. All gave the same reply: 'I don't know.'

'See', Mā said laughing, 'your head, your arms and your legs or feet have a considerable weight, but you don't know anything about it. You don't feel they are heavy because you do not regard them as a load, but as a living part of your own body which they are. So, I regard people who come to me as a part of my living body. You are my head, you my right arm, you my left arm, and you are my right leg and you my left . . . I don't feel you as a load, even if you hang on to me. So it is with everyone. Their worries and joys are mine. And their deeds, whatever they may be, are my deeds."

I discuss the topic of the so-called self-deliverance with my host. The West often assumes that Asia looks to it for its salvation. This does not apply to my Hindu friends. Babaji said:

"Mā teaches us that it is God's Grace when a man can pray and do *sādhana.* It is not enough to call the name of God a million times or live in a Himalayan cave for years. 'If there is no light, we are not enlightened', Mā says, 'and God alone can kindle this light. All ascetic and other religious efforts are only preliminary exercises to open ourselves to Grace which we have to await in hope."

Answering someone who asked her how to assume God's Grace, when destiny is predetermined by the *karma,* she told him:

"You must utilize our free will to find the Highest. All efforts you make to approach him are an expression of this free will. Your destiny (determined by your *karma*) can also be changed by God's Grace. A change is possible, if you firmly believe in it. Of course, there are laws in God's creation, and yet nothing is impossible for him.

If you believe that God's Grace rules your destiny, then it happens accordingly. If you are convinced, on the other hand, that God is more powerful than destiny (that is determined by the *karma*), then he will do everything for you (his Grace breaks through rigid contingency)."

Quite often I think, our Western ideas about Hinduism are one-sided and wrong. A handful of indologists and theologians have formed them, no doubt, on the basis of honest scientific studies, but mostly without any contact with believing Hindus. We have adopted these ideas, which then become clichés. How often do we not verify them from wrong examples? It is stunning to realize that Mā's insight about Grace is entirely different from what the specialists claim.

One could not help but ask: "Whether Mā has unwittingly Christian elements in her ideas?" I don't think so. She cannot read; she has never listened to Christian sermons or attended church, and has, I think, no idea at all about the Christian doctrine. The Christians who occasionally come to her do so for her teaching and not to talk about their tradition.

We have conquered the moon, but totally ignored the insights of our contemporaries in this part of the world.

The next day, Babaji came back to the topic of Grace: "Mā often talks about a mug in which we are supposed to Grace. 'Grace is flowing down to us all the time, but cannot enter us, because our mug is turned upside down. If we are open to Grace, we receive it.' Do you know, what Mā means by this? Holding the mug properly means focussing one's thoughts and feelings on God. It is true, Mā encourages self-confidence and the readiness for one's own efforts in those who think they act on their own, which everyone thinks at the outset. Only when the ego has experienced its own insufficiency and understands that there is only one who acts, then it becomes quiet and completely open to receive Grace. Then its actions cease; it is God who acts, and man is his instrument. Later, even this instrument ceases to exist, when there exists only the One."

Self-deliverance has this final thrust. "You know", Babaji said, "that, according to our view, only a very few people can attain perfection without the guidance of a *Guru* – an enlightened soul. Mā frequently speaks about the inner *Guru* and there is only one *Guru* who is a 'world teacher'. He can provide the individual with his guidance with the help of an enlightened teacher or also with the help of his voice in the soul or from an encounter with a sage who has lived centuries ago. Nearly all souls need guidance of one such *Guru*. Self-realization is not to be confused with self-deliverance. It means nothing else but the existential knowledge of my identification (*ātman*) with the Highest Self (*Brahman*). I need the Grace of *Brahman* to realize this. Mā often expresses it in a personified form: We know by God's Grace that we are one with him."

In the meanwhile, Mā has moved to a busy and central shopping street, invited by a young exporter for a *Gītā*-week. A huge paṇḍāla is erected behind his house with a dais for

Mā and the other prominent participants. The major part of the paṇḍāla is occupied by Mā's followers and local people.

Every morning begins with a communal reading of two or three hymns of the *Bhagavad Gītā*; this lasts for several hours. The participants read in low voice and in chorus. The text read in the morning is expounded by scholars in the afternoon and evening. In between for many days, Mā accepts the *praṇāma*, the adoration of countless people, hour by hour. Sometimes, the people's onslaught is quite ruthless. Children and women are trampled under foot. There are bruises, bleeding noses and tears. I was warned against going to Calcutta with Mā. A Bengali living in Bombay told me, the people from his home State "are savage and uncontrollable." It is true. I am amazed that my *sārī* was not in tatters in the mélée.

Often, Mā's personality is completely submerged, when she accepts such a "mass-*praṇāma*" as in this instance. She receives the adoration which is meant to be completely personal by most of them, because people love Mā as a *re-presentative* of God, i.e. as the God who is actually present in her. Everything that determines the purely personal charm of her contact with us recedes into the background. Her face, at times, is strangely "emptied"; there is no personal reaction. The *re-presented* God shows neither disinclination nor inclination, moods or desires.

There are, of course, occasional mass-*praṇāmas*, when Mā obviously cannot or will not refuse the need of her followers for personal attention, kindness and cheerfulness. Then she does not withdraw behind the representation of the deity, but "stays there" with all her charm.

I would like to quote what she said in this context: "If you want to do *praṇāma* to a deity or a living saint or a *Mahātmā*, then first take the *darśana* of his whole person. Begin from the feet and look upwards to the head, while slowly breathing in. Imagine that you are taking into yourself – along with your breath – the spiritual power of the one to whom you want to bow. Then let your look slide down slowly to the feet, while you breathe out. At the same time, offer yourself to God with all your being–good and bad. Empty yourself completely before him without any reservation whatsoever. When your forehead touches the feet of a god or a saint, his spiritual power enters you. When his hand touches your head, he transfers a part of this power.

To do *praṇāma* means handing oneself over to God or to one's *iṣṭa,* with total openness of what you are at this moment, in whatever condition, and then purified by his touch, you receive yourself back from him, as it were, as his *prasāda.*"

Someone asks, "Suppose one does *praṇāma* to someone who appears to be a saint, but in reality, is not; would this exert an evil influence upon me? How can one protect oneself from it?"

Mā replies: "By seeing in him the Highest Being. Everyone, irrespective of, whether he is good or bad, is His manifestation. If you remember this and do the *praṇāma* to the one alone, in whatever disguise he may be, then no calamity can befall you. *Praṇāma* has to be done only with this attitude in mind, always to the One, the Highest. To do *praṇāma* means offering one's ego to him, subjugating oneself to the One, so that he alone is there, and nothing of you."

I went to Kālī-ghāṭ yesterday afternoon; to the shrine of Goddess Kālī after whom Calcutta is named. The Goddess has been worshipped in this place for many centuries. The temple there is only a few decades old; architecturally not very interesting: a domed building whose external walls are decorated by colourful tiles. Immediately next to it is an open, rectangular hall, where the devotees it so that they face the idol of the Goddess in the temple which is the holiest of all. There are lodgings for pilgrims and shops for devotional articles round about the holy area.

When I leave the rickshaw, a man comes towards me speaking volumes in broken English. He assures me that he does not want a single paisa from me and intends only to show me the temple and its surroundings. Others are also wooing me and disturbing me as I go round in their intrusive prattle.

The man offering me his service has a face like a bird of prey, sharp-eyed, cunning and greedy. He calls two shopkeepers to prove that he is a priest and no tourist guide, and he only wants to be helpful to foreigners. It is true, he may be a *pūjārī* of the type about whom the Hindus complain bitterly, as they are so greedy for money. There is an army of such priests in India who have no regular income to support their families and they have to depend upon money they extract from the devotees – and the foreigners – often in a refined and sometimes in a brutal manner.

I press a rupee into his hand and say, "Leave me in peace and keep the others away." He performs this service to perfection. He prevents his colleagues from speaking to me.

The "tree of fertility" is in a corner of the temple area. Its trunk and branches are very black; there is no leaf or fruit, but the crippled branches are wrapped here and there in dirty red ribbons. A half-naked old woman is leaning against the trunk and begging. I have never seen such a dismal, dreary tree. Someone tells me that it has never borne leaves or fruit. Infertile women pray under this tree for fertility.

Devotees have gathered at the entrance of the temple. They bring their offerings of fruit and flowers to place them before the idol of the Goddess. I try twice to mix with those who are waiting, but I was brushed aside. My *pūjārī* comes leaping to explain that non-Hindus are not allowed inside the temple. Meditating and praying pilgrims, monks with begging bowls and women with sleeping children in their laps are sitting, all over the place in the hall of the temple.

There is a place for sacrifice behind the hall. Young billy-goats are sacrificed daily to the Goddess at sunrise. The stone is still blood-stained from the morning ritual and so also the wooden scaffolding on which the neck of the sacrificial animal is laid before the butcher severs the head from the trunk in one go. Several young billy-goats are tied to a side wall of the hall. They have eaten the last dried-up straw long ago and are now looking anxiously at the crowd of the pilgrims.

I observe an elderly couple leaning against a wall niche. They have come to sacrifice a billy goat to the goddess. It seems, they are farmers. They have lean worried faces and their hands look worn out by too much work. The woman is wearing round silver ornaments on her ankles and rings on several toes, her forearms are covered with colourful bangles. Both are squatting on their heels and the priest in front of them. He touches the black kid, then he strews yellow flowers on the head of the animal and draws a red mark on its forehead. While chanting the *mantras* in a low voice, he stops at intervals to haggle over the price they must dole out for the ritualistic preparation of the animal. He demands one rupee, but the farmer offers only five annas (about a third of a rupee). "*Ek rupayā*", he says, while bending down to the ear of the kid, to whisper a sacrificial *mantra* into it. "*Pāñca āṇe*", replies the farmer grumpily and pulls at the string tying the goat, as if he wanted to get up and go home. This is repeated several times. Finally, the woman says, "*Das āṇe!*", and the priest agrees. He rapidly mumbles the text of the prayers, pockets the money and goes away.

A young man with a broad knife has been waiting. Now he squats near the couple, and the haggling begins anew. The butcher gives in, when the farmer turns away and pulls the kid behind him. Cursing and swearing, he takes his money, grabs the kid, turns its forelegs with a quick grip on its back hooking them into one another. A yowling bleat, a muffled sound of the falling knife– the body of the animal rolls wriggling on the stones, and the butcher disappears with the head from which blood is dripping. The old people take the body. I do not know what happens to it. My *pūjārī* tells me that the meat is considered to be a *prasāda* of the Goddess and eaten by the devotees for whom the enjoyment of meat is otherwise forbidden.

I stay in my niche. The process of sacrificing is being repeated several times. Devotees and pilgrims walk past me in crowds. Many bend down to touch the bloody wooden scaffolding with their foreheads. The atmosphere is hot and dusty, filled with mustiness. It is hard to breathe. I see a burdensome mustiness on the faces of these people: mustiness and restlessness. Or should I say joylessness? Or fear? To whom do they pray? To the Great Mother, the Merciful or the Fearful? When going among them, I feel that they have surrendered themselves to her. They strive to appease the Goddess with pitiable gestures and so distort the real meaning of the sacrificial rite which they do not understand.

As I come back at the nightfall, I succeed in seeing the idol of the Goddess. Only her head stands on the ground of the holy shrine: a black mask with red-rimmed, white shining eyes and the third eye on the forehead. The mouth is a broad tongue of gold which is sticking out. The fire maintained by the priests in front of the shrine throws a flickering light on the rigid face of the Goddess. Is it smiling? Even its smile is frightful.

A few kilometers downstream, there is a temple in Dakshineshvara where Ramakrishna worshipped the Divine Mother. During his time, he was the greatest luminary saint of this country, and his life was an example of affection and steadfastness in love; as much as the love of a Christian saint to the Mother of God.

I tell my host in the evening how depressing I found the Kālī-ghāṭ. He says, "I also feel exactly as you. Hinduism is like a long flight of steps which leads via *Brahman* to the highest summit of enlightenment. The people you observed sacrificing the goat are at its foot. It is their *karma,* resulting from their ignorant behaviour of earlier lives that they remain there in gloomy surrender to the numinous powers. The Goddess of whom they are afraid, is the same Mother of Mercy whom Ramakrishna loved with sensuous fervour. But he stood on the upper edge of the flight of steps, and his eyes saw the light, where there is darkness for them. When they went to him, the mercy sometimes opened their eyes."

"Whose mercy?" I ask, "the mercy of the holy man or of the Goddess?"

"Don't you know, there is only one mercy?"

The old man continued at breakfast where we left our conversation last night.

"The variety of phenomena within our belief must confuse you. The One, the all-pervading, all-embracing presence of *Brahman,* is revealed in all his forms, in those which we call primitive and in those which appear to us to be spiritualized in the highest sense. Simple men pray to gods in whom they think, the cosmic powers are embodied. The sun is a deity for them, or the ocean or the fire. Some of them begin to suspect that behind these powers of the cosmos, is a last compelling mystery which encompasses and permeates all. Gradually, they turn to this supreme spirit. Their faith is purified of its anthopomorphic images. They no longer look for the external manifestations of the deities. Before their soul stands the unmoved Eternal residing in itself, the nameless One beyond existence and non-existence. They pray to it in the silence of their mind."

When I had gone to Dakshineshvara, a suburb of Calcutta, where Ramakrishna used to live, one of his monks told me that this significant Hindu saint had practised the Christian faith for a while, and at some other time, the Islamic faith, with such intensity that Christ and Mohammed had appeared to him. There are several parallels of this in Mā's life.

There was a Japanese in the group with this monk. He said, "The sages of this country know that religious faiths are only methods that are supposed to lead to enlightenment." This "only" in his remark made me think. It could mean that all religious phenomena are unimportant. And that is exactly the opposite of what those Indian sages mean who take all phenomena equally seriously.

It would be unthinkable for a convinced Christian to immerse himself with such a fervour in the spirit of an alien faith, imagining that he would be brought close to God by this "exercise". From his point of view, it would be more natural to fear that such acceptance of a religion would lead to an unreal faith, to acknowledging something as true with inner reservation, and therefore, farcical. Such an "exercise" would reduce the religion to the level of method. It would be nothing less than a method used to learn to read. One cannot believe today in the doctrine of the *Koran*, tomorrow in the *New Testament* and to worship day after tomorrow Kālī, "the Divine Mother of Mercy", whose priest Ramakrishna regarded himself.

As soon as I replace the word "one" by the word "we", it feels right. People of the West who are moulded by a Christian tradition, cannot, in fact, do it. Mā realizes this. It is not just an accident, that she constantly refers us to Christ.

But we should know that people like Ramakrishna and Mā can do it, because their religious tradition teaches that the Highest Reality or *Brahman* or God has infinitely many aspects. The divine truth assumes various forms in religious faiths. Each one of these opens a way to God, and this each one is a method of gaining an experience of God's reality. One who lives in this conviction can love God as Father of Christ or as Allah or as Mother of Mercy and get more and more deeply involved in his mystery by this love. According to an Indian view, right up to the threshold, the crossing of which is called in all religions salvation or enlightenment or knowledge. The mystics speak about it in East and West by using the imagery of God's marriage to the soul. One who has crossed this threshold, is, according to a Hindu doctrine, beyond "name and from" (*nāma-rūpa*). He sees that it is unimportant under what name a deity is worshipped. Such a manner of experiencing and thinking is not static, but dynamic concept of truth. Truth as an infinitely multiformed power of transformation of the Self to one's Self.

I was sitting early noon for a while in a travel agency beside an Italian priest who told me that he knows Mā. "No other woman here has reminded me of my mother as she", he said with a charming smile, but then his friendly face became stern, "she is really making a mistake – and with her all Hindus – , when she believes that the difference between religions is only a difference of way and that the goal is the same. It is not that simple. Christians and Hindus have their different images of gods".

It is an extremely important question for the dialogue of religions which cannot be and should not be avoided, and it is possible that the priest is right. I personally feel less urge for distinction and definition, and yet I wish so much that representatives from East and West whose vision is not blinkered by ideologies could establish contact with one another. I am strongly attracted by what unites and reconciles. A strong admiration and yet disquiet, when I look at the gigantic, complicated machinery of terminologies and doctrines, built up by major religions over the years, cutting man off from the surging infinity of existence. These walls are similar to the reefs of shell limestone from which life has almost completely withdrawn itself. How sad and absurd to fortify oneself behind them.

Let the formerly feuding parties go out and meet each other, protected only by the weapon of their unprejudiced openness to any manifestation of the Holy Spirit in the human heart and ready to be led, where they do not wish to go. If this were to happen, the landscape between the walls would revive wondrously, and even the reefs behind the courageous reveal many a zone of fresh blood and of great beauty.

Whatever Mā says about *Bhagavān*, corresponds to my image of God which is impressed upon me by a Christian faith, although not in the strict, dogmatic sense. "He, the Lord, the Father, the Beloved, who is all in all . . ." Sometimes she also says, "He is your father and mother." I assume a complicated theology of God worshipped only under the image of father, and not of mother, and that is there I found something lacking due to my Protestant origin. There was no Mother of God for me. God as father and mother may be impossible in a Christian dogmatic sense; it is an image of wonderful truth and power in my religious feeling.

After I had a long discussion with Mā on religious questions awhile back, she concluded:

"I hope, you have now understood that there are levels of knowledge on which problems cannot be solved in a particular way. Isn't it true that in the course of your life after careful trial, you come to a stage, when you have answers to the questions? But you must now realize that a solution is never complete. In other words, you have to cross the point when there is certainty and uncertainty. Every answer your mind has found arises from a certain point of view. As a result, there is a possible contradiction, because your answer represents only one aspect of the problem. What have you really solved? But you will find that there is a place, where all problems have only one universal solution, where there is no place for contradiction, no question of solution or no solution. Whether one says 'yes' or 'no'– everything is *tat.*"

It may be "existential experience" or knowledge at the basis of this attitude. That is why the wise men from the East give answers to the questions of those of the West, which they find "unsatisfactory". We insist upon a clear yes or no, where the enlightened one sees only the One (*tat*) that is above yes or no.

Today, I took my seat in the paṇḍāla at 2 p.m. although the *Gītā*-function begins only at 5 p.m. If you are late you do not get a seat. A young college teacher was sitting next to me. After exchanging a couple of words, she wished me a merry Christmas. Then she said, "If I could travel with Mā like you for months, everyday would be Christmas for me."

"In a real way, it is also true for me", I replied to her. "I am sure that I shall read the *Bible* with fresh eyes when I reach home. I often think that what I experience here with Mā may throw a light on the gospels."

My neighbour shuts the book she was reading. She wants to talk to me.

"The Christmas of the Hindus is celebrated in August or September", she ways, "We call it *Janmāṣṭamī*; it is the birthday festival of Śrī Kṛṣṇa. It is a pity, you could not understand what the speaker said about it yesterday."

"Could you tell me?"

"He said, it is the birth of divine wisdom in the soul of man which we celebrate every year. When the night of ignorance and suffering has reached its darkest hour, Śrī Kṛṣṇa comes to us as the light of wisdom. In its fire, all egoism is burnt, and its other name is love."

"That sounds quite like Christmas", I said, "only we celebrate the real, historical birth of Jesus, but we also believe that by it, the divine light has come into the darkness of the world."

"Śrī Kṛṣṇa's birth also has a real significance for Hindus. A doll representing the divine child Gopāl is ceremoniously bathed, clothed and put into a cradle and rocked in countless families."

As I was listening to the lady, my eye fell on the back of her book. There was a picture of the youthful God, the playmate of the cowherds of Vrindavan. Cross-legged, he stood leaning against a cow, playing his flute, while his splendid headdress consisting of peacock feathers bobbed boldly up and down. "As if from a colour film", I said pointing to the picture.

My neighbour looked at me with a searching glance. "Very colourful, yes! But the most important thing in the picture is that all details are significant for us. For example, the peacock feathers. They are a symbol of the beauty and wisdom of the God. Śrī Kṛṣṇa is the eternally handsome lover of beauty; and the glittering peacock eyes are a symbol for his wisdom that sees and knows everything."

"But what is the significance of the flute?"

"You should try and guess, but I shall tell you. A flute is a hollow reed, isn't it? The breath of the divine spirit flows into the soul which is emptied of its ego like a flute-reed of its middle. God sings in the heart that is hollowed out through suffering."

The young teacher reminds me of this remark, when we drink tea later in a small restaurant in the neighbourhood. The boy placed two cups before us; one of them had a broken rim. My companion took it and told me smiling, "There is a legend. It tells of Śrī Kṛṣṇa who was guest in the house of a rich man. One earthern utensil was mixed up with all the precious gold – and silverware. Its rim was broken. The guest immediately chose it. When his host tried to take it away, he said, 'If you had known me, you would have known that Śrī Kṛṣṇa attracts broken souls in all places!"

Pūjā is performed at the end of the *Gītā*-week. It lasts from 9 a.m. to 1.30 p.m. and ends with a sacrificial fire. Next day, there is a programme of twenty-four hour *kīrtana*-singing before Mā departs for Puri.

A two metre high pyramid of the pictures of Śrī Kṛṣṇa was erected in the midst of the dais and it was illuminated from inside and decorated with flowers. The *kīrtana*-singers will go round this pyramid. This expresses God as the centre of life around which they wander in tighter circles.

Kīrtana is sung by men during the day and by women

during the night. The same *mahāmantra* made up of three names of the God resounds throughout twenty-four hours. Its wording is: *Hare Kṛṣṇa, Hare Kṛṣṇa, Kṛṣṇa Kṛṣṇa, Hare Hare. Hare Rāma, Hare Rāma, Rāma Rāma, Hare Hare*! I am trying to fathom whether the sequence is significant. Someone tells me that the name "Hari Kṛṣṇa" expresses the attraction which the incarnate divinity has for us. "Hari Rāma" is the abundance of bliss we experience in the presence of God.

Something of this significance is felt in the joy which the *Kīrtana*-singers have and which is enlivened again and again. The *mahāmantra* is sung by a leading voice, a singer who is carrying and playing a harmonium, and each time, the chorus sings after him. The skill is in the leading voice changing the sequence of notes. Since he changes it fairly often, many singers have a chance to test their skill, some of them showing that they are real virtuosos. Several drums and different types of cymbals are beaten alongside the chorus. There are real artists among the drummers.

There is a particular charm in the rhythmical variety of singing; it determines the pace of the procession. The song begins again and again in a solemn stateliness to rise to the highest ecstasy. Then striding changes to dancing, then for a while, dancing on the spot with raised arms and heads tilting backwards.

Men are relieved by women at 10 in the night, and one hour later, all the men and boys have to disappear from the paṇḍāla. Mā's bed is carried to the paṇḍāla, and she stays there most of the night. It is less ecstatic with the women. When their circling movement round the pyramid changes to dancing, it is always with solemn and charming restraint. Gradually, the group of stalwarts is reduced to about hundred women, of whom only one-third circle the pyramid and the others sing along while sitting.

At first, I try to hide in the back row, because I don't want to be seen more than necessary. But Mā's eyes find me quickly. She asks me to take part in the procession. Twice she sings the *mahāmantra* to me; the third time, we sing together. Then she says smiling, "You know, don't you that Rāma, Kṛṣṇa and Christ are the names of the One who is above all names?"

By chance, a drum is free. I hang it around me and do not part with it for the rest of the night. I love to drum along in free rhythms, and it prevents me from getting tired.

Around 3 a.m., Mā left her bed and danced with us around the pyramid. She moves solemnly in circles with a complete natural charm; and suddenly she jumped from one to the other embracing each of us, while she continued to dance around the pyramid. A reverent, quite an impersonal tenderness was expressed in her beautiful gesture of affection. Ami called it: "God's love which loves itself in all" (Ami has been with us for past two weeks – a young Bengali girl whose family lives in Bombay. She has grown up in America. I notice often that we agree in our views and reactions.)

Chapter 10

Hindu and Christian Saintliness

The Missionaries of Charity have their inconspicuous Mother House in a small lane. It looks like a modest private house. The board at the gate has the name "Mother Teresa". Petitioners have gathered in front of the door; they are waiting for her. A young nun lets me in. At the same moment, Mother Teresa steps into the yard, a woman who looks like an ageing peasant at first glance; she is of medium size and is rather angular. Her hands and feet are those of someone who has worked physically hard all her life. Her face evokes similar impression. It is full of anxiety, with a crudely notched nose-lips-line, a furrowed forehead, eyes surrounded by wrinkles; the iris has a bright brown colour with a greenish tinge.

But what eyes! One loses one's breath looking into them. "She has the eyes of an angel", a young Indian girl told me later, and it is so to me. I have never seen anyone in whose eyes courage and love are expressed with such a power. These traits are found expressed in the life of this woman in a fascinating manner. For twenty years she belonged as a teacher to a religious order that runs schools in India. One day, she realized, she could no longer give Western education to children coming from the sparse upper strata of society in this country, where the misery of millions is crying out to heaven. She left the order, sought accommodation in a slum of Calcutta and began to teach a couple of beggars' children in the open.

That was is 1948. Since then, this woman has built up a work with a group without the initial capital of even a penny and without support, driven along by her obsession of compassion; it has become a life- saver for thousands. Her name is well-known throughout the world. Just recently, she has been asked to set up her organization similar to the Indian model in several South American states. 192 nuns (among them seven non-Indians) belong to her newly founded order; it works with several laymen and laywomen. A twenty-six-years old nun from Freiburg, Germany studies medicine in Calcutta at the cost of the order.

The work of the sisters extends over the realm of human and social help. They maintain children's and old peoples' homes, medical aid, schools, even Sunday-schools for adults, provide facilities for training the youth; they take the ambulance daily to different parts of the city to look after the lepers–they number 5,800 in Calcutta. At the moment (in the mid-sixties), she is building a lepers' village in an industrial area of West Bengal. She solicits, throughout world, the cooperation of people who are ready to take over the responsibility of financing a leper family in the village. With the help of such patronage, she has made it possible for many poor children to attend a good school.

She became famous through setting up an asylum for those dying on the streets. The first was established eleven years ago in a pilgrims' home in the holy area of Kālī-ghāṭ. At the beginning, Mother Teresa herself went with her sisters into the streets at night, picked up people who were dying, brought them to the home so that they did not have to die like the animals in gutters. Since then, 15,593 men and women have found a place in the asylum of *Kālī-ghāṭ*; 7,198 of them have died. The most common cause of death was malnutrition. The others could leave when they were strong enough.

Mother Teresa is about to leave her house. "Come with me", she says. We sit in the cabin of a delivery van. A few young men, volunteers, are sitting at the back of the van; they are being taken to their place of work for the day.

We come to the asylum for the dying on Kālī-ghāṭ. There are 132 men and women lying close to one another on low plank beds covered with grey blankets. It is cool, dim and silent; only at the back, where the mentally ill are lying, there is an occasional cry. Two small children are squatting on the plank-bed of their dying mother in the women's wing. Mother Teresa says, "We don't want to force them to go. If their mother dies, we shall find them a place in the Home."

Volunteers in the yard, some are medical students, make arrangements to bathe, shave and clothe the human wrecks who were picked up last night. They carefully remove stinking rags that are sticking to their scabby wounds. These peoples' hair is like black cement and has to be sawn off. A naked wreck of a body covered in blood, with idiotically staring eyes sits unsteadily on the step. Nobody knows his name. He may die today or tomorrow; will he become a human again?

Later I accompanied Mother Teresa back home; there we spent hours filling rice into bags. It had come in sacks, financed as a charitable gift from Paris. The poor in the locality were to receive a present of groceries in the evening.

When I took leave of Mother Teresa, she said, "It would be fine, if more young people could come and help us; they only need to be healthy and well-motivated. If they had a training, that would be invaluable." After I turned away, Mother Teresa called after me, "Ask the people to pray for us."

As we talked, I asked Mother Teresa, "What is your greatest worry; money?"

"No, we always get money. My only worry is that I am not a saint. People want this – they need it."

I remember the young doctor I had met in Banaras who suggested: "Go to Mother Teresa. She is a saint." He had grown up in a Christian family and attended a convent school and as a brāhmaṇa had returned to Hinduism at the age of almost thirty. Possibly in no other land do people know wholeheartedly their need of saints. Their spiritual *Geschick* (meaning in English fate and ability or skill) has sent them saints in every generation. They recognize their saints and love them irrespective of their creed.

Yesterday afternoon: Mā sat motionless for an hour on her bed completely withdrawn into herself. She raised her eyelids sometimes, but her look was as empty as a blind person. Focussed on the world, but oblivious to it. Yet her whole being was *contemplatio*: contemplation of God! Reflection of His light in the mirror of the soul. Something of this light is at times reflected in us. Only then, we see it.

Yesterday an elderly man was sitting in front of Mā's bed. I later heard, he was principal of a college. His face is suddenly like an open wound: suffering from himself, from the world and from God, nothing hidden, totally exposed. Later, when Mā "comes back" again, she gazed for a long time at the face of the man, and he suddenly began to weep. He closed his eyes. Tears gushed out from under his eyelids. After a while, he lay completely supine on the ground before Mā, then got up and went away.

Sometimes someone who takes leave of Mā like this man, transforms his house into an *āśrama* next day or becomes a monk. I have often heard, how Mā – without apparent action – intervenes in the life of people. Mostly in a hidden, but nevertheless effective way. Always drawing them towards the peak of the human existence: as she calls it – the realization of God in one's soul.

Strange enough, this non-acting action. A saintliness working because of itself, its very existence and its lustre.

Compare this to Mother Teresa and her holy fanatical altruism! Her dynamism is a sphere of activity, like highly motivated politicians. She changes the life of many by starving off hunger, curing diseases, giving homes to those who are homeless; by educating children, consoling those who are in despair and by giving work to the unemployed. It is, as if she has a thousand hands, because more and more people want to help her. To say that she is active, is saying nothing about her saintliness. She is saintly because of the driving force within her: for the sake of love which suffers because she feels, she is not saintly. She knows that people hunger for God, and she thinks, she can give them only bread. But that is her holy error.

Suffering seems an intrinsic part of Christian saintliness. I know little about it. I think, the presence of the Crucified somehow binds the saintliness and suffering permanently together. According to Catholic thought, even a saint is not beyond sin. He will always suffer because of his imperfection, although his purity may shine out for others.

The saint in the Indian mould realizes with his whole being the existential knowledge: *aham brahmāsmi* – I am *Brahman*. There is no shadow of self-doubt in such a being. He realizes absolute perfection within himself. Every self-doubt of any kind confirms an incomplete identity with *Brahman*.

I was invited to dinner with a family today. There a young girl asked me what I saw as the real difference between Mā and Mother Teresa. I said rather hastily – "In Mother Teresa's slogging day and night to fulfil the commandment of Christ 'Love your neighbour, as you love yourself."

"That is no difference", replied the girl. "Mā has been doing nothing else for the last forty years. She lives day and night for her fellow men. In fact, I think that if Mother Teresa is a saint, she should do what Mā does: lead human beings to God. All the creative activities she does are certainly vital, but one does not have to be a saint to do them."

For a moment, I imagined Mother Teresa in Mā's role and Mā in Mother Teresa's role. I had to laugh loudly at my thought.

Last summer I went for a walk with children. We stood still before a peacock butterfly. "Do you see the butterfly?"

I asked a boy, "That is not a butterfly", he said, "butterflies are yellow." So far he had seen only brimstones. My comparison is "childish", but it expresses what I want: there are people who think, saintliness is found only in one hue – according to their doctrine. I have the impression that this view is more widely spread among the religious people in the West than in Asia.

Often I wish, I was equipped with the solid armour of a specialist in (comparative) religious science. But I realize increasingly, I am better without such ballast; I am lighter, free-er. Concepts and categories do not affect my impartiality. A dialogue between the religions may be important and fruitful. But the real encounter takes place in a flash of intuitive knowledge throwing light into the depths of another religion, and we suddenly see there a reflection of the highest truth. Mā helps me more than an academic study of religions. I am lucky as I have no presuppositions to hinder me. I am reminded of the regret expressed by a theologian who said jocularly that the people in his subject are either too pious or too clever. In other words: they approach some other religion either with the prejudices of their own convictions or they adopt inappropriate methods lacking the flair to penetrate the peculiarity of religious problems.

January 5, 1964

In Calcutta: Mā today on the platform of Howrah station for long distance trains. Statistically, it has the highest traffic of any Asian railway station. One cannot imagine such a witches' cauldron in Europe Whole villages, whole jungle tribes, hundreds of soldiers, mendicants, coolies, aristocratic families, school children, groups of pilgrims, crippled beggars, beggars' children, ministerial messengers, traders of all sorts– all run about in confusion, stumbling against endless mountains of luggage and are incredibly noisy.

And Mā in the midst of this infernal chaos, mobbed by

countless inquisitive people, cheered by her followers. She stands there quietly, wrapped in her white clothes, with her hair flowing loosely and smiles – a near, but distant smile. Peace around her, peace in her eyes–*Nirvāṇa* in the midst of misery!

Purí is 399 kilometers south-west of Calcutta in the Bay of Bengal. The train brings us there in a night. Mā has a small *āśrama* here, very close to the shore; it is one of the last houses on the western border of this place.

Puri is paradise after the inescapable, noisy milling crowd of Calcutta. Especially the seaside, where my days are spent. I have never seen such a magnificent shore line. Its sand containing iron, has a faint reddish colour. The ocean is shallow in a broad coastal belt, but surges constantly against the stand with such savageness that if you dared to bathe, you would be tossed up and carried away by the waves like a toy.

Here and there, fishermen have spread out their long, brownish nets. Their boats are built today as they were built a thousand years ago. There are two types: the small one-man boats, the catamarans, a middle size between a boat and a float. Several thin, elastic tree trunks are tied together by ropes in such a way that they form the outer sides of the boats which are not very water-tight. These sides are also tied to one another by ropes at the bottom and at the points of trunks. Catamarans have the lightness of nutshells. When the fishermen go out to the sea in them, they are tossed around by the coastal surf like drifting tree barks. The bigger boats are seven to eight metres in length and have a high bow. No nail is used even for their building. The planks of the sides and the bottom are joined together by cross-stitches with coir-ropes. The gaps are filled up by thick straw-bulges. These are sewn in the cross-stitch.

The light boats go out occasionally during the day, but it seems that the heavy ones leave the shore only before sunrise. Sometimes, there is a long chain of boats quite far away on the sea. The fishermen's yield appears to be very negligible in relation to their input in courage, power and skill demanded of them everyday. Occasionally I see them returning with empty boats; sometimes, they pour out 2 to 3 kilos of silver fish of the size of sardines from their nets. Perhaps it is not the right season. One of the men explained to me in sign-language that they often catch bigger fish.

One evening a big boat returned to the shore after night-fall. In no time, a dozen men and women had gathered, and all were very happy. You could see a quantity of fish, like herrings in the bottom of the ship lit by a torch.

The landscape here: sea, shore and slightly ascending dunes; a brownish-green, strong brushwood growing on it. Ages pass by such a landscape without being noticed. Something of the archaic preservation of nature is expressed through the custom of the people living there, above all, in the religious form of their cult. Everyday, I observe some of their rites, when I go early in the morning along the beach to the *āśrama.* Nobody gives me exact information on this, but one of the monks indicates that *Brahman,* simultaneously visible and invisible to man, is invoked in all these forms of the cult.

All over India near the rivers, lakes and the artificial temple-ponds, one observes the same. Devout people stand in water with their hands raised and pray, eyes directed to the rising sun. I see them sometimes on part of the shore, which is washed by ebbing waves, kneeling or squatting in rows and writing signs with their right hand in the moist sand, which are washed off again by strong waves.

I recently saw a group of pilgrims, twelve Hindus (six men and six women); they (probably Tibetans) appeared to be performing a rite. A doctor in the *āśrama* told me that it was probably an ancestor cult. Men wore only a loincloth; women were in *sārīs* without blouses and petticoats. All the twelve were sitting on their heels next to one another looking at the sea. There was a palm-leaf in front of each with a few small heaps of condiments. Behind the palm-leaf, there was a green coconut, half buried in the sand; a thin branch was tied to its top. I have heard that this fruit is holy to Śiva. It may be that its use in this rite is supposed to represent a natural *liṅga*. The pilgrims are guided by a brāhmaṇa who has come with them from their native place, but here his only function is as helper to a native priest in the rite that is performed now. The *pūjārī* distributes rice to the pilgrims. It is kneaded in twelve balls and placed in heaps on the palm-leaves. While the leader of the group helps his companions in this work, the *pūjārī*, sitting in front of them, reads from a book. The pilgrims hold the rice-balls in their hands for some time, and then put them down. This part of the ceremony goes on so long that I do not have the patience to await its end.

Since we arrived, I have been watching another ritual every morning. It is performed by couples. It is not a fertility rite, because the couples I saw were without exception (was it a coincidence?) elderly people. They also squat on the shore, facing the sea, and a *pūjārī* squats in front of them and gazes at them. Husband and wife, with arms outstretched, hold a stone, a green coconut and a few flowers in their hands; their hands are back to back. The priest chants his *mantras* and pours water out of a coconut shell over their hands. After about five minutes, he is given some money, and the couple runs out to sea.

Very often I had the opportunity to watch a rite which first looks almost childish. Every morning, several *pūjārīs* appear pulling heifer calves behind them. While they hold the animal by a rope, the devotee pulls the calf by the tip of the tail – sometimes two or three people hold the tail firmly at the same time – and then the *pūjārī* chants his *mantras* in a distant, rhythmical voice. When the ceremony is over, the devotees touch the forelegs of the animals and then lift their hands to their forehead. Finally, the priest gets his fee. Sometimes he is not happy with the payment and protests loudly.

When I ask the doctor who is in charge of the *āśrama* about the meaning of the rites being performed year in, year out right in front of his door, he confesses to me that he had never consciously watched this, nor could he interpret what I had observed. This it typical. The educated, above all, the religiously educated Hindus, in my experience, know surprisingly little about what is happening in the life of a simple man in relation to religious rites. Meher told me now and again in Bombay with a sense of social guilt, "Sometimes I feel that we have only two types of people in our country, as it was during the British regime. A small section of rich people, who are masters, and the large masses of poor people." One notices something of this division too in the gulf between the spiritual and primitive Hindus. A brāhmaṇa in Calcutta (a senior official) actively interested in religion told me one day, "My family does not go to a temple any more. Our religious life takes place only at home." he found that what was happening in the temples was "too primitive".

The doctor in the *āśrama* was seventy-year-old; I thought he was only fifty. Again and again, I derive lot of pleasure from the diversity of characters from among Mā's followers. I have here thus a new "character". He stands at the extreme left, if strictly orthodox people among Mā's followers were placed at the right wing. It is surprising that he is a chain smoker. When I ask him about it, he says smiling:

"I have given up all vices one after the other. I am not for forcibly suppressing them. They must fade away on their own, otherwise they disturb us unnecessarily."

When I cautiously venture to criticise the doctor who has not been practising his profession now for over fifteen years, even though he is mentally and physically fit, but lives a contemplative and very comfortable life, he says:

"One has to obey one's inner instinct. We need people whose work for others is to contemplate. I am unfit for practical service. My thoughts are often carried away, so intensely occupied on this plane that they make me hopeless for practical things."

When I ask, what is on his mind, he replies, "I have to fathom what is *mind* (was he trying to fathom the soul or the mind?). I am less interested in examining its function than its nature." He has tested and analysed different ways and methods of meditation for years and occasionally writes for an American scientific periodical on questions which crop up while considering problems of Western psychology and Yoga.

I do not think, his is a religious approach to Yoga. His viewpoints are of philosophical and scientific nature. But a casual remark by him reveals that he has practised *Bhakti-Yoga* for years. He knows, thus, the religious side from his own experience.

"I don't know, who or what is God", he says, "and people who think that they know him, surprise me. I don't believe in doctrines, like, say, the rebirth of the soul or another form of eternity. I leave these things completely open. Only one thing that I know for sure is that our path leads to it!" Little doctor, as I call him in between because of his frail physique, points with a stern smile to the window. Very close to the *āśrama*, there is a cremation ground, and the smoke of a pyre is seen rising to the sky.

"And what does Mā mean to you?"

"Exactly what this name says, mother, neither more nor less. Even for an adult, it is good to have a mother. But Mā is the only one, I don't try to analyse, nor do I talk about her."

Later I have an opportunity to see him in the company of Mā. He is not lacking in reverence, but he is free-er and more detached than others who approach her, and Mā understands his nature completely.

One evening I asked little doctor about the fruits of his years of monastic seclusion in this house by the sea. It is hardly suitable for one who intends to study the human *mind*; he can study here only his own *mind*, and has almost no exchange of ideas with scientific thinkers who wrestle with the same questions.

Little doctor who sits on his bed with crossed legs, smiles as if he feels that he is "caught" because the real motive of this seclusion is now revealed. He says, "What we have to learn gradually is our detachment from the worldly is that we must become content."

"Why?"

"Only then is our spirit really empty and receptive."

"I feel, you have no religious goals. To what should your mind be receptive?" – "To peace."

Little doctor represents a type of modern mentality which succeeds in living without violating tradition. Where he is now, he has reached a different path from the pilgrims' religious path, but he says exactly the same thing as they: "I don't want to attain anything more. Nor do I seek God any more." If I have begun to understand his nature. I think, his psychic complexity must have made his way to detachment difficult. He could never have taken this path naturally without the background of his religious tradition. He somehow shares the religio-philosophical insecurity of the present-day Western man, but has been able to achieve peace in spite of this. I think, primarily through Mā's help, he makes efforts to consolidate this peace by performing spiritual exercises everyday, tried and valid over the centuries.

I do not think, I am justified in expressing my views, as to whether this is an egoistical way of life. According to Hindu thought, everyone who obtains self-realization serves the process of enlightenment for all human souls.

Yesterday I travelled by bus to the Sūrya-temple in Konarka. Departure at the first grey-purple light of the morning by a rickshaw to the bus-stand. We started an hour late, because the driver was lying asleep behind a hut. The "adorable vehicle!" was started with thc help of a handle; this was repeated at every halt and there was suspense each time, because the motor needed five minutes before it began to chug, and gave out a plaintive cry which showed that it was almost dying.

I saw the most impressive architectural monument of the land in Puri: a temple dedicated to the Sun-god. Its grandiose massiveness constructed in powerful rhythms is overwhelming: it is secluded and set in forest dunes. When it was built in the thirteenth century, it was by the sea. The tower was destroyed or was never completed, but the cube of the hall does not appear to have suffered much damage. The architecture represents a reproduction of the wooden processional chariot, the vehicle of the Sun-god, having twelve wheels and drawn by seven horses. Each of the gigantic wheels is completely covered by ornaments; it is a marvellous work of art. What liveliness of the animals on the elephantine frieze at the foundation! Each one of the mighty sculptures is full of vitality and, at the same time, worked in detail in a masterly fashion and has an astonishing grace. Above all, it is true of the gigantic figures of female musicians and dancers in the region of the roof. It is remarkable that such a massive ursine heaviness moves so splendidly and one "hears" the sound of their drums and cymbals. Many faces have an expression of eavesdropping and are so animated that one is surprised at the unexpected contrast of the heavy imperviousness of the bodies.

The *leitmotiv* of the statuary architecture of the temple is amazing; it recurs in countless variations; they are sometimes tiny, sometimes larger than the life-size. The sexual union between man and woman is reproduced in full detail and with ingenious diversity. If you are without any bias, you are neither embarrassed nor inclined to moralize. They have in them something of that luxurious proliferation of vital power; as when one walks through a jungle during the rainy season. Perhaps the author of a book on art rightly says: "The temples are covered by the carpet of blossoming life, under which, the holy is mysteriously preserved, like the magic of *māyā*, which, while offering itself to senses, conceals the true existence of the world."

While lying on the shore in the shadow of a big boat, I have read a treatise of Śrī Gopinath Kaviraj on the topic of how the phenomenon Mā is interpreted by Hindu philosophy. While reading this work, I had an insight into the volume of scholastic literature of different schools of thinking on the problem of "saints" alone (as we call this species which is quite inappropriate and too simplistic for Eastern concepts). I will mention only some of it.

G.K. examines at first the usual way in which a man can attain enlightenment and concludes that Mā has followed none of these ways (her *sādhana* was only "feigned"). Is she then one of those who are spiritually great, who have the enlightenment and the spiritual power within themselves (*akalpita*), without the guidance of a *Guru* and without Yoga-training? He thinks, he must deny this, because an *akalpita* cannot attain "self-radiation" without mercy. Mercy works in nine different ways. After examining these ways, G.K. concludes that none of them has contributed to what Mā is.

Is it possible that she is an *avatāra*? A divine being "climbing down from the Highest Heaven to bring peace of *Brahman* into the tormented world?" Even this question is answered negatively by the philosopher. Mā's image lacks duality between the source of the divine energy (in the Highest Heaven) and the bearer of this energy in the form of an *avatāra* working in the world.

Or is Mā a *vilasa* (a self-projection of the eternal divine in space and time)? "Is she a visible expression of the absolute? Is she an external manifestation – wearing a self-imposed mask – of the Inner *ātman* of the world – revealed to us – disguised in human form to draw us to her, away from the bustle of the shattering earthly existence?" This question is left undecided.

G.K. examines next, whether Mā is, what is called *Bodhisattva* in Buddhist conception and similarly understood by Vaiṣṇavas: as an enlightened one, who returns from the threshold of *Nirvāṇa* out of love for humanity, wanting to work for the salvation of the world before he goes into the bliss of eternal peace. The complete absence of intention in Mā's actions speaks against this interpretation. One does not get the impression that she is fulfilling such a mission in the strict sense of the term.

Each one of these interpretations have enthusiastic advocates among Mā's followers, only the supporters of different interpretations do not quarrel with one another. G. K. concludes this study by observing that Mā herself only claims "to be herself . . . In one way, she is indeed the truth that is proclaimed by the teachers of different views."

Then he turns to a question which is alien to the Western observer. He asks, namely: "Has Mā a body in our sense? Since every existence of man, according to Hindu thought, depends upon the accumulation of *karma* caused in earlier lives, and since Mā frequently emphasizes that her existence is independent of every *karma*, the involuntary conclusion of a thinking Hindu is: Mā cannot have, then, a body in the usual sense. What we call body, is a part of the realm of *māyā*, which conceals the real, the one existence of the Highest Reality behind the veil of the diversity of all phenomena. A Hindu is quite content to see Mā's body and to touch it and yet claim that it is not a usual body (usually it appears only to unenlightened eyes which allow themselves to be deceived by *māyā*).

This sounds like Docetism, says the author of the treatise; but there are many references that show even other Enlightened Ones – like Buddha and Christ – have appeared in a human body which was not usual. In fact, one has to have a clarity of vision to experience this. This "non-corporeality of the body" plays an important role in esotericism, and I have no reason to dismiss *a priori* as nonsense what our usual categories of thinking fail to describe. I myself can only say– this does not really hit the nail on the head – that even a person who does not have a clarity of vision, has, at times, the impression that Mā has another body! Her physical appearance is transformed by the spiritual. She appears, at times, so delicate and transparent, that one is forced to ask (in defiance of scepticism), whether she is about to "evaporate" altogether.

I would like to add here a few observations made by the principal of a college in Banaras. After long thinking, he cannot find a place for her in any philosophical system. Howsoever many-sided and ingenious all these systems may be, they are too narrow for the living numinous quality learned men encounter in Mā.

". . . . Mā has an unusual talent. She remembers people she has met and knows even those she is going to meet. Past and future have merged in her consciousness and have become one in her present. It is not a question here of memory, but of something we could call 'knowledge of existence', a process which is a result of a non-dualistic condition of consciousness . . . . Mā has repeatedly asserted that she does not make use of her intellect. I suppose it means that her intellect does not pursue its own independent endeavours, but is a focal point for universal life (another name for Highest Reality), which shows through her without any resistance. The concept that one has to silence one's intellect to achieve consciousness of a higher degree is not perceived by someone who has no experience of supramental sphere . . . Yet one recognizes in Mā that the intellect is a killer of the real, and when that happens, the real, the eternal, is born."

The only one for whom the question about the nature of the phenomenon of Mā never comes up is Mā herself. She seldom has the *khyāla* to say something about herself, even when she is asked.

How can the self, resting in itself, have an aspect that questions itself about itself?

Puri is regarded as one of the holiest cities in India. The temple to which thousands of pilgrims stream every year, is said to be 800-year-old. It was an early Buddhist religious centre. The present temple is a shrine of Lord Jagannātha (Śrī Kṛṣṇa) who is an incarnation of the highest Lord of the world, Viṣṇu. Puri is, thus, a centre of the Vaiṣṇavas, but it is visited by the pilgrims belonging to different faiths of Hinduism. One of the exceptions of this temple, which only the Hindus can enter, is that people of all castes and Hindu-sects can accept the *prasāda*-feast together.

The temple complex is enclosed by a high double-wall which is broken by large gates facing the four directions. Many people talked to me at the lion-gate, the main entrance. They assured me that efforts were made to permit non-Hindus to enter the holy complex.

Opposite to the entrance, there is a library which is managed by monks. You can get a view from the roof of this building into the holy area in which there are more than hundred shrines dedicated to different deities. The actual shrine of God Jagannātha is at the base of a 59 metre high tower that is shaped like a cylinder which tapers gradually. It is crowned by a fiery wheel and a big red flag; both are the symbols of Viṣṇu. A big building serves as a sacrificial hall. It is pyramidical in shape with a rather blunt end and its walls are terraced. Besides this, there are smaller, tower-like structures.

The monk who comes onto the roof of the library with me–armed with a long stick to chase away the monkeys – tells me that the President of the Federal Republic of Germany who presented a superb microscope to the library sat some years ago on this roof for two days to meditate and to draw. "Never", the monk says, "have I seen the stars in the Indian sky shining so brightly as then."

My days here are a great relief to me. Mā usually emerges from the house shortly before sunset and sits on a cement-pedestal that was erected for her *darśana*. There are about a dozen people who seldom speak. Mā herself is very quiet. Not pensive and introspective, but wide open and receptive to the surroundings, in silent dialogue with the cosmic powers.

Yesterday it was already night before she went back into the house. She was sitting on her pedestal for three hours, completely withdrawn. She did not even notice the people who knelt down before her to do *praṇāma.* Ami whispered to me, "We are only a dim flickering at the edge of her field of vision which reaches into the depths of the universe." As long as the evening sky was shining, one could see the reflection of this death in Mā's eyes and her face.

When I saw her for the first time two years ago, I was reminded of a huge tree. Something of this tree-nature could be seen in her again. The tree, with all its leaves, holding out its branches to the wind, the roar of the surf, the rain and the light of the stars. Their many-voiced message penetrates its innermost being, the sap and substance, down into its roots and becomes one with it.

Last night Mā had the same openness to the cosmos. She is part of its existence. How could it be otherwise? For one who has realized *aham brahmāsmi*, the ocean, the sun, the evening star and the wind are the beings to whom he talks in a universal language of trust. Perhaps this is not the right image. Perhaps Mā would say that she is not having a dialogue with the ocean. That is dualistic thinking.

This evening Mā talked for some time to people who came from nearby city. Then she kept silence for a long period; we felt as if we were all included in her own conversation with the ocean and the sky.

When Mā went into the house, Ami said using her Hindu terminology, "How good it is that God is not water alone (i.e. without form), but is revealed also as ice (i.e. with form), for example in Mā. If he were to be only water, I would be afraid of him. Who could bear his voice?" She interrupted herself, listened to the ocean down below, white from the foaming waves, roaring against the shore. "It speaks to us through Mā in a way that we can understand and love it."

Ami echoed my own thoughts with these remarks. One who sees in this phenomenon only an embodiment of cosmic powers, sees only the half. My host in Calcutta said, "The same divine spirit, which is revealed in Christ, Buddha, Mohammed and Śrī Kṛṣṇa and many enlightened persons, speaks through Mā. We don't know its name." This utterance refers to the other aspect of the phenomenon Mā: the acosmic phenomenon.

But as a matter of fact, it is just the cosmic that becomes particularly clear here. There was another indication this morning of the concrete and lively communion with the cosmos that is Mā's. We went for a walk on the seashore. I noticed how the girls and some monks bent down, took a handful of sand several times from Mā's footprints and threw it over their shoulders. After some time, Mā stood still on the wet strip of the sand which was regularly washed over by waves. For a good while, she gazed with quiet attention across the ocean. Suddenly her face became relaxed and giving a radiant smile, she said, "The ocean gives *darśana* to this body"; and when a little later a wave washed her feet, "With this touch it greets the little child." All this was neither solemn, not theatrical or playful: it was perfectly natural.

Often I sit for a long time on the seashore after nightfall. Small fires burn scattered in the distance. Fishermen prepare their meals on them. Sometimes one of them suddenly emerges from the darkness without a sound, looks at me and disappears again also without a sound. It is quiet around me, although the roaring of the surf does not cease for a moment. Perhaps because I am quiet within. I am living, as it were, mindlessly, only seeing and listening, with my antennae out which receive something beyond all naming and definition.

While walking around in Puri, I came upon a tiny temple

or shrine, hidden beside a line of low, miserable houses-there are countless such temples in Indian cities. I saw a woman with a child on her arm entering the space. Two boys, not even 10-years-old, were walking along with her. Inside, they sit with their mother in front of a crude, gaudy mural, depicting Goddess Kālī: a garland of thirteen skulls of the dead cover her black body. Her girdle is "ornamented" with chipped hands. A blood-stained chopper sways in her one hand, and in her second a severed head from which blood trickles down to the ground. A small dog is drinking from the pool of blood. The Goddess is dancing on the ashen-coloured body of her husband Śiva. She is wearing a shining crown. Her golden tongue is hanging right out of her mouth; the eye on her forehead is glittering. A shining aura is blazing behind her. Dark clouds flinch from the shining and fearful Goddess; her face expresses neither cruelty, nor pity, only her might.

The children look at the picture as our children look at gruesome illustrations of fairytales: with factual interest, perhaps with a little mingling of reverential awe, but not with horror or fear. Perhaps they have known it long since. One cannot fathom the face of the woman. Her eyes are focussed on the picture, without really seeing it. Only when she gets up, I discover a little grateful smile. On other occasions I have seen worshippers sitting in front of similar pictures. Expressions on their faces reminded me of women from Nepal worshipping before a statue of Virgin Mary, full of trust, love and gratefulness.

The *tremendum* of the divine appears to be equally present as its *fascinans* for a Hindu – even for a highbrow Hindu– Both are implanted in the soul of children, and that gives their faith a workability which preserves them from the fate of many Western believers: from the total collapse of faith, when the "dear God" turns out to be a touching, but a wholly unreal, legendary figure.

Recently someone translated a prayer to Kālī for me: "O Mother, in whom an infinite mercy is incarnated, I have gone on a wrong path, for, your face was hidden from me by the dust of my toilsome paths, so I could not recognize it. Let me return home to your holy feet and find peace in your immortal love."

It may be, that the horror of God is supposed to be banished by such euphemistic songs of praise. But the divine must be, both in its form of wrath as well in its form of mercy, an experience for the one who says this prayer in front of such an awful image of the deity. I think, an exceptional strength of Indian religious feeling and thinking lies in such an overall view. How often do I hear, in songs and lectures, the Sanskrit term *mātā-pitā.* God as "mother - father", not as mother and father, but as the one, the complex numinous mātā-pitā. Something of this complexity is also in Kālī, who creates life from her womb, nourishes it with inexhaustible motherliness only to devour again what has become a form.

I remember a man because he had talked to me about his travels to Europe earlier on. He tells me now, together with his wife, the following: "One day, when we visited Mā, she said to my son, 'What's wrong with your left eye? Take care, it is bad.' Two days later the boy's eye was injured in a sports' event and its lens was broken."

Or: "Some time ago, Mā was guest in our house. She distributed the *prasāda* of fruits from a basket. Both the women (members of the family), who had helped her with it, did not receive any fruit, At the end, there was only one fruit in the basket. Both saw it and thought, 'To whom of us will Mā give it?' Mā put her hand into the basket and gave each one of them a fruit." The narrator's comment: "As a matter of fact, such occurrences are unimportant for us. Many people do similar things in India. We come to Mā for other reasons."

A Bengali, who is basically friendly and has travelled abroad, recently complained that foreigners from the West in Calcutta are "not interested in spiritual things". He is working in a British firm. Many of his colleagues have been in India for years, but nobody has once bothered, even in passing, to explore the religious life of the country. "They know nothing about us, and yet they look down on our religion with an arrogant, or at best, sympathetic smile."

I had a long talk with the man. I found that he has a massive prejudice, when he refers to the "complete unspirituality of the West". Both sides suffer from the same evil: a remarkable lack of factual knowledge about what is available from the other. Every kind of generalization is dangerous.

Yet there are basic principles in the procedures covering a large area. And they can be recognized. For instance the aspiration rooted in mankind to achieve perfection has taken opposite directions in the West and East, and both have attained something that is impressive.

The man in the West has the mission "to subjugate the world", thanks to the development of his technical and organizational talent which is so great that he has ventured even into the cosmos itself.

The man in the East has focussed his urge for knowledge almost completely on the research of the cosmos within his soul. He has developed fine techniques for his diverse spiritual endeavours and has produced in every generation religious genii who are – according to Indian thought – shining incarnations of the deity.

Both the spearheads of aspiration for perfection are shot into the air from a small foundation. The West has allowed the Eastern side of its soul to waste away, and the East the Western side. What both have achieved had to be paid with one-sidedness. The East is inclined to despise the West for its barbaric superficiality, and the West finds that the East is barbaric in its neglect of external life. Both should now endeavour for a future synthesis. Both should realize, they are two branches growing on the trunk of one tree.

I think, it will be more difficult for the West to face this task because its progress in comparison with the East is much more spectacular, and the superiority of the East is much more hidden. But this may be, because I myself come from the West. The progress in the external world of the West may seem rather irrelevant, something that can only reluctantly be given equal importance. Now it is difficult to foresee in which way the Western and the Eastern aspiration for perfection can find a universal improvement for fusion of both the trends. Such an aim may be utopian and yet crucial to the development of integration which is seen in almost all walks of life.

For the time being only individuals can strive for such unification. I know from my own experience, it is not easy. Strangely, I have to overcome my anti-Western prejudices as much as my anti-Eastern. But it is not just the matter of overcoming this "anti". We should pay less attention to the failure of both sides, and look to the achievements of their aspiration for perfection and anticipate the totalitty of their objective appreciation and admiration. Our common heritage lies more in the assimilation of the Eastern half by the Western and *vice-versa.*

I have a great admiration for Didimā, Mā's ninety-year-old mother. With what dignity and wisdom she fulfils the role she has in the large community of Mā's followers. The more it is astonishing, if one bears in mind that she was brought up in a Bengali village where life was ordinary and horizons limited to village banality. Since then, she has assumed, as it were, the role of a Queen Mother in the realm of spirituality. She enjoys the veneration she receives from people coming from all the strata of the population. I do not know, how many of them look upon her as their *Guru,* from whom they have got their *dīkṣā*; probably they may be many. Years ago Didimā was elevated to the highest rank, a Hindu can attain, the rank of *saṃnyāsin,* and I have talked to a number of people who also think, she is a saint.

But all this has made no difference to her simplicity and modesty. She has learnt long ago to move with dignity and genuine self-confidence among all sorts of prominent people who visit Mā, but she always stays in the background. Her presence is inconspicuous, but something would be missing, if she wasn't there. In a real way, Didimā's presence assumes that Mā stays within the intimate human sphere and is familiar to each one of us. There is no fear that Mā's estrangement from this realm would cause her to slip from our grasp, for she has not fallen to the earth like a meteor from another planet, but was born of this loving, clever and modest woman who simply likes to laugh and is an untiring reconciler of tensions.

Didimā is beaming with happiness today. Her son from Banaras has come on a visit. At ninety, she is still his mother, and he her son. I would like to find out how the feelings of a mother – for, Mā is also afterall her child – are combined with the reverence for a being that says about itself, "*Brahman* I am". But probably, this would be different only for someone from the West. Countless Indians worship the divine child Gopāl as their "beloved deity" (*iṣṭa*). One reads occasionally: "It is all the same, whether you see in God your father, your mother, your friend, your beloved, your son . . . " besides, Didimā's undisturbed equilibrium proves it – this synthesis succeeds without any effort.

I hardly dare to confess that the Asian indifference to human misery has already infected me. I am reminded of my horror of the slums in Lodz (Poland), and qualms of remorse which every tattered man in West Germany gave me. I see thousands of poor people in Calcutta during day and walk during night over countless homeless people who sleep on the streets. Horsror and sympathy alone should kill me, but I notice that I am shamelessly getting used to the sight of misery.

Why? Because it is not a scandalous exception here which can horrify with a fairly concrete hope that it will be removed. Misery here is commonplace. It is obvious in a terribly harsh way. Today, every poor man in Europe is a social indictment, although he himself does not blame anyone. The poor here have an aura of resigned misery. Although they themselves could not say so, they are conscious that suffering is a consequence of earlier misdemeanors and has to be endured, if new *karma*-seeds are not sprout.

Perhaps they are right? This thought influences my fear that the Asian indifference is threatening to infect me.

But I am fighting against it. I want that these people get food, clothes and homes to live in and to work. It remains to be seen, whether they would exchange their misery for more subtle forms of suffering. One who withstands subtle suffering, also has subtle possibilities of overcoming suffering and has subtle joys.

The principle of 'love thy neighbour' cannot be totally achieved in the practical coexistence of people. One should not so absolutize the religious ideal that one suspects every decision to lead a contemplative life is disguised spiritual egoism. This is a danger of Western religiosity today. The danger of Eastern religiosity is the opposite. A look that is completely focussed on God, often does not notice the plight of fellow men, or see in this a God-given task.

January 11, 1964

Mā is staying for three days with one of her friends in a posh locality of Calcutta. The family lives in an apartment. It has an elegant, blue-white paṇḍāla erected on the top terrace of the house. Mā gives *darśana* there at noon after our arrival. She was bubbling with wit and vivacity, but now she is calm; this calmness is completely radiant for hours. She remains in a trance for hours, but her radiance does not diminish. She regains consciousness two or three times for a moment. Her look wanders beyond us. When it meets the eyes of a young man, who sits in front of me, he covers them quickly with both hands. I had to suppress the same impulse several times, and I knew, what must have happened to him. One feels that one is standing before a "fire" and suddenly notices how the flame dazzles one's eyes blindingly.

It is wonderfully quiet in the paṇḍāla. Perhaps nobody knows Mā is already here. Only a third of the seats are occupied, and nobody disturbs Mā in her contemplation.

Occasionally one hears across the roof tops powerful explosions and sounds like rifle fire. Perhaps there are military training grounds in the vicinity? . . . The calmness emanating from Mā has a quality that is not touched even by such noise, which is a horrible reminder of war for me.

As we later come down into the house, we hear that there are bloody riots in several areas of the city. A hair of Prophet Mohammed was stolen from a mosque in Srinagar in Kashmir. The theft of the relic, albeit by an unknown culprit, led to severe excesses in East Pakistan (Now Bangla Desh) against Hindus. Allegedly, over a thousand people were killed. The Government imposed a curfew upon the city of Calcutta and had to hand over the control of the city to the army because of Hindu/Muslim riots in parts of the town.

A few weeks ago I talked to an elderly man about the tolerance of Indians. At that time he was too sure of it. He now comes to me with a worried look: "You will now say, this is your Indian tolerance, won't you?" I answer with a vague movement of my hand. The man sits next to me on the couch. "These riots are no doubt regrettable and shameful", he says, "but they have little to do anything with tolerance. The reason is the political tension between India and Pakistan and the shocking misery of millions of Hindu refugees who have had to leave their homeland in the last years. Many of them have not yet been socially integrated. Nearly all of them belong to the lower strata of the population, and some are foolish enough to believe that the world would be better if they thrash some poor Muslims. And the Muslims are instigated by Pakistan."

The visitors come very late on the next day – it is Sunday. It seems that the public transport is more or less suspended. The family of our hosts begins the day by performing *āratī*. Mā sits in her room in an armchair. The hostess has dressed her in a lilac-silk *sārī* and put a garland of big white flowers around her neck. It reaches down to the floor. When the ceremony is over, Mā remains motionless for a long time. She tilts her head slightly to one side, her folded hands are raised. I cannot remember having ever seen her so radient.

Professor Chakrawarty who is to give a talk in the afternoon, cannot come on account of the political unrest. *Kīrtana* will be sung for an hour instead. I am again surprised at the many trained and beautiful voices. I ask for the text of the song from a woman who so fervently sang it, but quite without any sentimentality. She says, "I did not have the text of the song in the Western sense. I improvised new variations as I sang: 'I thought I had lost everything, but I have found everything in you, Mother'"!

While listening to the singers, the wind carries the constant rattling of guns across the roof tops. When I look around, I see that nobody feels he is disturbed. Later I express astonishment in a conversation with a woman. She replies, "What should we have done? Should we weep and lament? That would make the things worse. Mā once said in a similar context that there is no evil which we must watch passively. 'Purify yourself, fight against the evil within you, then fight against the evil in the world.' And we exactly do this, when we gather around Mā."

Although it appears as if Mā does not take notice of the bloodshed in the city, I ask myself: "Is there a mysterious connection between these events and the heightened spiritual intensity radiating from her?"

The city is depressing. Whole areas appear as if dead because nobody is allowed to step into the street. The army is patrolling particularly the areas around the colleges. This suggests that students are seen as a threatening disturbance.

It must have been terribly bad during the night on one of the main exit streets. The footpath is strewn with the ruins of pitiable bazaar-stalls, furnishings of shops and windowpanes. Burnt out cars and dead cows on which vultures descend, make the picture more bleak. Even a small mosque has not escaped the wrath of arsonists.

I have now been travelling with Mā for four months, in constant contact with her, and I think I slowly perceive something of the nature of her work. When I asked my intelligent host who has been closely associated with her for ages how he would describe her religious doctrine, he answered:

"Mā does not have own doctrine. But she teaches us two things through her being: complete, loving submission to the will of God and to know and love in every other being that particular Self whose essence He is and who also works in us. But as for different religions, she wants to help every devotee further on his own path by being a Hindu with Hindus, a Christian with Christians, a Muslim with Muslims, a Parsi with Parsis and a Buddhist with Buddhists."

This attitude would be unthinkable without the realization of "*aham brahmāsmi*". Mā can say, "I am a Hindu, a Christian, a Muslim, a Buddhist . . ." by being *Brahman*, only because she knows existentially (in accordance with the doctrine of *Advaita Vedānta*) that there is nothing except the one, *Brahman*, that is transcendent and immanent, cosmic and acosmic. The same attitude enables her to recognize God in the leprosy-infested human wreck that begs on the road, as it enables her to worship God in a toad or a dog with a reverent gesture – *praṇāma*.

From the same conception (this word should be understood in the sense of "acceptance" of what has been revealed to her as truth), she can assist a primitive from the jungle on the path of his enlightenment, as she assists a civilized person on his spiritual path.

Mā repeatedly reminded me that I should not forget to meditate on Christ. She gave the following answer to some Europeans who asked her on what they should meditate:

"You perceive what you see because there is light. But there is only one light. Whatever a creature in the world sees – whether an animal or a man – sees it thanks to one light. The external light has its origin in the inner light of the Self which is everywhere and present in all. Whether you now pray to Christ, Kṛṣṇa, Kālī or Allah, you pray basically to that one light that is also in you, because it penetrates everything. Everything, what is, is in its essence light."

Śrī Gopinath Kaviraj says, "Mā encourages everyone to progress on his path of his origin. Individual paths may take opposite directions. That does not remove their special importance as the paths of knowledge. When an individual path is followed to its logical end, it does not lead one astray, although it leads the pilgrim to partial truth and not the whole. But if the pilgrim has an honest longing for the Highest Reality, he would recognize the partial truth as a step on the path to the whole."

Once Mā said to me, "Even if you still have not reached the level of knowledge, where you see nothing else but *Brahman*, practise to see only the good in everything." I made no secret of the fact the I would find it difficult, say, where defenceless people were murdered, and I gave Mā several examples (among others, the one of concentration camps). She looked at me in such a way that I saw that she understood me. Yet she replied after a rather long silence, "You cannot understand now that God is in everything. Also in him, who says, 'He is love', and yet he does not lie."

Later an elderly woman said to me, "If we were as enlightened as Mā is, we would see it without any effort. All the saints in the world are grateful to God for their diseases, deprivation and suffering. How many of them – even Mā herself – have known that what we call suffering is welcome to them as a joy. One has to take that quite literally."

"Good, I could try to accept it as valid for my suffering, but what about the suffering of others?"

"You know that we believe in the law of *karma.* Suffering liberates us from what you call sin. Besides – if you are wise– you would know that there is no difference between your suffering and the suffering of others. But are you surprised that you don't understand these things? We are ignorant because we are not Mā, but only us. Mā sees the good in all because she is enlightened. We have to try to see the good everywhere to prepare our enlightenment."

The most essential practical piece of advice Mā gives to everyone is:

"Dedicate everyday – and as far as possible always during the same hour – a period of time for a prayer or meditation. This period does not belong to you, but to God to whom you have offered it for ever. Begin with a quarter of an hour and then increase the period of time as much as you can. There are virtually no external conditions of life which prevent you from at least thinking the name of God. Even if you are not interested in praying, begin to do it, as you begin to take medicine. If you are consistent, you will grow into a proper *sādhana.*"

"Seek, as often as the opportunity knocks at your door, *satsaṅga,* i.e. the company of wise and enlightened people. Be imbued with the atmosphere they radiate. Avoid carefully those who distract you from the goal of your path, i.e. God."

"Endeavour to keep God's name alive in you. You must reach a point, where invocation of the name – *japa* – becomes as natural to you as breathing. When you practise *japa* for long and earnestly, this prayer will remain with you, even when you have to talk or think of other things. It will continue to pray within you even in sleep. You will learn all this more easily, if you avoid talking unnecessarily. What we say, should reach Him alone, everything else is nothing and brings suffering."

"Even when you work with your hands, learn to do it so, as if you are doing *pūjā*. Mā repeatedly recommends *Karma-Yoga,* i.e. the Yoga of service and work without self-interest. But she says explicitly:

"First try to realize God with all your energy. That is more important than anything else. Then see how you can serve mankind. A service to man which is not done as a service to God does not bring about lasting grace. Do all your worldly duties as a service to God. You must, thus, fulfil them with extreme care, and it must leave you completely unmoved, whether you receive praise or blame in it. Such a *sādhana* of service is very powerful as a spiritual help."

A very important part of Mā's "work of spiritual welfare" is in giving courage to the "wanderers on the path of enlightenment" who have become tired. Mā said to a woman who complained that she was progressing very slowly on her spiritual path and felt she was stagnating:

"Examine yourself to find out, whether worldly wishes are frequently aroused in you. If you seek worldly joys, God will grant them to you, but you will not feel satisfied. God's kingdom is a whole, and you will not be happy until you are part of this whole. You are a child of the Immortal, and you will never reconcile yourself to the kingdom of Death, nor will God permit you to stay in it. He himself kindles the feeling of lack in you, by giving you a small bite only to provoke your hunger for more. That is his way of hurrying you along. The wanderer finds that this way is hard, but one who has eyes to see, realizes that he is making progress. What hinders you on your spiritual path, bears in itself the seed of future suffering. But the pains which are a consequence of this are also a beginning of your awakening to knowledge."

Mā says again and again: "A man must do his utmost, otherwise he will not be liberated. Don't allow yourself to be deceived by partial results. When your *iṣṭa* appears to you, it does not mean that you have attained your goal; it is only an indication to show that you have found your way. Don't be satisfied with religious rapture. It can be a foretaste, a touch, but nothing more."

Obviously Mā considers it to be important to warn believers against occultism. "Do not succumb to your proneness to thinking of ghosts and apparitions. It is better to focus your mind on God alone and meditate on him. No other power can exist in his presence. Be firmly convinced of this. The moment you seek shelter in God's name, no other lesser power can touch you. If you still have fear, you can be sure, it is only a physical reaction that is disturbing you. . ."

Mā said to a young man who often went into religious ecstasy and had visions, "Realize that a *sādhaka* who loses control over his mind runs into danger. He can become a victim of illusions and could even be exposed to the influence of evil powers. That would obstruct his way. Besides, it could become a source of arrogance or of egoistic pleasure, when you have visions or when you hear voices, which talk to you. It is not desirable to lose control over oneself. When one seeks truth, one should not allow oneself to be overwhelmed by anything. One should rather observe every emerging phenomenon carefully when one is wide awake and stays fully aware, so that one has an absolute control over oneself . . . Let meditation open your nature to the light, to what is eternal. Every dimming of consciousness works against this goal."

Another danger threatens a *sādhaka* on his path of *Bhakti-Yoga.* Mā refers repeatedly to it. "As there is a condition of highest self-realization, there is also a condition of perfection on one's path to God's love. One finds there that the nectar of love is identical with the highest knowledge. But there is no place for emotional excitement. In fact, it would prevent the lighting up of the Highest Love. The excess of feeling is absent at the summit of love. Emotional excitement and Highest Love cannot be compared at all; they are completely different from one another."

Mā was unhappy with the religious self - contentment of her friends. A woman complained that her religious duties were conflicting with her duties as a housewife. Her heart is always "half here and half there".

"Oh no", Mā replied to her. "You are not half 'there', but even less than 'half', and with a little other-worldliness (what is meant is the religiosity of the woman) you can fulfil your duties as a housewife very well, even better than without it (religiosity). Reserve a few hours for meditation each day, and during rest of the time, do your work as a service to God. If you think of God throughout the day and consider everyone to be his incarnation, then you can do excellent work and make everyone happy. Keep to yourself what little you have obtained within you and serve your family. You shouldn't make a show of the little you have so far achieved. When one day you immerse yourself in the One, so that it is not possible for you to do your work, nobody will blame you. On the contrary, people will feel God's presence in you and be only too glad to serve you. But this is very different from what you know now. Then the world will not exist at all any more for you . . . ."

Mā tells those, who think that they deserve a place in heaven, when they perform certain religious rites, say *pūjā*:

"Don't think that it is enough to celebrate correct *pūjā* frequently. *Pūjā* (the external ritualistic routine) is performed so that real *pūjā* takes place within us. It is exactly like someone accepting the initiation of *saṃnyāsa*, so that the real *saṃnyāsa* takes place in his soul. What does it then mean, to celebrate *pūjā*? To surrender oneself completely to the one whom one worships. When we really do it, all *mudrās* and *āsanas* are performed on their own, we do not have to 'do' them. When our devotion is perfect, he (God) reveals himself. And to find him means to find oneself, as to find oneself means that one finds Him."

When it is emphasized that Mā has no ego, it does not mean that she has no personality. In fact, anyone who has met her doesn't think of such a thing. On the contrary, he finds himself facing a usually intense and powerful personality of compelling fascination, based on qualities which at once evoke sympathy, trust and veneration. At first glance I know straightaway how I was dealing with someone who is incapable of even the slightest flicker of egoism and who is incapable of the slightest deceit.

An old Hindu has a Muslim *Guru* who had died many years ago, but he felt that he was still in close contact with him. He said to me, "Don't think that a divine personality disappears in the mists of impersonality, when we can no longer perceive a human form." This is particularly true, for instance, when the ego retreats from an enlightened man or – as many of Mā' followers think – when it concerns the death of a person who is born enlightened.

What is more natural than to seek to establish a friendly and personal relationship with somebody whose extraordinary fascination is based on admirable and loveable qualities? But here one realizes the different quality encountered in Mā. One immediately feels that she disdains any expectations of this kind. She clings as little to possession, place or doctrine, as also to people.

Someone told me that her husband had once asked her in the presence of many people, "You always say, you love all people equally. Don't you love me a little more than others?" Mā answered – no doubt with an expression of immense kindness, but unmistakable – "No!"

A morning on the roof-garden of the *āśrama* I was struggling with my *sārī* because the wind was pulling at it. Mā was standing in the sun with her billowing robe and enjoying the spreading of storm. Suddenly our eyes met. Her look had an expression of all-encompassing love. It rested for a long period upon me. I felt that I was bound by it, but I felt at the same time, that it penetrated equally lovingly the trees behind me, the village, the clouds, the thief, who was coming up the way with his stolen she-goat. It was strange, but I did not feel that I was robbed of the love which benefited the trees, village and the thief. On the contrary, I felt, I was loved *more*. In Mā's love, mine also reached out to the horizon.

I had felt something of this when I saw Mā for the first time. But then I had no idea about her realization of the wisdom of *Advaita-Vedānta*, of the existential realization of this mode of knowledge, or of a spiritual adoption. For, it is obviously not the case of Mā being overtaken by a philosophical insight. Rather the last mysterious truth finds expression and form in Mā's life, as it has happened in chosen few for centuries in this country. It was formulated around 1100 years ago by an enlightened one– Śaṅkarācārya – in the doctrine of *Advaita-Vedānta*.

What happens in such a chosen soul? This question worries us time and again, but can we seriously think of lifting the veil from this secret? One could try to imagine it. I read recently about "the mirror in the soul" in a book of a Sufi-mystic: "When the last sparkle of egoïsm is extinguished in a soul, this mirror will not be darkened by the shadow of one's own figure. It will receive the eternal light and reflect it for us."

Such a mirror of God is found in all major religions. The fact that Mā represents Hinduism in its highest form, gives the mirror of her soul the highest degree of sensitivity to light. Because of this, she is different from the enlightened souls whose inner mirror reflects the rays of a particular colour – a prism of religions in which the transparent light of Eternal Truth is refracted and split into a colourful spectrum.

A young Indian pointed rather arrogantly to the fact in a dialogue in Calcutta that the most significant Christian saints had said: "The mirror of the soul of heretics is completely destroyed and cannot be restored". He was interrupted by a *sādhu*: "And you would not have made such a statement?" – "No." – "Why not?" – "Because we are more tolerant in our thinking!" –"Then I beseech you, do not talk about things the premises of which are not known to you."

Later I asked the learned monk about the premises he had in mind. He said something like this: "We must refrain from interpreting the frequently exclusive attitude of the Christians as personal narrow-mindedness. The Christian faith (with Creation, History of Salvation and Doomsday) is historically oriented. A religious thinking which is so strictly linear is more easily questioned, if it deviates from its direction substantially, than our thinking which recognizes the world affairs in their infinite cycles. Many, apparently contradictory, trends are possible within a cyclic movement. We would deny the foundation of the truth which God has revealed to us if we were not prepared to respect your way of thinking as his thinking about his Self."

A Frenchman who has lived long in India answered my question: what fascinates him most strongly there: "The contact with a dimension of the spiritual about which the Western thinking and worldly wisdom in the so-called modern times knows almost nothing and even earlier very little." The West did conquer, actually through thought, the world of tangible things. The East undertook its expedition of conquest in the world of the intangible and expanded its *lebensraum.* "Where our science invents ingenious instruments to control nature, Asian thinkers have been endlessly refining the instruments inside the soul of man. They see, where we are blind, hear, where we are deaf, and they wander through zones which are not even marked on our maps, because we do not have any idea of their existence. . ." What enriched him, i.e. the letter writer, most in his contact with the Indian life, was the expansion of consciousness which he had experienced in himself.

I was waiting for this key word. It expresses what I am myself experiencing – though less intensely – because of my mere superficial contact.

But what is the meaning of expansion of consciousness here? The Sanskrit word which can be used in this context is *cit*; it is not translation of the word " consciousness". An Indian philosopher has explained it to a Swiss psychiatrist as "the original rising up illumination, a free, redeeming opening" (Madard Boss, *Indienfahrt eines Psychiaters*, 1959). The last truth of reality is experienced in this "light" ("light" has to be understood here literally).

It is not a scientific explanation. But such an explanation cannot be given in the realm of a mystical experience of the world. It is a hint. The Western–tangible – thinking will be quick to ask: "Who illuminates or lights up whom? Who or what opens itself to whom? How is active and passive divided in illuminating and being illuminated?"

But these are mistaken questions. Only unity (*a-dvaita* = non-duality) is experienced where enlightenment has become reality. Mā says, "Where there is *tat*, who is there, who? Who asks and who gives an answer? And what is the understanding? He and He alone! The Self, the Great Light, the Divine Splendour, the Highest Spirit, God–call it by whatever name you like."

The infinitely expanded consciousness – that mysterious sensitiveness to the Great Light – appears to be reflecting infinite realms in Mā.

I have heard Mā saying that she had seen and worshipped the Great Light in plants and animals, when earlier she "played the game of duality" and when she herself used to pray. She talked and lived with the gods in whom the transcendent *Brahman* becomes phenomenal *Brahman* ("like water assuming the form of ice"), as if they were siblings, or to be more exact: she entered the gods and let them emerge from her. Śrī Kṛṣṇa became visible in her body during her ecstasy and was incarnated in her flesh. Not, because she herself called him. She does not have any more "I"-voice, that could call him. Because the Kṛṣṇa-*bhaktas* seeking enlightenment come to her and want to see Kṛṣṇa.

One who comes to Mā seeking self-realization on the level of the knowledge of *advaita*, directs the mirror in her towards the transcendent acosmic *Brahman*, and it will be reflected for him in her silence. Perhaps in an indication – which can only be understood by one who is initiated – "When was I not?" Or: "I myself rest in myself!" Perhaps also in a ray of light received by her inner mirror and sent further.

One cannot imagine a realm that would be unknown by such an infinitely expanded consciousness. Mā says, "Every house in this world is my house. Every self is my self. But my self is *tat sat* (that self).

One, who comes in contact with her, experiences a wealth of quietude that is quieter than the quietness between the cosmic tides, quieter than the quietness between the breaths of an ant and as quiet as the quietness in the heart of *Brahman*. There is a phrase in which Mā expresses the bliss of this quietude:

"The Self resting in itself, calls itself for its own revelation – that is *Brahman*."

Chapter 11

Bodh Gayā: The Place where Buddha Attained Buddhahood

January 26, 1964

Rajgir in Bihar is our next station after a brief halt in Agapara-*āśrama* near Calcutta. Mā also has an *āśrama* here. It is situated at the border of a miserable village, in a forest and hilly landscape. This region has a great tradition. It is said that Buddha lived here for a long time, the founder of Jaina-religion spent many rainy seasons here and Śrī Kṛṣṇa lived in the woods.

On one of the first days I go to BodhGayā, the place where Gautama became Buddha. The bus leaves Rajgir and goes for a long time through wooded mountains up to Gayā. I take a rickshaw there. The coolie has to pedal for one and half hours against a sharp icy wind. This landscape is strange. Its paradise on the right side of the road and a desert on the left; on the right rich green, well-irrigated rice and corn fields, palmtrees with tapping pitchers on the notched trunks, wells, small shrines, and huts at a distance. On the left, a strip of desert, a bleak, steep mass of mountains on the horizon. Occasionally herds of black buffalos march across the white land without a herdsman, wading slowly and endlessly behind one another through the sand.

BodhGayā: a poor village with dirty lanes, noisy traders, milling crowds between ox-driven carts and tea-stalls. Suddenly the holy region grows up through an invisible wall, protected from every disturbance. The street here is wide and deserted. The Mahābodhi-temple, a small pyramid which tapers to a round point is situated in a terrace-shaped depression. The same smaller pyramid is repeated at the four corners of the temple premises. The temple-towers are divided by broad, round ornamental bands which circle them.

It is said that the main tower is 2100-year-old in its original state. It is surrounded by *stūpas* and multi-shaped votive stones of prominent pilgrims over the ages. Young Tibetan monks in dark-red habits prostrate themselves on wooden planks in front of the temple. Sometimes they do this prostration exercise for hours. They are all totally engrossed.

Older monks slowly circumambulate the temple on a red carpet, with bowed head, arms hanging down and rosary in hand. I adjust myself to their quiet stride. After a while, a monk who is walking in front of me turns to the right. His round, cropped head bows to a stone slab; its gold-coating is worn off by the pressure of countless foreheads. The tree of Enlightenment spread its mighty branches over us. Its leaves are grey-green and heart-shaped; they are as broad as a palm of a hand and taper at the end. The trunk is grey-brown and the bark is smooth. The sun sparkles its shafts of light through the branches and on the sand on which the immortal foot-prints of Buddha are imprinted.

I enter the temple hesitantly. The sudden change from light to dark dazzles me. Gradually I see a simple barrel vault with grey, unadorned walls. A golden Buddha sits enthroned at the front over an altar-like table. His eyes are blue and the hair stranding in turquoise curls. His torso is covered with a yellow cloth; a white linen cloth hangs over his left shoulder, and his right hand carries a black bowl containing oranges.

It is cool and .gloomy, and my eyes are strained by the sun's rays, but my whole attention is focussed on listening. A strange sound vibrates under the vault. I look back and discover that I am not alone. A woman and a young monk are sitting at the rear of the temple. The rhythmical chanting of their prayers fills the place with sound; its strange loveliness fascinates me. I go and sit next to the worshippers.

The woman is tall and slender. She has a pale, fine face with strongly defined Mongolian features. Two pigtails fall onto her breast. A bulging linen shirt is tucked into the waistband of her wide, dark-green skirt; there is a wine-red shawl made of the material used for monk's cowls lying on the top of skirt. She holds a rosary in her left hand and a brass-plate with an upturned edge.

One of the mystic diagrams called "*Śrī yantra*" from the Indian *Tantras* (geometric representation of *mantra*) can be faintly seen on the plate. A mixture of different grains, pips, suger-candy, colourful semi-precious stones and Tibetan golden coins lie in her lap. She pulls out a small bottle containing a yellow-red oily liquid from the pocket of her skirt. She rubs a few drops onto the plate and polishes it with her right sleeve. Interrupting herself again and again, she looks at the Buddha and prays in a low voice. While the young monk is looking at her, she makes a pyramid-shaped *maṇḍala* of four *cakras* on the plate, each one of them consisting of a double circle of faint-red and pea-sized stones. She fills the empty space with the mixture on her lap and closes it at the apex with a *Dharma-cakra* (Wheel of Law) made in silverwork. While she holds the pyramid with both her hands towards the Buddha, her prayer becomes louder. The monk joins her in singing.

Then she pours whatever she has put on the plate into her lap and the organ-like tone of the *mantra* resounds again, softly swelling up and down. A monk tells me its meaning later: *oṃ vaijra bhunti ah huṃ.* He cannot translate it, but it is something like taking an oath to be instrumental in the spiritual liberation of the universe. The melody, swelling up and down, ends each time in a deep humming tone. The right hand of the woman is filled with the mixture from her lap; during the pauses at every syllable, her fist dabs at a particular spot of the mystic diagram; simultaneously a portion of the mixture of grains spills onto the plate. Her hand is completely empty at the last syllable and she rubs the plate clean, then reaches once more for the mixture of grains, and the tune becomes louder again.

I now sit very close to the worshippers, at a right angle to them, and share in their rite by picking up the grains which sometimes fall to the ground and throwing them back into the woman's lap. The young monk has his hands buried in the sleeves of his cowl. At times, he throws back his bald head. His face is bright, his cheeks are red, and he doesn't look Mongolian. In spite of his moustache, there is something childlike about him. When I pick up the grains, he looks at me and gestures at me to eat them.

Later in the front hall, I ask a monk wearing a yellow cowl (which indicates that he is not Tibetan) about the two and learn that the woman is a wife of a Tibetan Tantra-Lama of noble birth, and the woman is seen as "very holy" among her people. The young monk is a pupil and a *bhakta* of her husband. The couple is on a pilgrimage to the holy places of Buddhism. The Lama has gone ahead to Rajgir, but his wife has stayed behind as she has taken an oath to celebrate the rite 100 000 times which I watched.

This holy region comes to life at sunset. I have returned to the temple. When I start to sit on my coat, because of the stone-cold floor, the woman moves a little aside and makes a place for me on her mat.

The temple fills up. Tibetan monks in "yellow cowls" from the so-called "Chinese Monastery", old Tibetans in long, dark-red, greasy shining overcosts and heavy felt shoes, women whose pigtails are hanging down to their knees and who carry their children wrapped in a cloth on their back and Hindus are gathered here. The table under the Buddha idol is now full of ignited candles and joss-sticks. A brāhmaṇa whom I saw in the afternoon praying in front of the holy tree with his group of pilgrims is performing *pūjā* and distributing the *prasāda.* For Hindus, Buddha is not a founder of an alien religion, but an *avatāra* of the highest God. Two elderly Muslims of noble birth stand in prayer before the idol with burning candles in their hands. Someone gives me a candle. The spirit of the Enlightened One establishes harmony in the hearts of those who worship together.

Later in the evening, the temple is exclusively occupied by the Tibetans who have settled in hundreds in their tents at the border of the holy region and the pilgrims who come and go throughout the year. About a dozen monks are sitting in the area; most of them are reading and turning the prayer-mills at the same time, some of them are praying with a rosary. Two very tall pilgrims with thin moustaches and a long, thin goatee on their chins prostrate themselves groaning before the Buddha. All their possessions are stuffed in the chest of their padded overcoats. Knives are kept in the leg of their boots. The old lady next to me also has a knife in a beautiful silver-sheath stuck into her belt. The two giants bow reverently to her Buddha.

It is already night when I leave the temple. The street lights are extinguished. A procession of singing Tibetan women goes slowly round the temple. Some of them carry candles. Their songs have a fascinating melancholy. Children seek shelter in their broad coarse skirts from the icy wind blowing from Nepal. A group of young men with broad-rimmed hats and casque coats with belts of resistant felt, roam about aimlessly. Most have kerchiefs over their hats and knotted under their chin.

A dozen or more monks circumambulate the temple on a runner. They let their rosary fall at every fifth step, fold their hands over their head, touch with them their forehead and breast and then prostrate themselves on the ground with fervour, arms first like the swimmers who leap into the sea. There are old men among them. I hear them groaning gently, but I don't see any hesitation in flinging themselves onto their knees.

Three hundred oil-wicks in silver-cups burn in front of the Tree of Enlightenment. Foreheads of all worshippers bow to the gold-coated stone adorning the holy place.

Another path for the pilgrims winds round the temple area on lower slope and right at the top a third one. The three paths are full with singing, murmuring, whisperings and silent prayer. Here and there, someone carries a hurricane lamp and the holy tree blazes at the bottom of the valley in the light of the burning wicks flickering in the wind. Crimson rises the moon over the temple.

Next day I visit a Lama-monastery. It looks like an Asian fairytale. A broad house surrounded by a terrance on the groundfloor. The roof of a Chinese temple rises above the first floor. The front facing the street is covered by ornaments in a fantastic way: flowers, stars, fish, carved and painted ones, everything in shining colours, ornamental bands running horizontally and vertically, lots of red and blue. It is a jubilant expression of vital joy in the beauty of the world. At the same time, the skilful handiwork is completely rooted in tradition.

I climb one staircase. The layout of the first floor, I feel, is like a village square. There is a small temple in the middle. The "square" is uncovered. Around the periphery are the rows of houses. In fact, these are only the cells of the monks. Door after door in a low white wall.

A monk in a torn cowl and with a broad Mongolian peasant face walks beside me in the temple and talks for an hour almost without pause. I try to shake him off by sitting on a mat with eyes closed, but he waits patiently at the door, till I get up, and again runs after me.

The place is in semi-darkness. Here and there, an oil lamp burns in front of a Buddha statue. A silver-embossed bowl of the size of a baptismal font is filled with a mixture which looks like semi-liquid wax. A burning wick swims over its surface. The focal point of the temple is a massive, golden Buddha with a flaming crown covered in precious stones. Valuable old books, each tied in Chinese silk, are piled behind him. Precious silver goblets placed in front of him. The small Buddhas look like ancient dolls in their faded silken garments; they fill a large showcase – row after row. Paintings of the Buddhist *Heilsgeschichte* and mythology hang on the walls: scenes from the life of Gautama Buddha, *Bodhisattvas* playing music, mysterious *maṇḍalas* which have faded to dark-yellow, a demon; blazing in flames, priests giving instructions . . . The inmates of the monastery must have collected whatever they could from the priceless treasures of their native country. They must have brought the showcases containing pious rarities here. May be, there is an order behind this chaos in the semi-darkness, and it can only be recognized by the initiated.

The monk turns away when I put a coin in the collection box. He comes down to the groundfloor with me to the "prayer-mill": a room almost completely filled up by a brass-cylinder. I think, it is nearly one and half meters in diameter and two and half in height with handles at the lower edge. A notice in English informs me that this vessel is filled up with prayers to help purify the world of its sins. The monk asks me to grasp one of the handles. I follow his example, and we walk briskly around the cylinder which turns easily. Each time we go round, a bell chimes melodiously. Several monks join us. They circle the mighty prayer-mill pushing it with earnest faces and long, quick steps.

Later I return once more to the temple near the Bodhī-tree. It is quiet and cold there. I see the young monk outside performing the kneeling exercise on a plank. As I stand next to him, he looks through me as if looking through a glass-window.

My Tibetan friend moves a little aside on her mat without looking up. She knows from my step who is standing before her. The rite is in progress. The syllables of the *mantra* ascend and descend like singing waters of a fountain. Peace and cheerfulness flows strongly purifying the air we breathe. The Enlightened One bestows his blue-eyed smile upon us drawing into a unity what was separated by the deceptive mirror of *māyā*.

I am restless after my return from BodhGayā: I would like to meet the *Tantra*-Lama, the husband of my Tibetan friend. I know that he has to be in Rajgir to make a pilgrimage to the holy places where Buddha had exerted his influence.

My destiny leads me there. While climbing the mountain over the hot springs, I saw a Tibetan nun standing under a tree feeding peanuts to shrieking monkeys. Later I had to search for her for a long time, as on reaching the spot, the landscape had swallowed her up. I finally found a gate in a rock and a small yard. The nun stood there in front of an open fire. If I hadn't heard her talking to the monkeys, I would never have known whether I was standing before a man or a woman. While stirring a thick yellow porridge over the fire, she turned her round cropped head to me and looked with a searching gaze from her narrow Mongolian eyes.

"Is the *Tantra*-Lama here?" I asked her. She nodded and went into another yard. She stood before a door, pointed to the place and said beaming, "*Tantra*-Lama."

As I entered the semi-darkness, I fumbled my way around. The only source of light was a hatch-like window in the external wall that was on the other side. A royal figure sat on a "bed" that was hewn in the rock: a tall, broad-shouldered man, clothed in a yellow, silk waistcoat which was lined with fur, a red scarf, tucked into the neck. He turned his beautiful head with dignity to me. His wavy, silvery hair was flowing over his shoulders. Really, the fairytale king of my childhood dream smiled at me and bade me a gracious welcome! After I had bowed to him, he also bowed and offered me a place on a carpet with an inviting gesture. While I was sitting down, he seemed to have forgotten me. Later I realized that the Lama does not speak either Hindi or English, so he could not do anything more sensible than to immerse himself again in his book and leave me to my contemplation.

I looked around at the place which resembled a cave

rather than a room. Two iron boxes were kept on the right of the Lama's bed and they were covered with a carpet. On this provisional table stood a round teacup of wood decorated with inlaid work, a hand-bell, like the one in a Tibetan temple, a small double-drum (it is called *ḍamaru* and serves to drive away demons) and a kitchen alarm clock.

Where I sat down was obviously a sleeping place. It was upholstered with carpets and furs. A niche was carved in the wall behind the Lama where he kept his books.

The Lama sat cross-legged on his bed. A soft carpet covered his knees. His white hands lay on his lap. He was holding a book in them. Its pages are not turned from side to side, but from bottom to top. The Lama's hands are surprisingly long, powerful, but not plump. On his left hand he wears a gold-ring with a dull pearl of the size of a hazelnut. His nails extend beyond the finger-tips by more than a centimetre. The skin of his face is darker than that of his hands; it is of a bright gold-brown hue. It is fairly broad with a lofty forehead; cheekbones are not prominent; his nose is powerful and straight; mouth and chin rather delicate and the eyes are slightly Mongolian and so filled with light that I remember them as shining blue.

The expression on his face which I study often during the next days is what I was reminded of the kings in the fairytales of my childhood, when I first saw him. He has: cheerfulness, wisdom, patience, goodness, coupled with a powerful manliness residing in itself.

The nun brings for her master a fresh cup of tea. With the movement of his hand, he asks her to bring for me a cup too. On this occasion, I hear her address the Lama as "Rimpoche" (preciousness), and I make immediate use of this form.

After I have drunk my Tibetan tea (it tastes like sloppy bouillon) and sat quietly on my carpet for a while, and *Rimpoche* continues to read his book in gentle murmur, I bow to him and go to the *āśrama*.

I repeat these visits twice daily from now on. When I enter, *Rimpoche* laughs and nods at me, clasps both his hands, calls the nun so that she brings tea, says something which sounds friendly and soon immerses himself in his book. Sometimes he stops and prays gently. Yesterday morning he called me to his bed, and while he continued to pray, he took out a tin-box from the heap of books behind him and poured sugar candy into my hands. Sometimes a Tibetan monk sits on a small carpet which is opposite to the bed, and prays for a while turning his prayer-mill.

A group of Buddhistic pilgrims from Bhutan, three young men with their wives, came last night. Powerful, cheerful people in their colourful clothes, with attentive and intelligent faces. Each one of them knelt thrice in front of the Lama, then sat on a carpet and started a conversation which was often interrupted by laughter. Only the young people talked loudly. I never heard *Rimpoche* speak other than in a low tone, almost whispering in a thoughtful manner. His deep, gentle voice is pleasant and radiates peace.

When I came to the Lama this morning, I hardly believed my eyes: his wife, my friend from BothGayā, was sitting where I usually sit. We greeted each other ardently.

I discover now her name: Lamo! In the twinkling of an eye, she shows that the pilgrim's refuge has now a housewife. She spreads a thin carpet on the floor, fills a woven dish with dry dates and puts a box of roasted rice from Bhutan in front of me. Then she offers me the sugar candy in a silver-box. Later the nun gets us butter-tea.

In the meanwhile, Lamo holds both my hands, keeps hers next to mine and is happy to know that all four hands have the same hue. *Rimpoche* is informed about this and he nods approvingly, but the expression on his face reveals that his thoughts are far away.

The palm of my hand seems to fascinate Lamo. She looks at it for a long time and opens her left palm to compare it. Finally, she fetches her glasses and searches in a wooden box and finds a book that is wrapped in a yellow cloth. Later an Indian arrives who knows both Tibetan and English. He explains that it is a "textbook of divination". Less educated people call it "book of magic", and it contains texts and sketches about the magic wisdom of the Tibetan *tantras.* Lamo pages through it, observes my palm once more and asks the Indian to tell me that there is no doubt that I lived in Tibet in an earlier incarnation.

Rimpoche nods and laughs at the childlike eagerness of his wife to draw me into their family. When I meet the Indian again, he tells me, earlier on he was a monk in a Buddhist monastery which he left for political reasons. He is now busy studying ancient Tibetan writings. I ask him to interpret my conversation with my Tibetan friends. Now I learn that they have a daughter who studied in a college near Madras at the request of the Dalai Lama and that the family fled from the Chinese in 1959 (the parents of *Rimpoche* died while fleeing) and they are now in West Bengal. In Tibet, *Rimpoche* was an abbot of a monastery of 300 monks, following his father and grandfather.

When I ask Lamo what the Dalai Lama means to her, she says, "He is something like a king, and we obey his orders. We even call him God, but we only worship the Buddha."

"What sort of orders do you obey."

"Our daughter was about to marry a young Indian. But the Dalai Lama will not tolerate this. He wants our young people to marry only from our own community. How else can we preserve our customs?"

Rimpoche puts his book aside and listens to us. I now turn to him, "What do you think, *Rimpoche,* why have your people to suffer the fate of expulsion?"

The Lama nods his head enveloped in curly hair thoughtfully and then says gently, "It was like this. We have made Chinese suffer for generations. So we have to suffer now. But the Buddha teaches us that we should not hate them for it. Even he had to suffer without ever thinking of revenge. We consider that the Chinese are our brethren."

"Do you hope that you will return to Tibet one day?"

"If we succeed in preventing the feeling of hatred against the Chinese, the land will be open to us one day."

"How many Lamas were you in Tibet?"

"About a thousand. But most of them have been . . . " *Rimpoche* explains with a sharp movement of his right hand that they were beheaded.

We sit facing each other silently for a couple of minutes. The Lama reaches for his book. Resignation and humility are reflected in his face, although it is a distinctly manly, almost bold face. Before he begins to read again, I ask him, "*Rimpoche*, tell me the most important religious rule of your *Tantric* Buddhism."

He replies without thinking for a moment, "Our most important rule commands us to love the Buddha and show goodness to mankind."

He nods to me smiling, then shuts his eyes. For him, our conversation was over.

Lamo listened to us, as a child listens to the conversation of adults. Now she puts her hand around my shoulder and the Indian has to translate a small speech. She says, "I cannot talk to you, but I love you as my sister. It was nice that you sat next to me for hours in BodhGayā and prayed with me. If one has a friend, praying is the best thing one can do together."

I spend the day before our departure almost entirely with *Rimpoche* and Lamo. Now Mā is only ever available for a few minutes. We hear, she has not been feeling well. Also Lamo complains of agonizing headaches. I give her a tablet. Her pain subsides afterwards. She stretches out on her bed happily; she prays while holding a rosary and my left hand in both of hers till she falls asleep.

I stayed close to her till it started getting dark. Almost three hours passed. *Rimpoche* was reading during the whole period and nodding to me sometimes.

This faculty of sitting quietly for hours without thought, even without dreaming, with a feeling of inner void which is none the less complete fulfilment, without desire – shall I forget it again in Europe? Have I mastered it here? It comes as gift; I cannot summon it. Mā gives it to me sometimes, I find it in a place sometimes: the spiritual communicates with me.

People like *Rimpoche* and Lamo create an atmosphere in their presence where peace and tranquillity appear without effort. I talk to them as if through the pores of my skin, not from my brain, nor through speaking. It would certainly have been good, if we could have spoken to one another, as one normally does, still we are not bothered that we cannot understand one another, but take care that our mute conversation is not disturbed by idle talk.

When the nun came with a hurricane lamp, I got up. It was time to take leave. Lamo slept like a child, holding the rosary in her hand with both fists under her chin. I stroked her hair carefully, but she did not stir, so I let her sleep.

Rimpoche put away his book. He held my hands in his huge hands for a long time and shook them. While bowing down to me from his high bed, his curly hair fell over his face, and then his beaming smile appeared again like a king in a fairytale. At the end he put both his hands on my head and gently said the same thing thrice. I think, it was a blessing. The nun embraced me smiling in the dark yard and accompanied me up to the tree where she feeds peanuts to the monkeys every morning.

February 5, 1964

I had a long conversation with Mā yesterday. Among other things we talked about marriage and the relationship of the married couple with each other. I have the impression that orthodox Hindus attach greater importance to those who do not marry for religious reasons than those who marry, although the position of the house-father (and the house-mother) is definitely a stage in religious development. If I have rightly understood, Mā said,

"It is good to marry. One who marries can become a father or a mother of saints. But today young people do not recognize this."

Not long ago, the responsibilities inherent in establishing a good marriage were looked upon with respect. Above all, a young man and a girl would not meet before marriage. They were not allowed even to see each other. This had a profound meaning for the sanctification of marriage as an institution, the task of which is to serve the realization of God in the life of a man. Inherent in a young man and a young girl – as long as they are pure – is *Kumārī-Śakti*, a divine power, which gives them the capacity for successful spiritual development. When the partners do not see each other before marriage, the *Kumārī-Śakti* accumulates in them so that it becomes extremely intense. In the holy moment, when the man and the girl look into each other's eyes for the first time, an exchange of *Kumārī-Śakti* takes place. By this each of them is enriched by the *Kumārī-Śakti* of the other. The foundation of marriage as a religious institution is laid in this act. In fact, they develop themselves completely, when the partners have sex only to give birth to a child. After some children have been born, it is better for the spiritual development of both husband and wife, if they spend the rest of their life as brother and sister.

"Have you noticed that we put a flower on the fruit that is to be offered to God in *pūjā*?" Mā asked me. "In this way, it is already offered to God before the rite begins. According to our view, a fruit becomes impure, if a covetous look falls upon it; it cannot then be offered to God."

C. who helps me as translator added later: "When Mā's food is cooked, the kitchen door has to be closed the moment there are people in the vicinity. The aroma of food could arouse the desire of the people, then this food would be affected and impure, so that we could not present it to Mā as our offering."

Back to my conversation with Mā: she said further on the theme of marriage: "A girl should see the young man she marries, as her lord, as an incarnation of God. A young wife has a great religious opportunity. By marriage she practises and learns to conquer her ego and to subjugate herself lovingly to the divine will. If she has remained completely pure before the marriage, she can look upon herself as a fruit that is offered to her lord at the moment, when the eyes of the partners first meet. If a young man sees the girl whom he wants to marry beforehand; it taints the fruit that it to be offered to God as if pecked at by a bird or subjected to a covetous look. We say then: it is half eaten."

Ami climbs the mountain over the hot springs with me. We leave the pilgrim-path which leads to the peak and follow a narrow side-lane. It ends near three temple ruins which are almost swallowed by a jungle. They are dark reddish-brown brick walls which enclose small rectangular chambers. There are about five or six *bodhisattvas* in niches in the walls next to each other, weather-beaten and entwined by creepers of red blossom.

A space in the larger ruin is taken over by the Hindus as a Śiva temple: a *liṅga,* a crudely chiselled Nadi-bull, wilted marigold garlands of the last *pūjā*; scurrying squirrels in the corners; rustling and hissing under a heap of dry branches.

Ami is afraid of serpents. We sit on a wall with our legs up. One has a view of the land from here. My companion is silent as usual. I see that she is thinking, and I would like to know what about.

"Can you think aloud?" I ask her.

She pulls the *sāṛī-pallv* over her head and looks at me abashed. "My thoughts are quite ordinary, but you know I have difficulty with the basic concepts of pious people."

"That is why I am interested to know what you are thinking."

"All right. I was thinking about *māyā.* A short while ago, as we were standing in front of the hibiscus, I had a momentous perception. I saw the blossoming bush in front of the ruins and thought: how beautiful you are, *Bhagavān.* Then I looked at the *bodhisattva* whose head is knocked off, and I had the same thought: how beautiful you are, *Bhagavān.* When I looked at the wilted flowers before the *liṅga* I had again the same thought, and so it was with everything I saw. It was irrational because I saw the hibiscus, the faceless *bodhisattva* and the wilted marigolds, but I did not see them, I saw Him. His beauty. It pierced my heart like a knife. Do you understand what I say?"

"I think, I understand, but can you be more precise? Did you see God in all things, or were the things in God? Or was everything around you suddenly God?"

Ami raised her head annoyed. "You do not understand. The pedantry of people who know God only second-hand speaks through you. Look at the tree with brown fruits. If God had touched your heart, so that you could see Him in the tree, do you think it would make any difference whether you see the tree in God or God in the tree? I tell you, you would see the tree and only think, God, God, God!"

Ami did not talk for a while, but then said, "This happens, when the veil of ignorance is torn away. You suddenly know that everything is God, and you understand that if we could see Him, we would find Him everywhere."

"Is it because of our blindness or because of the veil of *māyā?*"

"It is our blindness we call the veil; it is ignorance which makes us think that a tree is nothing but a tree."

"But you are born with your blindness. It is a part of being a human."

"Yes, God has caused it like everything else. We don't know why, but He also removes it from me. Now sometimes for seconds. One day it will be permanent. Mā always sees a tree as it really is, and it is God."

Ami returns to our conversation later on the way coming down. We sit on a rock taking a rest. She points to one of the wooded mountain-tops on the other side of the street that leads to BothGayā.

"Look at the mountain. God is like this mountain from which trees, bushes, grass, flowers, whatever you like, emerge, as your hair, nails, etc. growing from your body. We do not believe in a single act of Creation like you, but we believe that the universe has grown out of *Brahman*. Trees and bushes, creepers and all sorts of grass–everything springs directly from God, like the hair from our body.

But God–the mountain – likes to play a game of *māyā* with every part of his self which is represented here in trees, bushes and other plants. And that is why, the plants fight with one another for place, food, light and shadow; and strong ones displace weak ones. They are afraid, they would starve, because of the threat of death. They think: 'If I am uprooted or if I wither, my life will end.'

Only those among them who have overcome ignorance do not fear. They know: I – that is not this tree, when it grows, blossoms for a couple of decades and bears fruit. I– that is the mountain! And when the tree dies, the mountain does not suffer more than your body suffers when it loses a hair. Do you understand?

The tree must know that it is the mountain. Then it also knows that all trees, bushes, grass, creepers and flowers are nothing else, but the mountain, and there is nothing else at all, but the mountain. Mā is such a tree and she knows that we are one with her. That is why, she has no fear. For her everything is mountain, that means God or *Brahman*."

A question often crops up in my mind: what is Mā's position in the Indian society? When I watch people coming to her everywhere in large numbers, hundreds in a village and thousands in a metropolitan city, then I see that her devotees come from all strata of the society. I see petty bourgeoisie and industrialists, officials, traders, farmers and academics.

Of course, I seldom see peole from the lowest strata. Occasionally an old man and a very young woman with a child (who are unrelated) shared a room with me. I was told they were beggars. The man never left his bed even during daytime. Someone used to bring him food. He had only sought free lodging and board. I saw the beggar woman often sitting with the audience during the lectures.

I would like to know, whether a phenomenon like Mā is an isolated case, quasi as a remnant of the past, or whether this phenomenon can belong completely to the present-day situation.

An atheistic doctor in Ahmedabad has called Mā a living fossil from the religious middle ages. I have asked cautiously here and there, but those who were asked did not come up with a uniform answer. Of course, I only see a fairly small section of Indian life. Even less can I myself answer this question of Mā's position in society. I must leave it unanswered like so many other questions. There is also another question which often comes to mind, when I occasionally hear someone complaining about the complexity and elaborateness of the orthodox rites which have become "obsolete long ago". Namely: is this orthodoxy the fertile soil on which phenomena like Mā grow? It is true, this does not "explain" such a phenomenon. Nor does an average talent of a musical family explain the appearance of a musical genius among them. But it may be no accident that Mā was not born in a Western family of intellectuals or industrialists or a European family which is indifferent to religion.

I am sitting in the waiting hall in Patna. I left Rajgir at 5 o'clock by bus. Shortly after 1 o'clock I shall board an express train to Banaras. Mā and most of her followers are travelling by same train. A devotee drove Mā in her car to Bakhtiarpur, where she has boarded the train I am waiting for. The other āśramites have engaged taxis to get to the train.

When others leave at 10 a.m., I had to get up at 3 a.m.

to catch the early bus. Twelve-year-old Ram Prasad, another servant, Dasu, who brings me food, two old women who work in the *āśrama*-kitchen and two of Mā's girls travelled with me. Besides us, the huge mountain of the *āśrama*-luggage travelled on the rooftop of the bus. I only learnt by chance too late that I could have had the comfort of travelling by taxi.

The seat next to mine in the bus is unoccupied, when Ram Prasad, who I know is a strict orthodox, boards it. Dasu, who looks after him, says, "Take your seat next to Memsahib."

The face of the boy expresses a mixture of horror and anger. You can see what he thinks: "Of all the people you have left that seat for me!" After a while he sits down, annoyed and grumbles aloud to himself. Of course, he takes care to sit as away as possible from me and does not deign to look at me. Ram Prasad gets tired after the bus starts. I am sure, he has not slept at all during the night. I think, he was looking after the luggage at the bus station. Whenever he becomes conscious of my presence next to him, he moves to the extreme edge of the bench to avoid touching me.

But finally, fatigue overcomes him. He falls asleep and puts his head on my shoulder. I decide to let him sleep in peace as long as possible. "Misfortune" has happened, it cannot be undone, even if I wake him. After a while he starts up with a gentle cry. He looks at me angrily and scolds me, as if I had stolen his golden watch while he sleeps. Then he puts a bundle between me and him and sits at the extreme end of the bench.

But again sleep is stronger than the anger of a brāhmaṇa youth: he sits too much to the right and finds himself suddenly on the floor between the rows of the benches. With a sigh he takes his seat again on the bench. In the meantime I have an idea, but it was a mistake. I put his bundle on my shoulder and tell him, "You can lean here. I shall take care not to touch you." Even before I finish my sentence, he tears the bundle away from me. Probably, it contains his clothes. Who knows, how badly these must have been contaminated on my shoulder?

It appears to be indeed no small thing to be a brāhmaṇa. And in all my innocence, I force the poor boy into a further hard test of character. I take out a roll of cookies from my pocket. It is broken. As I hold it to him, he observes it with lively interest, but then turns his head away a little. Perhaps to see whether Desu is observing him. But as he moves, he feels ashamed and turns away with an angry sound. As long as I eat them, he sits with his back to me.

I reward him for his strength of character at the next main station. We go to a stall of sweets, and he chooses something good that is not touched by me.

There are moments when I feel that my life inside and outside the community of the āśramites has something eerie about it. For a while, I feel ambiguity, wherever I set my foot. If I were quite naive, I would feel that the life here – apart from a few practices, mostly connected with food–is not so different from that of a religious community from the West. But that is probably a mistake. Buaji's behaviour makes me think.

She teaches English in Allahabad University and spends her vacations with Mā. There is no doubt that she is not only well-bred, intelligent, well-informed about Mā's philosophical position, but also an enthusiastic pilgrim on her path to enlightenment, and humanly very nice. I thought I had a friendly relation with her. This and the fact that she is a more mature and an older person, from whom one can expect a useful advice, has occasionally persuaded me to express my difficulties to her in "the weak moments" of my bad feelings. So I complained to her about the arrangement made in R. concerning my supper.

Since the door of the *āśrama* was near the kitchen-region, I was not allowed to enter the house for reasons of ritualistic purity. It was said among other things during the first days that I should wait for my supper, which often lasted two to three hours, in the garden, where it was terribly cold (India was experiencing then a cold spell). Sometimes icy wind would blow away my leaf-plate together with the food. The food was then eaten up by dogs prowling hungrily around me and growling.

I did not hide my ill-feeling, when I came to know that Buaji and most of the others would go by taxis to catch the train, whereas I was asked to take the early 5 o'clock bus. I was not annoyed because of having an uncomfortable bus-journey, but they disregarded me as a guest which hurt me. And it pains me again only, because I would have liked a pleasant experience in Mā's environs.

Buaji reacted to my complaint by disappearing. During the last days, she was not available to me. She stayed either in the *āśrama* or behind the house in an area which I could not enter.

Basically I am grateful that I am not appeased with excuses. For example, I am amazed when Svāmījī forbids me to sit in a corner of a room to read, without any explanation, where everyone else moves freely. But if no explanation is given, then this laconic forbiddance is the best.

I remember how P. asked me in the *āśrama* in Banaras to eat out in town, because the cook was overburdened with providing food for 150 to 200 people. I immediately felt that this was an excuse. One who cooks for 150 to 200 people is not burdened by one more guest. I was upset because he did not give me the real reason. But I also felt that P. gave this flimsy reason out of kindness. The stringent rule concerning the meals in the *āśrama* was not the only reason why he wanted to exclude me.

Svāmījī accomplishes this curtness with his quiet self-confidence, and he can afford it too. And I do not feel personal unfriendliness in it.

The question is: why do I increasingly feel ambiguous

about my experience here. I am sure, if I could answer the question, I would immediately understand the behaviour of the āśramites. In a way, they look at reality differently from me. I live with them, as if my reality is also theirs, although I feel, it is not so. When I judge their behaviour from the point of view of my "reality", I try to measure the temperature of the atmosphere in centimetres. That does not lead anywhere.

Mā interrupts me laughing – and yet with a painful expression in her eyes. "Yes, yes, with all this outcast treatment, inconveniences and difficulties you have had to suffer. And you have travelled far for all this, haven't you? You had to withstand heat in Puri and cold here. And all for my sake."

Mā looked at me with a smile. It told me, she completely understood the situation. Suddenly she became serious. "When I saw you standing outside, I had tears in my eyes", she said, "It is indeed God, who comes in disguise of a stranger. She kept quiet again for a moment and added referring to what I had said: "Yes, one has to learn to accept sorrow and joy with the same indifference.

I had resisted the temptation of complaining to Mā about my superficial difficulties for a long time. Unfortunately, I deviated from my principle only a few days ago. The "punishment" could not wait: Mā was not diverted from the unpleasant theme for nearly one and half hours. I did not want it to last for more than five minutes. Her explanation answered my "level of ignorance", i.e. she told me, what anyone could have done. The instrument produced the music I played. If I had put the question differently, I would have got a different answer. But I was not in a position to do so. I groped in the dark so much in respect of that aspect of reality, I did not share with the āśramites, so I could not really formulate my question properly. If I had done so, it would have raised the problem to its true level.

Incidentally, I do not feel ambiguous with Mā.

Chapter 12

Tapasyā, Kuṇḍalinī and the Theory of Vibrations

Tapasyā is translated by the words "fire, heat and thermal energy" in my Sanskrit-dictionary. At the same time, it is invariably translated as "asceticism" in its active linguistic sense. The term often comes in the Vedic myths of gods. I have a selection of these in English rendition. For example: this or that ascetic "accumulated" so much *tapasyā* that the gods feared that he would burn them in his all-consuming fire of accumulated energy. One of them takes on the form of a seductress, deflects the absorption of the *tapasyā*-energy by stimulating his desire, and the power of this heat evaporates. The spiritual fire is transformed into a fire of sensuous passion that sinks to a sexual urge.

I am sure, there are concrete experiences behind these images. What is this *tapasyā*? one of the monks told me recently, "A number of people have quite perceptible electric radiation. It is called 'magnetic power' by the amateur." I have also heard, there are vibration-units which can be physically measured.

At times, I feel, I have these energies within myself–they radiate from the sacrum to the rest of the body. One has a sense of well-being of a strong life force during these times. My experience is that emotional shocks drive them out of the body, you are drained and the last spark extinguishes and you feel you will die.

According to a view of the *Śāktas*, the *kuṇḍalinī* also "sleeps" below the sacrum. One of the first aims of *Kuṇḍalinī-Yoga* is to revive it. Once it is aroused and flows through the *cakras* in the upward direction, a powerful heat is produced in each of the *cakras* that are penetrated by it. The struggle to revive *kuṇḍalinī* and to push it up, may well be identical with the process of accumulating *tapasyā*. One can further conclude that this method– to put it in Western terms – serves to intensify the magnetic power, the root of which is in the region of the sacrum (and so could be identical with the root *cakra*) and forces its radiation upwards in a straight thrust (i.e. not diffusely) through certain nerve-centres. I do not venture to conjecture what may happen physically in the so-called marriage of Śiva and Śakti (when the *kuṇḍalinī* has reached the highest head-*cakra*), but it is a process that is supposed to lead to an incredibly ecstatic expansion of consciousness.

The powerful movement of *kuṇḍalinī*, or the magnetic power takes place in psycho-physical frontiers. One does not feel it "physically" but "also physically". This has nothing to do with being ethical or religious. Even an evil man can accumulate *tapasyā* or radiate magnetic power. Abundance of *tapasyā* is not identical with saintliness or kindness.

And yet, there is a zone of contact between a *tapasyā* "having no ulterior motive" and striving for truth or for divine fulfilment. A man who is filled with a burning longing for God is favourably disposed to accumulate *tapasyā* or– if he is a *kuṇḍalinī-yogī* – for the realization of marriage of Śiva and Śakti. He abandons all worldly desires. He "starves and thirsts" (fasts) in a concrete way for God and "burns" in his longing.

One who is concerned with demonic power over human beings and things can do so equally well: a magician, even a black magician. Indian tradition teaches that *siddhis* – supernatural powers – accrue to one who has enough *tapasyā*. He can work miracles, say, cure an incurably ill man. For a Christian, such a cure would be supernatural, an act of sacrificial love. This has nothing to do with prehistory and the mechanics of the process of miracles (i.e. the development of *siddhis*). We call them supernatural because we know almost nothing about their nature, whereas I would call *siddhis* "Natural powers".

I would definitely call Mā's "miracles" an act of "holiness". I was suffering from insomnia for many years. She cured it literally overnight by working a miracle on me. I call her act "holy" because she is someone who knows that she is united to God. Religious teachers or saints like her know that this requires strict purification and self-discipline and that a *yogī* who abuses his *siddhis* is immediately deprived of an spiritual progress.

February 12, 1964

Some time ago, a Muslim woman familiar with Indian epistemology referred me to the theory of vibrations. Although I know I must learn to understand the secret of this phenomenon, I reacted with a feeling of ambiguity.

I understand that everything goes back to the phenomenon of vibration for the one who lives in the mystic tradition of the Indian world-experience. Whereas Western natural sciences speak about the vibratory character of light and have focussed their attention increasingly on the problem of vibrations, Indian thinkers defined all the phenomena of reality – whether visible or invisible – ages ago, as a vibration or an effect of vibration.

I sense that behind this key word 'vibration' an extremely ramified and complicated landscape is opened for the one who has the opportunity of studying it.

I did not have this opportunity for several reasons, and I can only explain a little without fully comprehending it.

Everything is vibration, but every vibration varies from the other because of its length, breadth, period, colour, rhythm, sound, etc. Besides, there are many stages of fine and crude vibrations, also a type of vibration that leads to these phenomena in the sphere of minerals, plants, animals and human beings.

Man himself is an extremely complex creation of vibrations and he lives in this medium like a fish in water. To make a distinction, an emotional vibration is received and transmitted through the soul and the contemplative one through the senses, although unrecognized as such, viz. one of matter or of forms of phenomena like that of light.

The finer the vibration, the longer its reach. The spoken word, e.g. has a fairly crude vibration, reaching only from mouth to ear, whereas a thought has a finer vibration which can be transmitted throughout the whole world.

One who is finely tuned picks up the vibrations of the man in whose room he has been staying, of the bed, on which he has been lying, of his clothes, and tree whose shade protects him from the sun. Everyone registers these vibrations unconsciously with varying intensity. The emanation from holy places is based on the echo of vibrations which the holy man has left behind and on those of all devout souls which come after. In India, the presence of a saint is as important for the destiny of the country, city, etc. as a good Government. The saint transmits his peace through such vibrations throughout the land. One who strives for enlightenment, serves his own interest best by seeking the presence of enlightened people or saints, to be "tuned" in their vibrations. And that is why, Mā repeatedly recommends *satsaṅga.*

Perhaps it is not naive optimism, when Mā says: "Keep to what is good in man and protect yourself and your fellow men, as best as you can, from every evil thought." Acute sensitivity can discover from countless concrete experiences that vibrations of good thoughts and feelings produce goodness, and that the contrary is true for evil influences.

One who knows and recognizes the law of vibrations, knows that everything that appears to be separate on the surface of things, is one on the inner level, because it is vibration. To that extent, there is endless communication between everything. That is why, an evil thought or feeling disturbs everything else. Each one of us is responsible for our thoughts and actions and equally for everything that happens in the world.

Since everything is vibration, the usual distinction between body and mind is insufficient. Ages ago, India knew a great deal about the interaction between the two which the modern Western psychosomatics have only now discovered.

When I asked an old man in Vindhyachal, why he cooked his own food, he replied:

"You people from the West have no idea at all about the spiritual effect of the food you eat. you observe its effect on your body, but you do not want to know its effect on your soul. I take in the feelings, moods and a part of the thoughts of the cook with the food I eat. All that is transmitted from him to the food as a vibration, and from the food to me." That is why, only people with a certain spiritual maturity are allowed to cook in the *āśrama,* and very special conditions have to be fulfilled by those who cook for Mā.

People for whom the key word "hygiene" is handy and think it is merely a matter of observing certain spiritual taboos, are naive and totally ignorant. I have always suspected it and now I know it is true.

One who lives in a desert or a Himalayan cave gets rid of the disturbing vibrations of his fellow beings, anyway of the crude disturbances of proximity. According to a Hindu view, there is a spiritual risk caused by these vibrations. Vibrations of a man can also be in his look or his clothes. A *sādhu,* therefore, never wears clothes which are worn by others, except when they are presented to him by an enlightened person. That is why, no āśramite ever takes my jacket to keep (recently, I kept it on the roof of the *āśrama* as nobody could be "affected" by it there). And it is felt that by merely looking at the food of someone else in some cases, it might be contaminated.

The most intense influence of vibrations is through physical contact. Probably, this is the reason why the āśramites hesitate to go in the same taxi with me. Indian taxis are almost always crowded. So it would be virtually impossible to sit there without touching me.

Obviously contact with certain parts of the body causes particular impure (*juta*) vibrations. The mouth is one of them. Thus when I drink from a vessel, it becomes impure, and has to be ritually washed, in case I do not throw it away before someone else uses it. Or I pour the liquid into my mouth without touching the vessel with my lips, as many people do. Whenever *prasāda* is distributed, you can see it thrown directly into the mouth by people for the same reason.

Probably, the theory of vibrations and orthodox practices have a close connection with the caste-system. An orthodox brāhmaṇa would never eat food that is not cooked by a brāhmaṇa, and there are further distinctions within the brāhmaṇa caste. In big festivals, brāhmaṇas of different sub-castes cook separately for persons coming from their sub-castes.

Casteless people – every non-Hindu – often give out particularly disturbing vibrations. I am, therefore, not allowed to enter small *āśramas* which are already crowded with too many āśramites. Verandahs are exceptions because they are at least open on one side. If we take the theory of vibrations as the basis, then their influence quickly becomes diffuse under the open sky. But it is not the case with all vibrations. For example, walls are not a hindrance for very fine vibrations of thought.

My observations are amateurish and, therefore, perhaps too bold. All the same, I now understand why those who have grown up in the reality of these concepts and their practical application have a far greater awareness than I have.

Hindus are convinced that Mā has a direct knowledge of the complex relations in this field, that she feels these vibrations and can "work" with them, say, in cures or in spiritual influence. Obviously she herself is not endangered by my vibrations, like the āśramites, because she allowed me to put my chain I wore for years around her neck, and she often touches me. This may be the reason why I do not have this feeling of "ambiguity" in relation to her. She also respects the rules concerning the food, not because she is afraid of becoming impure, but out of consideration for her orthodox followers. For the same reason, Mā takes upon herself the painful situation of allowing "the God in disguise of a stranger" to stand in the tropical sun and in icy wind in front of her house.

I don't feel competent to criticize this situation. I have superficial understanding in this field and have no criteria for being objective enough.

I can understand that the āśramites do not talk about the theory of vibrations. They may have unpleasant experiences from West and their "liberal" country men. One needs little imagination to realize that most "modern" people would refuse to take such thing seriously

I am reminded of a young Swiss who said with respect to the rules concerning the food: "What queer, nonsensical rules! I replied to him, "How narrow-minded you are!" This was evidence of the limited horizon of the Western mind. My first reaction was very similar. We are always in danger of condemning alien phenomena whose background or context we fail to comprehend. Above all, in the realm of non-Christian religions.

They are "heathen" religions for the average Western man, and for him, paganism means primitive, backward, archaic . . ., whereas the Christian religion, the religion of the highly civilized Western world, is considered to be "progressive" even by those people, who have nothing to do with it. Decide to start from the fact that the Eastern interpretation of the world with tis concepts of vibration relates to an experience of the world that is inaccessible to me and look at those manifestations without any prejudice.

One thing is gradually becoming clearer to me: how naive we are, when we presume that the reality we encounter is identical with the reality of another culture. The theory of vibrations is a striking example of this. Basically it gives added dimension to every dimension, and we have no faculty to perceive it. Even the emptiness of a room– if the theory is correct – can be filled with the "lingering potency" of a man who was there. If I was receptive enough, I could receive in New Delhi the vibrations of an idea coming from Berlin.

Or take basic difference in experiencing reality. There has to be a difference because the traditional concept of *māyā* is still valid, or – in modern thinking – has its aftereffects: the whole plurality of all phenomena of the "changing world" is nothing but illusion!

Or take the concept of *līlā*: the concept of world affairs as an endless spontaneous play of the highest Self with It-Self. Or take infinity of time: time is limited for a Christian, looking back to the past through the concept of Creation and looking ahead to the future through the concept of God's Kingdom. When I immerse myself in the Hindu-concept of the eternal recurrence of worlds without any beginning or without any end, I feel how protected we are by our views and concepts. We ram them like bullwarks into the raging river of a faceless infinity.

How different must be the psychic structures of people whose concept of reality is so different from ours.

I was on a train to Vrindavan. It halted in Patna for eight minutes. I succeeded again with the help of a few coolies– a small miracle – : in hurriedly throwing colossal pieces of luggage into an already crowded third-class compartment and finally boarding the train myself over the mountains of bedrolls, bundles, buckets and boxes which almost blocked the door. It took a long time for everything to be packed, and then everyone found a place on the pieces of luggage.

I was lucky at the next larger station; I saw an old Muslim who was lying on the luggage-rack tying up his bundle and getting down. I succeeded in reserving the place and could keep all my luggage on the broad plank and also stretch out myself.

The weather has changed. Suddenly it is a tropical heat. All windows are open. Grimy dust lies on the face and hands, on clothes and luggage. It reminds me how unpleasant I found it during my first travels through India and how I let everything wash over me. What senseless loss of energy, when earlier I used to take a wash every hour. One learns to resist overwhelming conditions only when it is sensible.

The jabbering of half a dozen dialects sounds like one language to my ears, and although I scarcely understand a thing, it gives me a feeling of intimacy. Odour engulfing me has the same effect. Months ago it used to cause nausea. It smells of dust and perspiration, of cheap hair-oils, of fruits which I have never eaten and whose names I do not know, of exotic sweets, of rancid ghee and sandalwood fragrance, of joss sticks sticking to the cowl of a monk.

I must have slept for a long time. When I wake up, the train is halting at a station. Shrill calls of traders pierce through the window: *chai, chai* (tea); *cigret, cigret; doodh, doodh* (milk) . . ., crying of children and the noise of a group of soldiers who are changing trains. Sleepily, I let myself slide down from the luggage rack. The moment I come to the door of the compartment, I see Mā on the platform walking past me, a yellow turkish towel loosely thrown over her head. She looks at me wide-eyed. Someone walking behind her pours nut kernels into my hand.

I turn back then and there and climb onto my plank. The moment our eyes (Mā's and mine) met, I recognized something which took my breath away. I am at a loss for words. While stretching out again on the plank, I decide to leave Mā this very week.

I shall tell her: "The moment has come. I shall cease to

look for you in *āśramas* or in trains or during *Gītā*-weeks in the houses of your followers, patiently or impatiently. I was happy when I could see you and disappointed when I was blind and restless for something I looked for; I was grateful to you when you helped me in overcoming my bad moods. It was good to go with you, as I have gone so far. But from this day onward, I know that I should look to myself for what I sought in you."

February 15, 1964

I am now in Vrindavan. Mā has another large *āśrama* here which is situated in the midst of a garden. I am accommodated in a pilgrims' home.

Vrindavan is a holy place of Śrī Kṛṣṇa and I have bought a small idol of Gopāl which is cast in metal. He stands naked on my suitcase. When I returned from the *āśrama* yesterday, the woman who looks after the home made it clear to me that I cannot possibly let Gopāljī stand there naked, and if I intend to take him to Germany, where it would be too cold for him. Anxiously I have to admit that I really want to do so. The woman shakes her head worriedly. She accompanies me to my room: Gopāl is wrapped in a piece of cloth from a monk's garment. She takes him with a sigh and disappears. This evening, Gopāl stands in front of my bed beautifully dressed. He wears a shirt of wine-red silk, a yellow gown and a crown of pearls.

When I thank the woman, she interrupts me reproachfully: "I hope, you don't think that I have dressed Gopāljī so beautifully for your sake? Not at all! He is more than all the kings of the world, and you wanted him to travel naked to Europe with you!"

Gopāl shows his grace to his faithful devotee on one of the next nights. As I stand in front of my door after coming back, I notice that I have snapped the padlock shut, leaving the key inside. I have to wake up the woman and ask her to help me. She gives me a few keys, but no key is suitable.

Later she tries it herself, and while putting the first key into the lock she says the name of the child-God: "Gopāla, Gopāla, Gopāla . . .". And look, the lock opens easily.

A legend narrates that Śrī Kṛṣṇa spent his childhood and youth here, on the banks of the Jamunā among the herdsmen of Vrindavan. His name is synonymous for his worshippers with the idea of "heaven" or "place of bliss". It is said that there are more than 5000 temples here dedicated to him, although Vrindavan appears to be only a small town. It is possible, many insignificant shrines are included in them.

I see, there are really many temples. Many of them are behind a high wall. I was denied access to them by fairly furious watchmen. The beggars were more obliging! Sometimes, twenty, thirty and more swarmed around the gates of the temples, and the moment I returned, they dogged my heels, crying loudly. I noticed that only women were begging in front of some temples. They were particularly aggressive.

As I was drinking tea yesterday at a stall in the bazaar, a soft, coloured trunk of an elephant suddenly pushed from behind over my shoulder and groped for my hand with which I was holding the tumbler. People burst out laughing when I jumped up in fright. The elephant's forehead and ears were artistically decorated with ornaments and they were resplendent in all colours. It is nice that this town has so many animals. One meets camels passing with their noses in the air. A petite brown peahen wanders in my *dharmaśālā* (pilgrims' home) and pecks curiously at the bedding and suitcases. I call her Krishni. The peacock is the bird of Śrī Kṛṣṇa. It lives protected in the woods around Vrindavan. When it is evening, one hears its piercing plaintive cry from the garden behind the *āśrama.* There are very large pilgrims' homes in which many thousands find shelter during certain seasons. Now everything there is deserted under a yellowish layer of dust. The birds make noise only in the treetops, and sometimes herds of monkeys attack the deserted garden looking for the last fruits which have dried on the branches.

Ami, who has been brought up in a Christian country (U.S.A.) and has a small New Testament in her luggage, appears to be fascinated by the figurine of Śrī Kṛṣṇa. At present, she is collecting legends from his life, which are reminiscent of Christian motifs. Today she read a chapter from the *Purāṇas* to me, where is a mention of the human-mother of the God.

"Nobody could look at Devakī without being blinded by her dazzling light. Men and women lost consciousness overcome by the light, but the gods praised her day and night. She bore the Highest Lord in her womb. They said to her: 'You are a holy sacrifice, filled with wisdom and nectar of immortality. You are the light of heaven. He who will protect the whole world has entered your body. O divine One, you bring us salvation. For the sake of love, bear the divine Lord who will carry the whole world."

"Isn't it like the song of the angels praising Virgin Mary?" Ami asked. I remembered in the same context a familiar description of the first days on earth of the boy Kṛṣṇa. It is said, when his foster mother Yaśodā, the wife of herdsman Nanda, offered her breast to child kṛṣṇa to drink milk, she had sudden revelation: she saw the whole world, the infinite universe within the child in her lap. When the sight began to overwhelm her, the child covered her eyes again with the veil of *māyā.*

This flowery language! Ami read to me from a *bhakta* to whom the God had appeared: "Breathless and wide-eyed, he observed the face of the God . And the Lord of the world, the Ocean of mercy, filled his heart tenderly, yet more tenderly with the nectar of his smile. He, the matchless friend of his people, took him to his lap, fanned him and touched him again and again. He embraced him like his mother." – This is pure *bhakti*! I have always laughed to myself at the presumption of may of Mā's friends in regarding her as "omniscient". This was in the early days of my stay when such suggestions were made in Mā' ambience. Only now in the last weeks, I have started asking without prejudice about this claim and how people could have arrived at such an assumption. A world-renowned scientist told me in Calcutta that Mā had predicted the events in his family four years in advance. I have heard of many such instances.

I have a conversation with Ami in the last week in which this complex question was alluded to. Then I made it clear to her that I have myself frequently experienced moments which are "beyond time" since my later childhood, and presumably that could be the case with anyone. They possess a quality which cannot be compared to usual experience. Obviously they take place in particularly important times of our life and in situations which are extremely trivial, even banal. What remains as the after-effect is emphasized more clearly in important moments, say while taking leave of someone close to you. One feels suddenly: this is timeless moment. It can never be lost because it is outside time.

But I remember having experienced the same clarity on seeing a piece of yellow paper on the street wet with rain. And who has not experienced suddenly knowing in advance without rhyme or reason in this way how a particular thing would end?

Ami said something abruptly that was very peculiar. Our conversation started it. We were standing in front of a tea-stall, and at first, she spoke so softly that I could hardly hear her.

"Do you remember the time when you were a stone? Or later a conch? Or the age of grass? Or the taste of the bark in the years you lived as an animal in a forest?"

I was not sure whether she was joking and I pointed to the elephant which was coming along the street. "How would you like to feel the world with a trunk?"

"I was never an elephant", Ami said seriously, "but you have not yet answered my question."

"I don't remember my earlier lives", I replied. "Do you remember them?" How strange that your memory is consistent with the Western theory of evolution. You must know that the Indian sages, *munis*, speak about a falling development."

Ami nodded. I did not see her face. As always, she hid it behind her *sārī* when we had an important discussion. She said after a while:

"Something within me reminds me at times of these earlier lives; it is a physical perception and not a spiritual one. The memories are sharply demarcated from one another. They are not chronologically arranged. Sometimes, I seem to be all of them at once: stone and grass, animal and human being. Do you understand? Not a mixture of all of them, rather all in isolated form, but simultaneously. And yet not in sequence, but . . ."

We stood up. Ami pulled me to a quiet side street. Only after some minutes, she continued the conversation.

"I cannot describe how I feel this simultaneously within me, or know it is so. In fact, I wanted to tell you something entirely different. Sometimes, in a flash my whole life unfolds before my eyes, everything that will happen in the normal course of our existence. I have a prior insight that already I am what I shall be. I am already there, where Mā is now and beyond. I feel it as an embrace in a dream what one knows is true, and yet not true. When I wake up, I am only Ami who finds it difficult to concentrate in meditation even for five minutes. But at that moment, the embrace and a reality."

I ask myself what is going on in Ami when she suddenly experiences previous existence and future perception of her life. The collective unconscious comes to mind, but perhaps it can more aptly be described as a secret "knowledge" suddenly reaching the surface of your consciousness from a deep level, so we have perceptions which transcend time and space.

I am telling this as it gives me a clue to what is perhaps the precondition for Mā's clear-sightedness in both the dimensions of time. A Director of a College called it: "Mā's existential knowledge". Perhaps even ordinary people like Ami or extremely ordinary people like me share this in momentary flashes.

But what is existence? Who can tell me in a way that would satisfy our Western scientific thinking? Perhaps nobody. One can only say metaphorically that it must be a "sphere" in which time has not yet unfolded between past, present and future in which spatial demarcations are invalid. Yesterday and tomorrow are today. And there is here. Perhaps, each one of us shares this "sphere of existence" from which knowledge reaches out to consciousness under certain preconditions, but of what kind? It is not received like ordinary knowledge into "forms of intuition of space and time" (Kant). It has not gone through the graded filter of our view, but it is a direct communication from "subconscious" existence.

With these I grope my way forward cautiously, always threatened by the possibility of mistake. I think, it is not impossible that a conscience in which the borders of egoism have fallen knows its identification with the universal consciousness of the Highest Reality (of *Brahman*), has a continuous and direct access to that "sphere of existence" from which consciousness transcending time and space emerges. It is surely equally obvious that each *cogito* (I think) presupposes a state of consciousness which receives matter that is offered only in the form of an idea (of time and space). The thinking ego is localized in respect of the "sphere of existence". The rare moments in which an ordinary man who thinks as "I" can receive knowledge from there, only occur when the *cogito* is silent.

Yesterday I brought Ami to the bus. Her husband has returned from America. Her normal routine in Bombay begins for her again.

We were an hour too early at the bus-stop. A small pond which the Indians call *kuṇḍa* is about a couple of hundred metres away. We looked for a place to sit here. Ami was quiet as at most of times. As long as we were together, she rarely asked me a question, a situation which forced me to control my urge to ask her questions. Then minutes before the departure, she began to speak. She said abruptly:

"I feel, I have to leave Mā, but I know that she will not leave me. We have a proverb in India which says, 'It is as difficult to escape the grace of a *Guru*, as the revenge of a tiger."

I was happy that Ami began to speak. It gave me courage to ask her: ,"Are you able to explain what particular knowledge of experience you owe to the period you spent with Mā?"

She pulled the *pallū* of her *sārī* over her head with an almost angry gesture, as she always did, whenever she was afraid that she had to disclose something that she would prefer to keep to herself. But I knew that she would talk in spite of inner resistance.

After a while she said, "There are many things. I still do not know what was the most important; perhaps I shall understand in a couple of years that I have learnt something of more intrinsic value than I tell you today. Three things appear to me to be the most important: it seems to me that I am a crow living in a flock of crows from the day it came out of the egg and which has never met any other birds. One day, a white eagle flies down to the tree and settles itself on it. The crow is so much frightened that it fears that it will die of fright. Hidden within the eagle is indescribable joy, and suddenly the crow feels, it could also be an eagle. 'Don't be afraid' it heard the mighty bird say, 'soon you will know that you were only in the disguise of a crow, in reality, you are a white eagle. One could also says, *māyā* made you believe that you were a crow.'

'One day', but that does not mean within this life span. And that is the second thing I begin to understand, not with my intellect, but existentially, as you sometimes call it: that we have time, whereas in reality there is no time. Time it man's invention; he has also invented miles, pounds and temperatures. What does it mean for the sun when we calculate how far we may be from it? Nothing! What does it mean for my self, if I find out that I will perhaps live in this body for seventy years? Nothing? If time were not a fiction, I would say, 'The self has endless time.' But I say more correctly, 'It has eternity. In it, seventy years are less than a drop of water in the ocean.'

You know that I have been brought up in America and studied there. I believe till now in time. Life for me is what it is for you: this is a life span of perhaps seventy years. But from the time I have met Mā, I know that looking at this life is looking at a drop of water through a microscope. I don't want to admit that this drop is only a tiny part of the infinite ocean. Perhaps, because we cannot put this ocean under our microscope.

From the time I have been with Mā, I have a growing sense of eternity. Do you understand? I begin to feel the eternal present. I cannot describe it more accurately. I could say in your usual mode of expression that I suddenly feel something of the infinite past which is behind me, and something of the infinite future which is ahead of me. That would be accurate, because I begin to feel through the faculty of my perception that my existence is extending itself in both directions. But on a higher level – not of thinking, but of perceiving (i.e. through seeing and hearing rather than through a logical conclusion) – both the dimensions of my existence, past and future, are united at this point, however improbable it may sound to you."

Ami let the *pallū* of her *sārī* slip from her head again and looked at me mockingly. "And now you want to determine this point geometrically?" she asked laughing. "Don't waste your energy! It can be determined as little as the point at which a drop of rain falls into the sea." "We must go", I said, "the bus leaves in ten minutes. Couldn't you have begun speaking earlier? Your wanted to tell me three things."

Ami adjusted her *sārī* calmly. "The third can be explained in a second", she said, "I see now that my inner *Guru* has been working in me as far as I can remember. And I think, he is identical with Mā. There is only one. And it is a great Grace when he will be revealed one day, as he has revealed himself to me in Mā, so I can see him and love him."

Ami took leave of the *āśrama* only a few hours before I did. Mā is constantly with us on the last day of my stay, whereas she was not around for days before that. We were able to see her when one of the *puṇḍits* or *svāmīs* from the surrounding *āśramas* visited her. I have a long final conversation with her; but our real exchange is a silent one. Then she lets me go with so many presents that I cannot carry them alone.

I know at once – while I am afraid that the very next day, I shall not be able to see Mā – that the separation is merely an illusion. An old Muslim told me in Calcutta, "My son has been in America for thirty years. And yet he is always with me. His physical absence is like the absence of the moon when there is eclipse."

For a moment, Mā's light hand rests on my head, then it moves over my forehead, my cheeks, touches my shoulders, breast and the back. I stand up quickly and go to the door. While I am holding the knob, Mā says thrice: "Take care of yourself and come back safely; take care of yourself and come back safely; take care of yourself and come back safely."

Chapter 13

West/East Realities

February 25, 1964

I had heard the name Raihana Tyabji many years ago in Germany. Someone told me that she was an associate of Gandhi and she was also in prison with him. She came from a Muslim aristocratic family which has given many leading personalities to the country, and she was regarded not only as an exceptionally intelligent woman, but also as one of the wise people of the country. Many Europeans obtained a deep understanding of the Indian disposition through her, because she was able to bring Western people spiritually close to Eastern ones, and Eastern to the Western. Added to which, she was Well-versed in para-psychology.

The house in New Delhi where she lives--I think, she is occupying only one room – belongs to an aged colleague of Gandhi. It is small and in Western terms extremely modest. I went round the house several times. I did not actually ring the bell because I was not sure whether I would disturb the occupant in her siesta. When I again came near the door of the house, someone shot out, seized my hand and pulled me in behind her. Only when I had entered, did I realize that Raihana T. herself did this. I recognized her from the patchy pigmentation of her face which someone had mentioned to me.

Raihana T. asked me to sit on a wooden stool; she sat on her bed. She was about to drink her tea.

The room was sparsely furnished. When I looked around, I remembered having heard of a close relative of Raihana who had bequeathed part of her priceless antique furniture to a museum. Her grandmother had nineteen children and lived in a palatial building. (A college is now housed in its side wing) She used to dress like a mediaeval princess and whenever she travelled to her country-seat in a palanquin, a caravans of more than hundred servants used to carry her luggage. The country house had a perron of twenty steps, and there was a Chinese vase on each on of them. Today, one would pay about twenty-five thousand *Deutsche Mark* for each one of them.

These stories came to my mind as I looked around in the room and observed Raihana who was quietly drinking her tea. The deliberate poverty of this dwelling was also reflected in her dress. She wore something which looked like a brown cardigan with long sleeves. Over it was a bright-blue woollen cloth which was knotted over one shoulder, while her other shoulder was free. She wore on her head a thick pointed woollen cap. It looked like two caps over each other which were tied under her chin. Probably, this lady dispensed with every adornment, not only out of her conviction, but because she was entirely indifferent as to her appearance.

If one considers what we normally understand by the word beauty, then Raihana is astonishingly ugly; but she has at the same time such an overwhelming charm, such a warmth, scintillating spirituality and lovable frankness that one suddenly finds, this face is beautiful after observing it for a while. Its skin is white. There is a bright-brown pigmentation only near her eyes and on her chin. It is broad and short because her mouth is so thin. One can see her eyes almost disappear in the wrinkles of her skin, especially when she laughs– which she does quite often – but when her face becomes stern and serious, they have a piercing penetration.

Raihana offered me tea, but I declined. After she slowly finished hers, I took cup and saucer from her hand and told her that I had brought her *praṇāmas* from Mā.

Mā's name works like a magic word. The room is suddenly "electrified". A dozen questions are shot at me, and I try to answer them as best as I can. While answering her questions, I take out a sandalwood-garland which Mā has presented to me. I cannot accommodate it in my luggage, and it is my pleasure to pass it onto Raihanaji. Raihana thanks me by raising her folded hands to her forehead. "If the garland has come from Śrī Mā, I will hang it in my *pūjā*-place."

Now I notice an Indian house-altar in the corner of her room. I want to save her the trouble of hanging it, but an energetic "Stop, stop!" holds me back. "You have your shoes on", says Raihanaji patiently, "besides, I would prefer to do it myself". She climbs down from her bed and takes the garland from me. Holding it in her raised hands, she stands very straight in front of her *pūjā*-place, and I hear a gentle chanting which reminds me of the song of *Mullahs.* The voice of this lady, about whom I still know so little, may be she is old and in need of rest, becomes increasingly a powerful, metallic sound of sombre beauty, which makes me sit up and take notice. Several times, I hear her invoking the name of Allah and Śrī Kṛṣṇa, and suddenly I remember that although Raihanaji is a Muslim, she is regarded as a fervent devotee of the Hindu god Śrī Kṛṣṇa.

I wait standing, till she hangs the garland up and returns to her bed. The pathos in her voice and the attitude while she was singing has disappeared, and she laughs a little mockingly at my surprise. "So you come from Śrī Mā, she says, 'Śrī Mā has been making use of me as her mouthpiece for many years. She has been often sending me one or two. If you have questions, please ask."

"I would like to know what she means to you."

"I have seen a number of saints in the course of my life. Śrī Mā is different from all of them because she always shines. The others shine only sporadically. Besides, I think, she belongs to those *avatāras,* through whose charisma, every believer recognizes his *iṣṭa.* A worshipper of Śiva sees Śiva in her and a worshipper of Buddha, Buddha. If you are worshipper of Christ, you must have actually seen Christ in her.

Avatāras of such great spirituality are sent to the humanity only in critical times, and we can never thank God enough that Śrī Mā has come to us. This also has a complete concrete side. Śrī Mā is sent wherever there is great danger. I have been observing this for years. How often I have breathed a sigh of relief, whenever she came to Delhi in critical times."

"What kind of danger do you mean?"

"Of different kinds. We had a series of explosions in one year, and they stopped at once when Mā came. Or calamities such as floods or political unrest."

I suddenly remember that Mā had gone with us to Calcutta exactly at a time when there were bloody Hindu-Muslim riots. When I mention this, Raihanaji said, "How will I know this! I had no idea that she was in Calcutta this winter. You can be certain, if she had not gone there, there would have been more bloodshed."

"How can I explain it, Raihanaji? Indeed, it occurred to me that Mā's spiritual emanation at that time in Calcutta was very powerful, and I recollect that I had connected this fact with the riots in my consciousness."

"I cannot give you an explanation that would satisfy your Western rationalism. Your science has not progressed in its epistemology so far that it can throw light into these mysterious connections. But the East knows that the saints are in complete harmony with the whole universe: with the stars and animals, plants and the ocean, wind and human beings, with all; with those who are intelligent or foolish, good or evil, living or dead. And therefore, emanation of their peace is more powerful than desires and thoughts of ordinary people.

"I have often heard that since childhood Mā has lived in the same state of consciousness as she does today. According to a philosophical theory of Hindus, the enlightened spirit is immutable, reposing in itself. People perhaps think about Mā's utterances in her childhood because one would like to connect all her utterances with certain theories. I think, Indian thought is occasionally reverse to that of the West. Many people say for example: 'Mā cannot have a body like ordinary people. Therefore, she must be a *jīvanmukta*."

"She probably does not have an ordinary body", Raihana says laughing. I embrace her, whenever I meet her. But what I hold in my arms, is actually no body. And what is said about Mā's childhood, may be connected with certain theories. As for me, I am sure that it also corresponds to the concrete reality.

I have known several children in my life, who were probably like Mā when she was a child. I lived for some period in a street, where a child like her used to stay with its parents. It was a boy. When he was three, four-year-old, children from the neighbourhood used to come to him to seek his blessing before going to school, even those who were fourteen-year-old. He was a saint for these children. I know a small girl who was already the *Guru* of her parents before she could even read. The parents had completely distanced themselves from religion. But this child recited Sanskrit-*mantras,* although she had never heard the language; this reveals religious wisdom of an enlightened one. Many of these children die early.

It is true that the Hindus teach that an *avatāra* like Śrī Mā has an immutable intellect. They are not unenlightened when they are born. They make use of child's body to be revealed to people in a form which is acceptable. Believe me, such an enlightened soul would not like to be incarnated in the West. Western parents who had such a child would be afraid. If they understood their child, they would be rightly afraid of what could happen to it in your world. If they couldn't understand their child, they would feel uneasy and take it to a psychiatrist and the damage would be done.

We know that there are such children. It is natural for us, and we will also understand how to deal with such children as long as we remain uninfluenced by Western ideas."

Raihanaji speaks so fast and with such an intense and rapidly changing expression and gesticulations that I find it difficult to grasp both fully at the same time. Suddenly she interrupts herself and says: "Sit here" and showd me a place at the foot of her bed. When I am seated cross-legged so that we are very close to each other, she takes a tin-box from the window-sill and snuffs leisurely.

I would like to ask her a dozen more questions, but she continues to speak so vehemently that I cannot do it, as everything she says captures my attention afresh.

"You told me earlier that Śrī Mā presented you with the idol of Śiva as a parting gift. I know, he is weird to many Western people. For Hindus: he is a creator, a beneficent Lord, a divine physician, God of Death and at the same time, conqueror of Death and much more. I tell you: Śiva stands for the Holy Spirit in the *Trimūrti*; one can compare this with the Trinity of the Christian faith. Perhaps, it is in this way you should know how the God of creation Brahmā corresponds to God the Father, Viṣṇu who repeatedly embodies the saviour God for us in his *avatāras* corresponds to the Son and Śiva the Holy Spirit. He incarnates the Highest Knowledge, the divine wisdom which vanquishes all the darkness in the world. Gaṅgā, the holy river, has its origin in the head of the God in the corresponding picture. You should read the myths connected with it. What the myth expresses in a hidden way is this: the Holy Spirit flows ceaselessly from its divine origin into the human world, as the Gaṅgā flows ceaselessly through our land."

"Isn't Śrī Kṛṣṇa, Raihanaji, *iṣṭa*? I heard you earlier invoking his name. I have no *iṣṭa*, and I don't want one. Gods don't interest me. What I seek is the last and highest reality. As far as I am concerned, you may call it God ."

Raihanaji grins from ear to ear. Her eyes disappear completely between the wrinkles. For a while, she does not utter a word, but her body is swaying fiercely from right to left. Finally she asks me, "Have you noticed what happens, if one holds a bowl under the Niagara Falls? There won't be a drop of water in the container for you to drink. You are one of those who would like to swallow the ocean in one gulp. My advice is: 'Fill up your vessel. The water is the same.' And after a pause she asks, "Do you claim to love God?"

I nod.

"It would mean in Hindu-terminology that you don't love one of the deities, but you love *Brahman, tat,* the Highest Reality, don't you?"

I nod once more.

"So you love complete silence and çoolness. Some people say, 'Nothingness that is, at the same time, everything.' Examine yourself. Can you love the *tat*?"

We remain silent for a while. Raihanaji reaches again for her snuff. Finally she says, "I can't think of an answer I can give you. Thus you have not yet walked the real path of God's love (*bhakti*). It would help you very much if you did."

"I cannot call Śiva my *iṣṭa* nor Śrī Kṛṣṇa."

"Did not Mā repeatedly tell you that names and forms of all *iṣṭas* are only like a disguise of the One, who is all in all, form, formlessness and everything beyond it, about which one can think or cannot think? But the human soul is so constituted that it can approach the One most successfully in its spiritual childhood by turning lovingly to one of the divine forms which incarnate Him."

"What do you think then, I should do?"

"Adhere to your *Guru,* to Mā. One day, the iṣṭa will come on its own. I also advise you to read the *Bible.* But read it in such a way, as if it were totally new. Try to wipe out all you remember of it. Before you begin to read, pray to Christ: "Reveal yourself, and let me understand you as you want me to see you and understand you, not as I want to see and understand you, or as I have learnt through schooling and the church."

As we go on talking, Raihanaji tells me about experiences from her own life. I do not make notes of them because they are so personal. She mentions her *Guru* several times in it. When I ask her about her *Guru,* she answer, "He was not my *Guru,* he is my *Guru*", and after a little hesitation, she says, "He lived on this earth 600 years ago."

"But didn't you say, you have talked to him."

"Of course, I often talk to him."

"But what do you mean?"

"I hear his voice, as I hear your voice. I can ask him questions, and I get answers from him. Whenever he wants to say something to me, he speaks to me. In fact, I meditated upon his spiritual path for years, before he talked to me."

There is a picture in the *pūjā*-place. I had glanced at it and immediately had the impression that I knew it. I mean it is the picture of an Arabian Sufi. When I ask Raihanaji about it, she smiles without saying anything.

"Are there records of what your *Guru* has taught you?"

"Oh yes!"

"Then can I ask you who he is and what I can find in his work?"

The smile on the broad, intelligent face becomes more and more mysterious. Raihanaji's body begins to shake again vehemently. After while she says, "I won't tell you his name now. You would not yet understand any of this. It would not help you; it would only confuse you at present."

Already three hours have passed. "We are lucky", says Raihanaji, "for months, I have not had such an undisturbed afternoon as this." She embraces me at the door of her house. While going away, I say half jocularly, "I feel I have met you many times before. I hate the idea of our being separated by the ocean in a couple of days."

Raihanaji gives an understanding nod. She then says, "I don't doubt that you lived earlier in India or that you will return."

On the next day, my last in Delhi, I cannot resist the

temptation of visiting Raihanaji again, although we had taken leave of each other "for good".

This time, we are disturbed; a middle-aged Muslim wants to bid her goodbye. He is to fly to America in a few days, but he assures me that he simply wants to sit with Raihana for a while, and I can ask her questions and ignore his presence.

We had just talked about *karma.* Raihana called it "the law of unlimited chance." It was, she said, the real reason, why there is no existential despair for an Indian – Sanskrit has no term that corresponds to the Western word "despair".

"The threat of eternal damnation plays an important part in Christian thinking. Even a man from the West who no longer believes in God has an inkling of this concept, and he is convinced he has only one life. When he realizes at the end that he has wasted or misused it, then it surely resembles the plight of eternal damnation. We do not have such absolute hopelessness in our experience of the world. We know, we always have the chance of fulfilling our divine destiny, thanks to our law of *karma.*

My next question concerns the law of *māyā.* "It is difficult to understand", Raihana says, "I always advise my friends from the West to study thoroughly the idea of three-dimensionality of time. This is one way which leads to understanding. The mystery of *māyā* is: what is now is real. Another "now" is real the next moment, and what was just real, has become unreal. Think about this."

One day Mā said to me, "Once you have realized God, good and evil are two hairstyles. It is up to you to choose which style you want.' Could you explain this?"

Raihana runs her hand through her close-cropped, unkempt hair– she is not wearing her cap today. "One can begin to understand it only when one has experienced at least for a moment one's own self and the divine as one and the same. It may help you perhaps, if you imagine yourself peering at the world with a microscope, while Mā in unity with the Highest Self looks through a telescope. You see nothing but tiny details in their alterable, momentary reality; for example: the evil and good in a man. Mā sees the whole truth from a further perspective of his life, not the good or evil he has done yesterday, does today and will do tomorrow. She sees his divine self which bears no scars and if he has chased a hungry fellow away from his door, or he gives away his last piece of bread tomorrow.

A further thought: what is good and evil in your own life here and now? I was in prison earlier on. One says objectively, "People who robbed me of my freedom, treated me badly, and it was bad for me to be imprisoned." But I did not experience it that way. On the contrary, this period was good for me and I felt happy."

We are disturbed at this point by a visitor who quickly takes leave. But alas, we lose the thread of our train of thought. In the meanwhile, it occurs to me that I wanted to ask Raihanaji's opinion of a popular Indian philosopher who is also well-known in the West. Would it be rewarding to attend his lectures? As I have the opportunity? Raihana answers:

"My *Guru* forbade me for a long time at the beginning to listen to lectures or to read the books of such people. So I advise you not to. You will stuff your brain with strange ideas. Examine yourself. That is more important. You will be surprised how much time and energy this will take. But if you are very curious about this man, then go and see it as an intellectual exercise, not more than that. You are now on a definite path and it would be confusing, if you allow yourself to be drawn to any other path."

I am afraid I have taken too much of Raihana's time without thinking of her and, therefore, ask her, "Is there something particularly important that you would finally like to tell me?"

The small shining eyes are focussed on me with penetrating clarity.

"The most important thing is that you learn to believe. It is difficult for you people in the West. You have made a god out of despair. Your despair has religious pathos. If you don't want to appear old-fashioned, you have to bow to general consensus that faith is impossible, and everything believing people say has its psychological cause. An autonomous man!

I know that there is magic in thinking that man has attained his majority after a long evolution and reached where he himself has made his own laws. He considers that he is mature and does not know that spiritually he is a child, a mere toddler who shakes off his mother's helping hand. When he is older, he laughs at his childish defiance and knows the need of parents and teachers to walk in the spiritual world as well.

A sharp knife is useful for cutting fruit, but it is useless to play a song on it. So it is with the intellect. It is appropriate when explaining the theory of aerodynamics, for overcoming the forces of gravity. But the keenest intellect and the thorough knowledge of such laws cannot help to work out a method of bodily levitation. Time and again, I am reminded how my *Guru* taught me: "Stop arguing about spiritual things. The intellect knows as little about it as a knife about playing a flute. Keep quiet, where there is nothing to say."

One could say metaphorically that the East embraces feminine perception. It seeks peace, subjugation to the divine spirit and loves to dream. The West embodies a male principle. It has a keen intellect and energy and with increasing technical skill, it wants to rule the world. Today the West is poised to invade the East. Who can say what will happen. Perhaps the man who now rules supreme will eventually find himself subservient to "the woman".

I am at a loss realizing that faith without tradition is impossible. For India, it is absolutely essential. But in reality, it is so for all and you who are about to destroy your tradition will become blind, tear off your own eyes — to the way of faith. Even in the future, if you increase your perception, say, of hearing, touch and smell, this will penetrate no further than the material order, like groping in the dark night of the new moon."

Raihanaji has spoken with great intensity. Finally, I ask her a question; but she misunderstands it and applies it to Mā, whereas I was thinking of someone else.

"Wait", says Raihanaji, "I shall ask Mā about it."

For about two minutes, she sits there with her eyes closed, and her face has an expression of effortless concentration. Suddenly, she looks at me quietly and explains, "Śrī Mā says. . ."

It had happened like this several times in the course of our conversation. She had "asked Mā" three or four times what reply she should give me. Once she even astonished me by referring to what happened in the last hour of my stay in the *āśrama,* about which she could have had no idea and about which I assumed that even Mā could not know. Her telepathic communications had nothing of the occult about them. They took place as obviously and as naturally as everything else in the ambience of this remarkable lady.

When I thank her while taking leave of her, Raihanaji says laughing, "But for what? It was, in fact, wonderful for me to be with Mā."

Chapter 14

Thus Speaks Ānandamayī Mā

Who is Ānandamayī Mā, who is Ānanamayī–imbued with bliss? He is in all figures and forms, eternally enthroned in the hearts of all beings. It is true, HE lives everywhere. Once one has achieved to see this, then one has seen and achieved everything. It means, to be fearless, sure, devoid of all conflicts, completely silent, imperishable.

There is only one thing. What is thus wrong in allowing people to do what they would like to do? If one still lives in duality and does not perceive the One in everyone and everything, only then it is wrong to permit people that they worship one.

You and I are two persons in your eyes, and yet You and I are one and even the distance between us is me myself. There is no question of (being) two here. Bond and hatred result from the feeling of duality.

Peace can be promised only then, when the mind is concentrated on what gives us peace, and the eyes rest upon what strengthens peace, when ears listen to what fills the heart with peace and when you hear at all times the answer of the One who IS himself peace.

The feeling of deficiency awakens spontaneously. It is the divine that arouses this feeling. To lose everything means to obtain everything. HE is merciful. Whatever HE does in some moment is blessed, although it is sometimes certainly painful. If HE is revealed as a complete loss, there is hope that HE will be revealed as a complete gain. It is beneficial to long for the one who helps us to find the light of truth, because he arouses our attention to truth.

To lose hope is to lose everything. But was there really a total loss? Does not your heart still surge with wishes and hopes? Complete resignation means the most profound joy. Accept it as your only source of strength. Whatever God does at any time is fully beneficial. If you can accept this, you will find peace.

Do your best not to succumb to anybody's influence. One must be centred in God to live faithfully and peacefully. One must be deeply earnest, full of courage with a sound personality and pure and holy from one's own strength.

It may be tiresome in the beginning to live in harmony with the highest ideals, but finally, it leads to a genuine sense of well-being and peace. One must learn to find joy in the sublime. If one is blessed with a *human* body, it is wrong not to live accordingly. Why should one go after animal instincts?

It is the duty of man to choose what is extraordinary and to push aside what is only entertaining. Let our mind be like a beautiful flower which can be offered to God in a prayer. Really, the only duty of man is to seek self-realization. You must, my friend, try to avoid, together with the one Highest Friend, the fetters of worldly friendship.

Children of the Eternal must concentrate their thoughts on HIM. Separated from HIM, they have not even a chance of peace–never, never, never! Only by living in God, man can find peace, the veil will be torn and the chaser of worries will be revealed. He alone is the vanquisher of the evil. HE is yours, the only Beloved of human heart.

It is all the same at what time what work is done; give it your full attention and do it thoroughly. Rely on God in all circumstances. It is true: HE permeates everything, and therefore, you can find HIM everywhere, even in your work. Call the Lord of life with your whole being.

Serve the Lord and HIM alone in perfect inner peace by regarding all creatures as His form. Love and devotion to HIM and unconditional faith in HIM will be awakened in you in proportion to your capacity of serving God, becoming more and more perfect.

A man, who does not accept with joyful heart every responsibility given to him at any time and for the love of God, will find that life is a burden and will never be capable of achieving something that is important. It is the duty of the people, above all of those, who have made the Highest question their one and only aim, to work joyfully for the spiritual "upliftment" of the world, with a conviction that service of all is His service. Work that is done with this sense in mind purifies the heart and mind.

You emphatically declared some time ago that, if you succeed in finding the right work, you would go about it extremely earnestly, even to develop the spiritual side of your life, beside the enjoyment of material comforts and pleasures.

It is only too obvious that you have kept your word with respect to mundane joys. But in what dark cave, in which inaccessible abyss have you hidden the delicate plant of your spiritual endeavour? When will you exert yourself in bringing light to this dark cave? Precious time is fleeting. Dedicate your days to the effort of approaching the Lord of the humble. You will be too weak in your very old age to concentrate on the name of God. How will you make up then what you have missed to do in good time?

Now is the time to mould yourself. You will have to take refuge in renunciation and inner strength. Then you can be liberated from the negative tendencies you have acquired in your earlier life and which have led you to pain and suffering. Try to make your heart a dedicated shrine of all-bountiful, and wish for yourself wishlessness. This only is feeling oneself drawn to God. Be unfailing in your service. Whatever has to be done for someone, do it in the spirit of joyful service.

One more thing to which you must give special attention: every kind of negligence must completely stop. Wherever it is a question of doing something good or practising spiritual things, aversion and inertia have to be unconditionally wiped out.

Do not allow yourself to be overwhelmed by despair. In spite of everything: trust HIM. You should call HIM in happiness and sorrow. If you have fallen, use your fall as a kind of handle to lift yourself up again. It is man's duty to strive hard irrespective of what he undertakes.

Try to go through life by imposing your burden in His hands. HE is the preserver, He shows you the way. HE is everything in all.

Let patience be your motto at all times. Tell yourself: O Lord, whatever YOU do, is for the Highest Welfare. Pray for strength to last to the end. Nothing happens that is not an expression of God's Grace. Believe me, all is His Grace. Anchored in patience, enduring everything, keep to His name and live in happiness.

Depend upon Him and Him alone. In whatever circumstances you are, remember Him. In every moment. Let this be your prayer: O Lord, YOU have liked to come to me in the form of illness. Give me strength to endure it, give me patience and help me to know that it is YOU who are living in this disguise in me.

Self (*ātmā*) reposing in itself, calls It-Self, to its own revelation – this is *ānanda* (joy)!

The intense wish for the realization of God is itself the path to it. God, the Self, is all-permeating. Where is HE not? In all forms and what is formless, in all names and what is nameless, in all places and under all conditions – HE is. When a desire for self-realization is awakened, then it is HIS real manifestation, manifestation of the Undivisible. HE lets Himself be recognized in all names, since all names are His names. A burning desire to reach the goal must be conceived. The fact that self-realization is your goal, means that it is to be sought and found.

Be truthful in everything. One cannot approach the divine without purity.

The truth itself will help him in every way, who has taken off in search of truth.

Nobody remains unscathed in his journey through life. A pilgrimage to the summit of human existence is the only path to happiness. Try to go on this path on which there is no question of sorrow or happiness. It is the path which leads to freedom from egoism and to the Highest joy.

One must endure all hardship and be always patient to reach the truth. In fact it is the obstacle which helps in the birth of patience.

Write to my friend that he has to become a wanderer on the path on which peace is found. He has to start his pilgrimage to a place, where there is no death and decay, where everyone is always present. Who it is, who dies, and who it is, who appears in the disguise of death? If these things are not understood by direct perception, then there cannot be a liberation from the ocean of suffering. Let my friend strive uninterrupted for staying in the (spiritual) presence before the one, whose memory (through a *japam*) ends the suffering for ever.

He who longs for HIM, finds HIM, and the Death dies for him, who has found him. One should long for God who is the death of the Death and occupy his mind at all times with the things which prepare such a show. You do not know in what way or in what form God is with you yourself. Try to spend the whole day in contemplation of the Highest Being, in repeating God's name or in studying books of wisdom. The one makes His presence felt by a divine atmosphere or phenomenon even through tears which are shed in one's longing for HIM.

In all and each one, is only the one self. Try constantly to be aware of the fact that whatever is perceived whenever and in whatever way, it is a manifestation of the Highest Being. How could the one who perceives be excluded? Excluding and not-excluding are nothing else, but HE. Even the feeling of absence of God is His manifestation – so that His presence may be manifested.

Write to him that he has no reason to be frightened. He who has made realization of God his one and the only goal, has already found a refuge in HIM, although HE may be seen present in his absence.

Where there is a constant endeavour to guard in the perception of what IS, there is hope that this perception will become permanent one day.

Corresponding to one's own capacity, one should try to reserve one day for strict self-discipline. If not once every week, then once every fortnight, or at least, once in a mouth. Everything what we do – eating, drinking, talking, moving, visiting people –, simply everything with which we are busy, must be carefully controlled on this day. One can gradually succeed in one's endeavour for self-control by it. Finally one will live in harmony with the rules, without an effort, even for two or three months in a year.

If you feel that energy (*śakti*) is growing in you, if new light shines to you from within, it will gain more intensity, the more you keep yourself protected in highest peace and silence within you. Even if it gets the slightest opening, there is always a danger that it would escape. Be vigilant. HE Himself will take care of everything that is important: *dīkṣā*, instruction –whatever it may be.

It has to be your only and constant effort with the intensity of the one who is obsessed to keep the mind in equilibrium with the Self – wide-awake in the current of reality, where the unfathomable and the infinite is revealed.

God alone is truth, joy and bliss. Hope for nothing else but for the Highest bliss (*paramānanda*) of the Self. Nothing else exists in reality, nothing else has reality. What appears to exist besides it is only illusion (*māyā*). Try to find your Self (*ātmā*). All this noise is only natural for man. He shouts again and again in his craze for getting rid of the feeling of void.

One's mind must immerse itself in worship of the beloved (*iṣṭa*) to wipe out completely what is harmful and what is undesirable. The idea that HE is far away must be abolished once and for all. "You are within and without, in every vein, in every leaf and blade of grass, in the world and beyond the world." Awakening of a feeling of deficiency is to be welcomed. It opens the path. HE is there at every step to make a knower from the one who is inept: "YOU appear as a feeling of deficiency and void, and nobody else. YOU are always near, Lord, I take refuge in YOU."

HE and nobody else resides also in the realm, where vain solutions, vain sorrows, vain joys, which appear to be completely senseless, are experienced - even in disguise of vainness. There the question about a senseless or some other realm does not arise. There is *everything*, although there is nothing. There everyone's own, true Self is Self that reposes in It-Self.

If you can love God, there will not be any more worries for you. Even the feeling of separation from HIM is joy. For, you will be conscious of the pain of separation only because of your love for HIM. Only the man, in whom God resides in a special way, is capable of the painful knowledge of separation from HIM.

Do not waste even a thought on results. Be engrossed in HIM and HIM alone. Results may not be always bad. When the right time comes, the Self is revealed to It-Self. You are a child of immortality.

The realm of the spirit in enveloped by the body. Even if you may wish to change your spirit into what is non-corporeal – will it renounce its realm voluntarily? Its natural movement is parting, and wandering forward and backward again and again. Your only duty is to realize: "You alone are within and without, as well in abundance as in deficiency and void, in fact, in all possible circumstances that can be thought of. One has to concentrate on the invocation of the beloved (*iṣṭa*), on the one who is desired, to disperse what is not worthy of desire.

Watch carefully everything, whatever you do. How you

eat, sleep, go around and sit. Besides, all exercises you do to seek freedom from all bonds, must be done with faith and love. No spiritual exercise should ever be done without reverence, because it is HE Himself who has come to you in disguise of exercise.

Even if someone does something bad, you should feel for him nothing else but affection and goodwill. Think: "Lord, this is also one of YOUR manifestations." The more friendly you can feel towards everyone and behave, the more swiftly will open the path for you to the One who is an epitome of goodness.

When the relationship between the *Guru* and his pupil is dependable, then the *Guru* can never be forsaken. He is always present for his pupil. God alone is man's *Guru.* One should completely trust HIM.

The relationship between the *Guru* and his pupil deserves to be regarded as only eternal, if the *Guru* possesses a divine power (*śakti*) and imparts this power to his pupil, when initiating him. Since this power is eternal, the relationship between the *Guru* and his pupil, which is established in such a way, is also eternal. The *mantra* given to the pupil during the initiation-ceremony (*dīkṣā*), should not be a dead word, but must have a syllable or a series of syllables which are charged with life and spiritual energy and are capable or working actively in the psycho-physical organism of the pupil. If the faith of the pupil in his *Guru* is genuine, then some sort of limitation in the *Guru* is no obstacle. But if this faith is shaken, whatever may then be the reason, then difficulties must arise. There is no other way to eternalize the relationship with the *Guru* except by faith, and it is its nature, to invoke God's Grace, and which does not depend upon the merit of the *Guru.*

A man, who seeks truth, will find his own true self in himself with the help of the instruction of his *Guru.* The *Guru* is always present in a *mantra* which he gives to him. You may see his body dying, but the *Guru* will never forsake you.

If there is no opportunity to attain the corporeal presence of the wise and the saintly, one should meditate on Vāsudeva, the divine dweller of every human heart. One prepares oneself by cherishing his presence. One must look for activities and ambience which are fit to imbue oneself with thoughts and aspirations which lead one to the divine.

It is quite natural that more and more joy is experienced, when one practises Yoga. Distractions come till the One has revealed Oneself. But it is the *Guru* alone who can say, whether one is progressing in the right manner. Transformation means that there are no more worldly interests. One progresses towards the real joy in proportion to one's becoming indifferent towards mundane things.

Where there is Buddha-nature – enlightenment – there, pity will do its work even from the *Nirvāṇa.*

Mā's answer to the question, "Who are you?", is:
"This: 'I, mine, you, yours and:
I am this, you are that . . .
defines only borders.
This body is insignificant (*elomelo*).
Exclude it.
Try to understand our own Self (*ātmā*).
You, I, beyond you and I –
This, that is infinite and the only One,
that, that, that – it is only THAT, whatever you may say."

The *ātmā* of this body is everyone's *ātmā.* It is not possible that someone, somewhere, does not belong to Mā.

Only for you all everything is real what this body (=Mā) says or does, its actions, its movements, its going hither or thither. It is you who are the reason whatever is done whenever by this body for your sake.

Events appear to you to be natural or supernatural, normal or supernormal – from the point of your view. But here (with Mā) is no *karma* and no desire. Here is everything that can be said: whatever happens, is welcome in the same way.

This body keeps its real being secret in its behaviour as in its words. This is a fact. It is certainly necessary, and therefore, it happens.

Nothing happens with this body unconsciously or by mistake. May it be here or elsewhere. Whether it is outwardly perceived or not – whatever is ordained to be, that happens, that takes place.

It is not a question here (with Mā) that suffering and sorrow of others is taken over by her. Here is only perfect unity, identity.

This body is not always consistent in what it says, as you would be. Everyone's changing thoughts and feelings are clearly visible to my eyes all the times.

To tell the truth: whereas a few people come to me no doubt to seek the Highest Truth, many come to me so that their wishes and aspirations are fulfilled.

Does his heart still hang to the world, although its true nature is clearly evident to him? He should do his best at this cross-roads to dedicate himself completely to service by considering that whatever he does is the service of the Lord. Ask him that he should strive to see, at any cost, that he does not get again involved in something, what belongs to the ocean of suffering (of the mundane world). It was his attachment to the world what caused such a profound affliction to the unfortunate fellow. Nothing but ignorance is the root of all that. He should continue to communicate with this body, because he has nobody else in whom he could confide.

Mā is with you in all your activities, even when you sing *kīrtana.* Sit quietly in complete peace and think: Mā is with me in the midst of void. That will give you joy (*ānanda*).

To know Mā means to realize Mā, to become Mā. Mā means *ātmā* . . . at all times in her arms, in the mother. Once the mother (God as Mother) is found, everything is found.

(Excerpts from the letters dictated by Mā. Quotes from: *Matri Vani,* 2 Vols., publ. by Shree Shree Anandamayee Charitable Society, Bhadaini, Varanasi, 1977.)

Many faiths and sects serve the purpose that HE offers Himself to Himself on different paths – each one has its own charm –, and that HE may be discovered as immanent, when HE reveals himself in countless ways and forms and in what is formless. As a path, he entices everyone in a particular direction, in harmony with the inclinations and tendencies of one's heart. The One is present in all, although there are conflicts in a few ceases which are to be traced back to the limitation of the ego.

This body (Mā) does not exclude anything. The one who belongs to a particular faith or sect, has to go ahead upon a point, where everything what his faith espouses, is completely familiar to him. If you are progressing on a definite line, in other words, if you are a follower of a particular religion, which you regard as completely different from all other religions and in conflict with them, then you must at first realize the perfection to which the founder of (your religion) points out, then only, what is beyond it, will be revealed to you.

What was explained right now, applies to all religions, but it is, of course, true that the summit of human life cannot be reached, if one is satisfied with what one can reach on one line. What is desired is a realization, which uproots conflicts and contradictions of opinion, that is, one is completely free.

If it is less than it, if means that the relevant experience was only partial and incomplete. One cannot fight any more with anyone in the case of a true realization. One is completely enlightened with respect to all religions and doctrines and considers that all paths are equally good. Only this is absolute and perfect realization.

But then one should have a firm belief, devoid of any doubt, in one's own beloved God (*iṣṭa*) and must go one's chosen path with persistence and concentration.

(Quoted from: Words of Sri Anandamayi Ma, publ. by Shree Anandamayee Sangha, Bhadaini, Varanasi, 1962.)

So far following books with text of or reports on Śrī Ānandamayī Mā have appeared in German:

Matri Darshan – *Ein Photo-Album über Shri Anandamayi Ma* (revised new edition 1988);

Matri Satsang – *Gespräche mit der Glückseligen Mutter Shri Anandamayi Ma* (1984);

Bhaiji – *Anandamayi Ma. Wie sie sich mir offenbarte* (1986);

Anandamayi Ma – *Worte der Glückseligen Mutter* (2 1985).

(All appeared in Mangalam Verlag S. Schang, Westerkappeln.)

Anandamayi Ma – *Leben der Hingabe*, Verlag Heilbronn, Heilbronn 1987.

Glossary of Sanskrit-Terms

Advaita	literally: "Non-duality"; a condition which can be ascribed only to God or to the Absolute. Referring here, above all, to the non-dualistic doctrine of *Vedānta*-philosopher, Śaṅkarācārya (A.D. 788-820).
Āratī	Rite done to worship gods, saints and holy scriptures in the form of *pūjā*.
Āsana	1. Different body-postures of *Haṭha-Yoga*. 2. Place or mat on which a person striving for spirituality sits.
Āśrama	Centre for religious studies and meditation; hermitage, Hindu-monastery.
Ātmā	The real, immortal Self of man (soul); it is identical with the Highest Self, i.e. *Brahman*.
Avatāra	literally: "descendant"; an incarnation of divine consciousness on earth. According to Hindu-tradition, only Viṣṇu has incarnations. Independent of this tradition, Hindus regard Jesus also as an A.
Bhagavad-Gītā	literally: "Song of the Sublime"; a philosophical didactic poem which is regarded as the "Gospel" of Hinduism. It is a part of the Indian national epic *Mahābhārata* (6th Book) which dates back to the period between fifth and second century B.C.
Bhagavān	literally : "Sublime, holy, the sublime One", name of a god, mostly of the highest World-Lord Viṣṇu; even great saints have this title (e.g. Bhagavān Ramaṇa Maharṣi).

Bhakta	A follower of the *Bhakti-Yoga*; generally a devotee.
Bhakti-Yoga	Path of salvation with the help of love of God; one of the four main Yogas or ways to merge with God.
Brahmacārī (*cāriṇī*)	A person aspiring for religious goal. He/She who has gone through a spiritual practice and who has taken the first vow (monk/nun).
Brahman	The eternal, imperishable absolute, the highest non-dualistic reality, also the "Highest Self".
Brāhmaṇa	A person belonging to the priest-caste, the top-most of the four castes.
Cakra	literally: "wheel, circle"; 1. A circle of god's worship in Hinduism; 2. Name of the centres of subtle or fine energy (*kuṇḍalinī*) in the energy-body (astral-body) of man. They gather, transform and distribute the energy permeating them.
Darśan(a)	literally: 1. "Look, seeing"; 2. A "system". Here: presence of the saint endowing blessing.
Dharma-cakra	The wheel of the doctrine; in Buddhism, a symbol for the doctrine proclaimed by Buddha.
Dhotī	Length of a material which can be worn as a loin-cloth or a *sārī*.
Dīkṣā	Initiation by a *Guru* of the one who chooses a spiritual path.
Durgā	literally: "the unfathomable One"; the oldest and most often used name of the Divine Mother, Śiva's consort.
Ghāṭ(a)	Steps on the river bank. Also bathing place.
Gopāl(a)	literally: "herdsman"; God Kṛṣṇa's name in his manifestation as a child (young Kṛṣṇa

	used to live among herdsmen of Vrindavan).
Guru	Teacher, particularly, spiritual master.
Hanumān	Deity in the form of a (King) of monkeys. He rescued God Rāma's wife Sītā from the demon Rāvaṇa (*Rāmāyaṇa*)
Iṣṭa	literally: 1. "Beloved"; 2. "wish". Always a particular, personal aspect of *Brahman,* incarnated in a deity with whom the *Bhakta* has to achieve a complete *union* to attain salvation.
Japa	Repetition of a *mantra* or God's name in a prayer.
juta	Impure in religious sense.
Kālī	literally: "The black One"; Bengali Mother Goddess.
Karma	literally: "deed; action"; also the law of causality of retribution, which determines man's fate and turns the wheel of rebirth.
Khyāla	A sudden psychic impulse; here: a sudden revelation of the divine in Mā's soul.
Kīrtana	A religious song; joint recitation, singing and dancing to show reverence to God which has a special role in *Bhakti-Yoga,* as it elevates the feelings of a *Bhakta* and thereby lets him progress on his path to God.
Kṛṣṇa	literally: "black" or "dark-blue"; Viṣṇu's eighth *Avatāra.* The most well-known of all Hindu-deities (see also Gopāl).
Kuṇḍalinī	literally: "serpent", also "serpent-power"; called so because this spiritual power rests coiled up sleeping in every man at the end of his spinal column. Once it is awakened, it finds its expression in the form of spiritual knowledge and mystic visions in

	its ascent through different centres (*cakras*).
Līlā	literally: "game"; God's game in the world of phenomena. The creation is regarded by *Vaiṣṇavas* as "God's *līlā*".
Liṅga	Phallus-shaped symbol (mostly in stone) of God Śiva; in esoterical interpretation regarded as a symbol of divine-creative light.
Mahābhārata	literally: "The great epic of the battle of the descendants of Bharata"; next to *Rāmāyaṇa*, the second (and simultaneously the most comprehensive) monumental heroic epic of the Indian literature, abounding in didactic poems, legends and fables.
Mahātmā	literally: "a great soul"; honorific title given to significant spiritual teachers and wise men (e.g. Gandhi).
Maṇḍala	literally: "circle, arch, section"; mostly a circular symbol developed from a representation of lotus, which serves as an aid in meditation.
Mantra	A word (name) which conjures up the presence of a deity through the medium of sound, partially, only a syllable or a series of syllables.
Māyā	literally: "Deception, illusion, appearance"; M. blurs the vision of man so that he sees only the plurality of the universe and not the *one* reality.
Mudrā	literally: "Seal, sign"; a body-posture (above all of arms and hands) or symbolic gesture which has a spiritual significance.
Nirvāṇa	literally: "dying out"; state of freedom from suffering, death and rebirth, as also all

other forms of worldly bond; merging of the individual ego with *Brahman.*

Praṇām(a) literally: "bowing"; reverential greeting of God as also of saints and respected people by folding the hands and joining the palms or by touching the feet of the other with the hand and then touching with it one's own forehead or lying prostrate before the other.

Prasād(a) 1. Grace or favour of a deity; 2. Clarity, purity, equanimity; 3. Sacrificial food that is offered to a deity or a saint and consecrated by him by blessing it.

Pūjā Worship, ceremony, ritualistic service of God with water, flowers, a ritualistic bell, joss-sticks and *mantras.*

Pūjārī A brāhmaṇa priest who performs *pūjā.*

Purāṇa "Ancient narrative works"; 18 P. deal with the legends of gods and are the main writings of the *Vaiṣṇavas.*

Rāmāyaṇa literally: "Biography of Rāma"; the most ancient epic of the Sanskrit literature (earliest version fourth century B.C.) in which the life of God Rāma and his consort Sītā is narrated.

Ṛṣi Seer, saint, inspired poet, to whom *mantras* and holy scriptures were revealed.

Rudra literally: "The howling, frightful"; an earlier name of Śiva in his destructive aspect.

Sādhanā As good as "means for perfection", religious practice, e.g. Yoga, fasting, silence, meditation, singing *kīrtana.*

Samādhi literally: "fix, make secure"; state of the deepest contemplation in which the identity of the individual self with the Highest Self (i.e. *Brahman*) is realized.

Saṃnyāsa literally: "renunciation"; highest ordination of a monk. Complete S. means knowledge of *Brahman* and absolute freedom (also from the rules, a monk has to observe).

Satsaṅga literally: "good association"; association of saints and wise men.

Śakti literally: "strength, power, energy"; Śiva's consort; personification of the original energy, of the power of *Brahman*; the dynamic aspect of God by which he creates, preserves and destroys.

Śāstra literally: "teaching, text-book"; holy scriptures of Hinduism, e.g. the *Vedas*.

Śiva literally: "One who is good and kind"; the third deity of Hindu-trinity (*Trimūrti*), in which he is the God of annihilation and destruction.

Siddhi as good as "complete capacity"; "supernatural" capacity which can come up on its own as a side-product of spiritual development, when forces, which open an access to cosmic realms, become free.

Stūpa literally: "knot of the hair"; characteristic form of expression of Buddhistic architecture, of the principal symbol of Buddhism and focal point of temples and monasteries; often a place to preserve relics.

Svāmi literally: "Lord"; A monk is addressed as S.

Tantra literally: "Web, context, continuum"; a manifestation of Śiva/Śakti-cult which is full of rites. Worship of great Mother-deities plays a great role in it. There is also a *tantric* manifestation in Tibetan Buddhism.

Tapas/Tapasyā	literally: "fire, heat, asceticism, mortification of flesh"; intense spiritual practice done out of burning desire of realizing God or *Brahman.*
Tat	literally: "that"; Name of Highest Reality, *Brahman,* God, the infinite absolute.
Trimūrti	literally: "having three forms"; threefold aspect of *Brahman* who is incarnated in three deities *Brahmā* (creation), Viṣṇu (preserver) and Śiva (destroyer).
Upaniṣads	literally: "sitting down near someone", i.e. to sit at the feet of a *Guru* to receive the secret doctrine; philosophical writings which interpret the *Vedas*; principal basis of *Vedānta*-philosophy.
Vaiṣṇava	Worshipper of Viṣṇu, follower of Vaiṣṇavism, one of the three trends of worshipping God in modern Hinduism.
Veda, Vedas	literally: "knowledge, holy doctrine"; a collection of the most ancient texts of Indian literature to which an orthodox Hindu ascribes superhuman origin and divine authority.
Vedānta	literally: "*Veda*-end", i.e. the final consideration of the *Vedas* as they were at first in the *Upaniṣads*; a non-dualistic doctrine which presumes that the highest world-process is the cause of all happening and all phenomena.
Viṣṇu	One of the principal gods of Hinduism; the highest Lord of the world hastens each time, when the world threatens to come apart, to help it and incarnates himself as an *Avatāra,* to show to humanity new ways of further development.

Index